GREEN MAN,
EARTH ANGEL

SUNY SERIES IN WESTERN ESOTERIC TRADITONS

David Appelbaum, editor

GREEN MAN, EARTH ANGEL

The Prophetic Tradition and the Battle for the Soul of the World

Tom Cheetham

Foreword by
Robert Sardello

STATE UNIVERSITY OF NEW YORK PRESS

Published by
STATE UNIVERSITY OF NEW YORK PRESS
ALBANY

© 2005 State University of New York

All rights reserved

Printed in the United States of America

For information, address
State University of New York Press
90 State Street, Suite 700, Albany, NY 12207

Production, Laurie Searl
Marketing, Fran Keneston

Library of Congress Cataloging-in-Publication Data

Cheetham, Tom.
    The prophetic tradition and the battle for the soul of the world / Tom Cheetham.
        p. cm. — (SUNY series in Western esoteric traditions)
    Includes bibliographical references (p.) and index.
    ISBN 0-7914-6269-2 (alk. paper) — ISBN 0-7914-6270-6 (pbk. : alk. paper)
        1. Spirituality—Psychology. 2. Corbin, Henry. 3. Mysticism—Islam. 4. Psychoanalysis
    and religion. 5. Jung, C. G. (Carl Gustav), 1875–1961. I. Title. II. Series.

BL624.C4515 2004
200'.1'9—dc22

                                                                                    2004041605

                        10   9   8   7   6   5   4   3   2   1

To Joan, Ben, and Amy

Henry Corbin

1903–1978

Director of Studies in Islam and the Religions of Arabia,
École practique des Hautes Études, Paris;
Professor of Islamic Philosophy at the University of Teheran, Iran;
Lecturer at the Eranos Conferences in Ascona, Switzerland;
Co-founder, University of St. John of Jerusalem.

CONTENTS

FOREWORD

Tom Cheetham has written a remarkable book that has the power of shifting our way of imagining the world. This power stems from his insight into a core longing felt within the heart of human beings, a longing for wholeness that feels as if it were a memory. We imagine that there was a time, long ago, when human beings lived reverently in relation to the earth and the cosmos. We felt, so the story says, whole, in our place, with God at the center and the periphery. Then the Great Disjunction happened. Matter and Spirit were split into two isolated realms. God was removed from the world and placed in His heaven and the earth, gradually at first, and then more and more rapidly, became the great supplier of commodities, mere material substance. Different thinkers locate this disjunction at different times and due to different factors, but it is always depicted as occurring sometime in actual history, and the story says we have been on a downward course ever since. This way of imagining the unfolding of evolution always looks to the past as the better time, and all our efforts need to be focused on retrieving the sensibility of the past. The more sophisticated tellers of this story do not imagine we can return to the past, but they do feel we can return to the values of the past, or find ways of living those past values, primarily by living in relative isolation from the present world dynamics, encompassed in a shield of fear.

Cheetham's first creative contribution lies in pointing out the obvious, but it is obvious only to one who has a living inner life. The longing for wholeness is an archetypal longing. It belongs to the essence of the soul to feel such longing. It will always be there. This longing motivates us to search for the ultimate inner meaning of our existence and to at least find ways to assure we do not go off on collective tangents that depart from world destiny. When we understand that the longing originates in the soul, new ways of imagining the world have to be sought, and these new ways have to be conscious soul ways. Here lies the second and truly great contribution of this book. Cheetham recognizes that a longing of the soul has to be responded to in kind. That is, only soul can respond to soul. Only soul understands soul. If we are to ever get anywhere with this archetypal longing, we have to approach it on its own terms. A metaphysics that excludes imagination, the hallmark of soul, as a world force, is fated to painful longing without the slightest possibility of resolution. Metaphysics that has no place for the category of imaginal being splits spirit from matter with no way for them to ever be linked. Longing becomes replaced by abstract thought that turns into systems of science and technology. Materialism characterizes the other side of the split. Materialism is the outlook that says that everything in the universe can be understood in terms of the arrangement and action of purely physical forces. And, more subversively, materialism offers the notion that all longings can be quieted through material means of every sort.

Cheetham develops a method of proceeding from longing to questions of metaphysics. His method consists of making us feel deeply all that we have lost with the way reality has been split up; the loss of the imagination, the loss of living speech, words as angels, the loss of reading that speaks from within reality rather than about it, and most of all, the loss of the sense of place. He throws us into the depth of loss, the depth of despair, really. We cannot recover what we cannot feel. Cheetham's method involves a descent into hell, a necessary descent, but one that distinguishes the hell we live—the literal, surface-bound, consuming, manic world, with the fructifying descent into the darkness where we await the voices and visions of the archetypal worlds.

Cheetham progresses in his method by seeing through the split of spirit and matter, seeking to establish what a metaphysics with imagination as the forming force of the world would mean. As long as we think only in terms of spirit and matter, and its two primary manifestations in the world, religion and science, we contribute to the loss of the subtle, participative sense. An archetypal metaphysics views creation as happening every moment. All is alive. And soul is not in us; in this metaphysics, we are in soul. The implications of such a view are enormous. However, it takes more than the idea of such a metaphysics to begin discovering the ways to live such a proposed reality. And here is the third great contribution of this book. Such a metaphysics exists. The outlines of it can be found by interpreting the work of C. G. Jung in a radical way, and the further outlines of it are found in the work of Henry Corbin, the primary emphasis of this book.

Cheetham makes a long and fruitful excursion into the work of C. G. Jung as a preparation for introducing the reader into imaginal metaphysics. We have come to think of Jung as the phenomenologist of the soul. When we come to Jung's work on alchemy, however, we find that the alchemists were seeking to make spirit conscious. They were working out an imaginal metaphysics of transformation in their theorizing–visioning, and they demonstrated the practicality of this metaphysics in the practice of alchemy. Jung did not quite see them this way, but, in truth, the alchemists were attempting to free spirit from matter and were not just projecting their fantasies onto matter. Alchemy was simultaneously a transformation of self and of world into completeness. Jung reads this completeness, this wholeness, as involving the incorporation of contradictories, the light and the shadow of soul reality. Cheetham's understanding of Jung's project and the limitations of that project is brilliant. Once those limitations are clear, he is able to establish an all important bridge from Jung to the astounding work of Henry Corbin, from depth psychology that never quite made the metaphysical leap, to Islamic mysticism's fully developed imaginal metaphysics.

Central to the movement from Jung to Corbin's creative interpretation of Islamic mysticism is the difference between the darkness of the Shadow in Jung and the luminous darkness of the divine Night. In Jung there exists a throwing together of soul experience and spirit experience without really seeing that there is a decided difference. Jung's adamant commitment to soul made it impossible for him to conceive of anything outside of soul, or to plead ignorance when it came to saying what was behind archetypes. Even spirit, for Jung, is the soul's perception of spirit. One result of this limitation of Jung, a limitation that still exists in present depth psychology and even in Archetypal Psychology as put forth by James Hillman, is that spirit experiences are not recognized as such. For example, there is no recognition that there are these two darknesses—the Shadow and the luminous darkness of the divine Night. The former is a soul experience, to be integrated into consciousness for completeness, the latter a spirit experience necessary to wholeness, not only of experience, but of the world. And without that recognition, it is really not possible to tell when one is conscious in soul and when one is conscious in spirit, and certainly, it is not possible to have any sense of the relation between the two. Hillman solves this dilemma by taking an adamant stance against spirit, as if that opposition would cancel the reality. At the same time, Hillman acknowledges a debt to Corbin for bringing forth the notion of the *Mundus Imaginalis*. Hillman interprets this as the imaginal world of the soul, saving depth psychology from sophisticated subjectivity. However, in Corbin, and even more importantly, in the Islamic sources of this term, the *Mundus Imaginalis* is the imaginal world of the spirit. The confusion wrought by interpreting spirit phenomena as soul phenomena has meant that depth psychology tends to honor the darkness of the descent into hell as if it were the realm of the holy. Depth psychology is unable to distinguish the realm of the unconscious and the realm of the superconscious. Hillman's interpretation of the *Mundus Imaginalis* is a misinterpretation. Cheetham's teasing out of all the exact quotations from Corbin that establish the clear difference between Shadow and Luminous Darkness constitutes one of the scholarly delights of this book that frees us enough from Jung to be appreciative of his efforts while reorienting the search that archetypal longing pulls us into.

While the soul realm is perceived through soul, it is more appropriate, says Cheetham, to say that the superconscious realm is perceived through the "supersensory senses." While soul is certainly an imaginal realm, the luminous darkness takes us into the imaginal world. These supersensory senses have to be prepared for through meditative disciplines that gradually bring about an alteration of our physiology, one of the effects of the meditation practices in the Islamic mystical tradition. The difference between soul sensing and super-sensory sensing distinguishes the darkness of the lower soul from the Black Light, which is the Light that itself cannot be seen but which makes everything else visible. What is first visible upon entry to the imaginal world are colors, but colors without matter. These colors are the mark of entering into the realm of the *Mundus Imaginalis*. They also mark entering into the non-knowing of the heart, the perceptual organ for sensing the spiritual worlds. One of the most beautiful sections of this book describes the seven prophetic colors and their functions.

In this imaginal metaphysics, all beings and things and places are mirrors of the spiritual worlds, illuminated by the Light that makes everything else visible. We are, in effect, then, composed of the artistic play of spiritual beings. The imaginal metaphysics of Ibn 'Arabi, as interpreted by Corbin, is a fruitful gnosis that accounts for the divine worlds and for the earthly world, but does not confuse them, nor does it separate them the way we do in the Western tradition. It is a fruitful gnosticism. I say fruitful in contrast to Jung's gnosticism which confusedly mixes soul and spirit and never resolves the intense archetypal longing.

The gnosis outlined by Corbin is in opposition to any kind of incarnational Christianity. For the metaphysics of Ibn 'Arabi and other Islamic mystics, the incarnation of Christ is an impossibility, for it historicizes God. Cheetham indicates that in this cosmology, to say that Christ *is* God incarnate, is equivalent to saying that God is dead. The entry of God materially, wholly, and substantially into historical, material, and public time and space is the archetypal act of secularization. In the gnosis of Islamic mysticism Christ is an ever-present reality of the soul. And, Christ did live, but, in this gnostic imagination, he did not die on the cross. One of the most interesting sentences in this book describes an intriguing imagination of what happened to Christ. Indeed, the chapter comparing Corbin's view of Christ with the view of Christianity is a pivotal chapter in this book. Corbin speaks of Christ as a man, but also as a figure of Light—both. Christ is also the Soul of the World. This theological chapter gives a basis for approaching the world as spiritual image, populated with Presences.

The doctrine of the Incarnation in the exoteric version of Christianity collapses any sensibility of the angelic hierarchies. The angelic realms no longer have the power they once did, and that can still be found in esoteric Christianity, which is far more compatible with the view put forth by Corbin. We find this collapse evident in religion these days, which no longer has a conception of the creating power of the angelic realms. So, there is an imaginal theology accompanying, even preceding, imaginal metaphysics. This theology is founded on Beauty rather than on Salvation. Cheetham puts his finger on the key element for responding rightly to archetypal longing, and his uncovering of the senses of Beauty in the work of Corbin is stunning.

Beauty is the strength of imaginal theology, and its hope—that which holds the possibility of guiding our longing to its destination. And Beauty is the core imagination for any culture seeking this destination. Beauty is not something given but strived for through purification of soul. Beauty here is completely objective, "subjectively objective." By this term I mean that in imaginal metaphysics all dualism is resolved so that there is no longer a subject-object distinction; rather, subject and object are one. Further, Beauty is not an abstract concept but rather the theophany of Sophia. And, while Beauty is a sort of destination, She is a destination that takes us always farther into the unknowing.

The path of Beauty is epistemologically complex because it is based in non-dualism of knowing. In imaginal knowing, you know only through the aspect of the known within you. But, it must also follow that an object known, knows when it is known. Beauty is understood completely interiorly but not subjectively.

The difference between a world based in Beauty and one based in a theology of Salvation is more than an interesting comparison of two cosmologies. Cheetham shows how destructive technology is tied to Christian theology of Salvation. Drawing on the philosopher Gianni Vattimo, Cheetham shows that radical freedom is the destiny of the Christian tradition, and that such freedom makes the earth a playground of destruction. There are no longer any boundaries. The section of this book concerned with technology is fascinating in that the view of freedom coming from Vattimo's understanding of Christianity is based upon the notion that with freedom there is always the risk that a choice to make a world in harmony with the spiritual worlds does not seem to be an option. The difference between freedom and nihilism collapses. Such a view commands a great deal of reflection, for powerful elements of this view can certainly be seen in the present world in which we find wars being fought pitting these two—freedom and nihilism—against each other, which may in fact, then, be wars of self-destruction. This country's battle cry is freedom and strikes out at the apparent nihilism of terrorism. But, what if freedom, as presently politically understood, is no more than a form of nihilism?

This view of freedom without limits as nihilism is not completely accurate. Freedom is nihilism only when it is not filled, completely, with the content of love. So, to read technology as the fulfillment of the Christian tradition, and the Christian tradition as finally nihilistic in its total freedom, leaves something out. It leaves out the option of the choice of love. The difference, then, between the Christian tradition and the kind of technological world it ultimately creates, and Islamic mysticism and the kind of world it imagines, hinges on the detailed process of metamorphosis and initiation into the source of love, the Beloved, described in such detail in Islamic mysticism. Exoteric Christianity lacks a necessary angelology as a way of proceeding to the Beloved, and without such an angelology it almost certainly does lead to nihilistic freedom. The intricate and careful way Cheetham works out these concerns is truly wondrous. In particular, his section on the radical work of Archetypal psychologist Wolfgang Giegerich is invaluable.

While James Hillman takes Jung toward the direction of Corbin but never reaches the autonomy of spirit, Giegerich takes Jung toward the direction of Jung's alchemical view of spirit freed from matter, which leaves matter, and indeed the world, open to the kind of nihilism suggested by Vattimo. We have rid the world of things from their status of being the appearance of the shining of the gods and the angels, says Giegerich. And we are left with only one god, the one we have created, technology, best exemplified by the bomb. It is not, however, particular technologies Giegerich is talking about, but rather the world-creating/destroying idea of technology as how we save ourselves. The description of the intricacies of this view and how Giegerich arrives at it are worth the price of admission to this book. Giegerich's view of the incarnation, however, is based on an incapacity to imagine that God became fully human in Christ. Fully human. For Geigerich, the incarnation of God is incarnation into a different kind of flesh than the rest of humans. Flesh from above, is, in Giegerich's view, not the same as natural flesh. It is, in effect, technological flesh. The event of this "technological" flesh has ultimately meant that abstract technology is our god.

Cheetham wants to make the most difficult case possible for valuing the world and then finding how it is possible to find meaning and avenues of responding to the longing for wholeness that will not go away. It is easy and rather cheap to begin with an abstract notion of wholeness. That approach, characteristic of the New Age movement and those captured by nostalgia for a past that never was, is abstract and begins by turning away from the world as it is now. Cheetham is one of the most courageous thinkers I have ever read. He shows the very basis of the now dominant worldview, and he shows how this basis is indeed nihilistic, and as he is doing so, he also shows us the way out, which is by going through the labyrinth, not ascending to thoughts that ignore our situation of being lost in the labyrinth. The way through the nihilistic, technological world, is twofold: love, described as an initiatory process with definite and clear steps of purification and perception, and the re-sanctification of the world. And this twofold path has, in addition, to be founded in a priority of the imaginal in order to avoid making a false dichotomy between spirit and matter.

The last section of the book concerns the word as the way out of nihilism and the way to rightly respond to archetypal longing for wholeness. The living, breathing word, not those collections of words found in the dictionary and strung together into dead sentences. Cheetham begins a reflection on the word based upon Ibn 'Arabi's view of language as the unique articulation of the divine Breath. Our breath, articulated, nondualistically, belonging both to us and to world, speaks human and cosmic reality simultaneously. This is poetic, creative speech, speaking without knowing in advance what one is going to say. Speaking that lives in the region of holy Silence. The excursion into spirit must always return to soul in order to be connected with sensuous reality, and it is with speech that this return continually occurs, embodying spirit without collapsing it into matter. We come, then, to a new understanding of soul, soul as the embodying process of spirit, and as the spiritualizing process of matter. These intertwining processes live together in word-breath. The world speaks and the symbols of its speaking are the breath of God. The discipline needed to hold technological destruction at bay is the capacity to read the world. This discipline requires, says Cheetham, an imaginal asceticism, an ongoing purification process that works to keep us from falling into the false desires of the present worldview and inspires courage to be fully present to what is present.

These few indications of what you will find in this book will, I hope, entice you to enter into a study of a work that certainly does not belong to the world of throwaway books. This book requires slow reading, for as you read these living words you are undergoing a transformation. At the end of reading, the world will not be the same.

ROBERT SARDELLO

ACKNOWLEDGMENTS

On occasion I have had the good fortune to teach some of this material at Wilson College in Pennsylvania and at the College of the Atlantic in Maine, and am deeply grateful to those students who shared their thoughts and enthusiasms with me. Jay Livernois has long been an important source of support and helped me to believe that I had something worth saying. Many thanks go to Rudolf Ritsema, Shantena Sabbadini, Benjamin Sells, Robert Bosnak, Gisela Binda, and the participants at the 2001 Eranos Conference in Ascona for inspiration and friendship. The encouragement of Elliott McLaughlin, David Miller, Robert Sardello, and Arthur Versluis has meant more than they know. The book was greatly improved by the thoughtful comments of several anonymous reviewers. I rely more than I have any right on the staff of the inter-library loan department of Bangor Public Library who somehow manage to find nearly everything I ask for, however obscure.

"You Are Now In Heaven" was presented under another title as *The Paul Swain Havens Memorial Lecture* at Wilson College, Chambersburg Pennsylvania, December 3, 1996.

A version of "Consuming Passions" was published in *Temenos Academy Review* 5: 117–37.

"Black Light" was published in *Spring: A Journal of Archetype and Culture—Jungian Fundamentalisms (and others)* 68: 59–104.

"Within This Darkness" appeared in the online journal *Esoterica: The Journal for Esoteric Studies* IV: 61–95.

References to Carl Jung are to *The Collected Works* (CW) (1953–92), Translated by R. F. C. Hull. Bollingen Series XX, vols. 1–20. Princeton: Princeton University Press. Citations are by paragraph.

Quotations from the Qur'an are from: Ali, Ahmed. *Al-Qur'an: A Contemporary Translation*. Princeton: Princeton University Press, 1984.

All of these essays have been revised for publication here. Translations from Henry Corbin's untranslated works are my own.

The photo of Henry Corbin is from the Eranos Foundation Archive and is used with permission of the Eranos Foundation, Ascona, Switzerland.

ONE

"We Are Now in Heaven"

The *Mundus Imaginalis* and the Catastrophe of Materialism

It is only the things that we don't understand that have any meaning.
—C. G. Jung

THIS STATEMENT OF Carl Jung's is a psychological as well as a metaphysical pronouncement, and I invoke that ambiguity at the outset. It is in this spirit that I want to think about matter. Because as a culture we don't understand it, our intuitions about it are confused, and we don't at all know what to make of it. Our modern approach to material reality is limited, constricting, confused, and dangerous, and the results of this are increasingly invasive and pervasive in our lives. For these reasons we are in danger of disappearing.

THE MUTABILITY OF EXPERIENCE
AND THE HISTORY OF STUFF

My first encounter with the idea that there is a history of perception occurred when, as an undergraduate, I attended the classes of the historian F. Edward Cranz.[1] He claimed, and it seemed shocking to me at the time, that over the course of Western European history from the ancient Greeks to the modern world there have been fundamental shifts in our perception of the relations between ourselves and the world. Thus, the experience of encountering and of knowing something, and correlatively the experience of consciousness and the self are historically variable. And further, there is nothing in particular to guarantee privilege to our modes of experience.

One important source for his thesis is Aristotle's *Peri Psyche;* in Latin, *de Anima;* in English, *On the Soul*. Cranz asked that we read the texts as if they mean what they say. So, when Aristotle says that "the soul *is* somehow, all things,"[2] and that in knowing something, we are somehow conjoined or united with it, we must not dismiss this as archaic foolishness. We must not assume that if Aristotle had read David Hume he would have got it right. But the experience that Aristotle describes, of some kind of union with the objects of knowledge, is clearly not ours. We know things by having accurate ideas of them somewhere in our heads. The things are, of course, "out there" and we are, somehow, "in here." Dr. Cranz called the former kind of knowing *conjunctive,* and the kind of self that experiences the world this way an *extensive* self. Our kind of knowing is *disjunctive,* and we are *intensive* selves. In the *Meditations* Descartes provided the paradigmatic example of the intensive self, sure of nothing but its own thoughts, and relying on God to provide the miraculous connection between the Soul and Matter somewhere deep in the pineal gland.

On Cranz's account, the textual evidence allows a surprisingly clear chronology for a shift from texts that suppose an experience of conjunctive knowing to those that assume the disjunctive mode. In Western Europe, the change occurred around the year 1100. In the twelfth century in any case. Although the subsequent history of this new sense of human being is complex and not well understood, the long-term consequences of the disjunction include, among other things, the modern experience of subjectivity and objectivity, and the modern conception of language as a system of human meanings.

I can quite clearly recall being very uneasy about all of this. I liked it because it seemed to hold out the promise of a kind of psychic emancipation which would be very liberating. But I was bothered too by the suggestion that our sense of objectivity is not normative, or perhaps even very common. Surely there are things "out there" about which we have "ideas." We need only look and there they are. I remember asking anxiously, "But Doctor Cranz, what about rocks?!" My recollection is that he smiled his wonderful smile and said that he was a historian and didn't know about rocks.

In language that I've learned since, this is the history of what the French call *mentalité,* and this shift in the relation between the subject and the object involves a "withdrawal of participation." Many people have discussed this phenomenon from a variety of viewpoints. For instance, you can analyze the Neolithic transition in terms of a kind of disjunction between humans and nature: outside the walls of the city lies the Wilderness, within them, the Tame. It has been argued that by a similar process, the immanent, female deities of Earth were severed from the remote and transcendent masculine gods of the Heavens.[3] Another disjunction, another loss of participation, accompanies the transition from oral to literate society. For European history the crucial transition occurs in Greece roughly between Homer and Plato. The techniques of alphabetic writing and reading for-ever changed the relation of humans to language and to the nonhuman world.[4] Socrates was very concerned about this new technology, and was afraid that it sig-naled the death of real thinking, and that education would suffer irreparably. In fact the great sweep of Western history as a whole has been read as a story of withdrawal and the progressive "death of nature," and the birth of a mechanistic cosmology based on abstract materialism.[5]

It was most interesting to me, with my background in Cranz's work, to notice that many scholars concerned with this history of our selves have also found the twelfth century to be of particular importance for us. They include Ivan Illich and Henry Corbin. It is Corbin's version of the story that I want to discuss here.[6]

Henry Corbin was a French philosopher, theologian, and scholar of Islamic thought, particularly Sufism and Iranian Shi'ism. It was Corbin's contention that European civilization experienced a "metaphysical catastrophe" as a result of what we might call the Great Disjunction. This was signaled by the final tri-umph of the Aristotelianism of Averroes over Platonic and neo-Platonic cos-mology championed by Avicenna. To the defeat of that cosmology is coupled the disappearance of the *anima mundi,* the Soul of the World. The catastrophic event that gave rise to modernity is the loss of the soul of the world.

The details of this history hinge on the fate of the Aristotelian *nous poi-etikos,* which became the Agent or Active Intellect in medieval Western philos-ophy. This Active Intellect operating through us was sometimes equated in Islamic thought with the Holy Spirit or Angel of Revelation, the Angel Gabriel. The realm of being to which this intellection gives access is the place of vision and symbol, what depth psychology calls the world of the psyche and of the imagination. Corbin called it the *mundus imaginalis,* the imaginal world, to underscore the fact that it is not *imaginary* or unreal. Through the agency of the active imagination we have access to an intermediate realm of subtle bod-ies, of real presences, situated between the sensible world and the intelligible. This is the realm of the *anima mundi.*

Lacking this tripartite cosmology we are left with a poisonous dualism of matter and spirit. "Stuff" is severed from Intellect, and both are incomplete and disoriented because the ground of their contact is gone. On Corbin's view all the dualisms of the modern world stem from the loss of the *mundus imaginalis:* matter is cut off from spirit, sensation from intellection, subject from object, inner from outer, myth from history, the individual from the divine.

There are, then, a number of ways of talking about the history of con-sciousness, and something like a disjunction, a withdrawal of participation has been detected by various people in different modes at various times and places. One must wonder whether they are all talking about the same thing, and if so, why this withdrawal or severance seems to appear in such a variety of guises. I believe they are all talking about roughly the same kind of thing, and that the reason it keeps appearing is because it is an archetypal phenomenon. This withdrawal is *always* present as a possibility. We are victims of a continuous withdrawal. But this implies the ever-present possibility of conjunction, of Return.

DUALISM AND NON-SENSE: WHAT'S THE MATTER WITH TRANSCENDENCE?

One of the most fundamental and pernicious effects of the polarized cosmology we've inherited is our inability to discriminate among various kinds of subtle realities. We think things are simple. Or, we think they are merely complex. Our senses for the subtle have atrophied. We recognize as fully real a very limited range of phenomena. We have no feeling for depth, no sense of the positive realities of mystery and enigma. Thoughts have no body; bodies have no animation. We are unable to understand either matter or mind, let alone their relations. This unknowing ignorance is catastrophic.

For instance, we tend to confuse, conflate, and identify truth, abstraction, transcendence, and the spirit. The history of mathematical physics illustrates these confusions. The scientific revolution begins with mathematical physics and it inaugurates the "reign of quantity." It was early established as the paradigmatic science, and has been for four hundred years the standard against which would-be "hard sciences" are measured. As the biologist Stephen Gould has quipped: all the other sciences have "physics envy." On this view, mathematics is the language in which God has written the universe, and the framework of the material world is laid bare in language that is timeless, abstract, universal, and formal.[7] Newton's $F = ma$, Einstein's $E = mc^2$, Schrödinger's wave equation—all these, understood as true statements about reality, have been, and still are, regarded as "Ideas in the Mind of God." Truth, abstraction, formal universality, and the transcendent God are all lumped together in one undifferentiated bundle.

The consequences of this are disastrous. To attain to a true vision of the world we must leave most of it out of account. Understanding requires absence. The truest ideas are the most abstract. The closest approach to God is via the timeless and the universal. The marginalized categories include the timely, the particular, the local, the vernacular, the concrete. These are unintelligible in themselves.

You might think that unless you are a mathematical physicist you can ignore all of this, but it applies to all of us because it determines the orientation of much of modern science and technology. It is a curious fact that the less subtle, and the more abstract our language becomes, the more literal and nakedly powerful it is. We are deluded into believing that knowledge reveals and illuminates the clear and distinct ideas of Truth; that it brings power and control. We persist in not understanding that the blinding clarity of transcendent abstract ideas both requires and produces the light of the fireball over Hiroshima, and is, as Blake foresaw, the Single Vision of Newton's Sleep. The limitless energy in matter, conceived in abstraction, confronts us with apocalypse as both a bang and a whimper: in the deadly illumination of the fire ignited at Trinity, and in the slow decisive poison which we try to conceal by naming it Waste, and which we can find nowhere to bury. The earth will not receive it.

For a while I tried to escape into biology. Here at least we do find attention to the particular, the timely, the local. Biologists must confront individuality and historical contingency in a way that physics can seemingly avoid. For traditional physics, all the interesting *history* happened in the first three minutes after the Big Bang, and it's been thermodynamically downhill ever since. But biology is less and less Natural History, as nature dwindles to a few isolated preserves bordered by parking lots and its seemingly intractably complex mysteries begin to yield to the very real powers of abstraction.

The major metaphors of theoretical biology are today derived from systems science. Biological objects are conceived in terms of dynamical systems theories which when coupled to Darwinian natural selection provide the framework for the eventual unification of the science. The order that we see is explicable as an emergent property, which appears as the crystallization of order from simple, local rules governing the interaction of system elements. The elements may be molecules, genes, neurons, organisms, species. The search is on for formal rules that apply across all scales and serve to unite all the various branches of the biological sciences. Animals no longer look for food: they engage in optimal foraging strategies. Cognition is understood as maximally adaptive neural network processing of sensory input. And so it goes.[8]

Theory in biology has become wholly continuous with the technologies of power in a way that we take for granted in the physical sciences. As physics is required for engineering, so now genetics is required for bioengineering. We are perhaps on the verge of technologies that will enable us to control matter in extraordinary ways, but as before in our history, this knowledge is founded upon an act of abstraction. It is, I think, crucial that we recognize that the metaphors that govern our discourse, both public and private, scientific and personal, are increasingly dependent upon and derived from that most abstract of all technologies, digital information processing. Computational language, the machine language of 0 and 1, is wholly logical, entirely formal. The embodiment of the language does not matter at all. You could, in theory, build a computer out of paper clips and rubber bands. What matters is the sequence of logical relations among the units. Premise: Genes encode information; Brains process information; Organisms are like computational devices. Premise: Discovering abstract laws is our highest, most god-like activity and we should do more of it. Conclusion: We should become computers. This may seem absurd. I hope it does. But it is the clearly stated position of Marvin Minsky at MIT and, I think, of a host of others less clear in intent and in their assumptions about the nature of humanity.[9] It is the logical outcome of modern materialism. We are matter in space. Exceedingly complex without a doubt, but matter in space nonetheless. And what kind of matter doesn't matter. We should remake ourselves into something more durable. We can then continue our inevitable evolutionary ascent toward the summit of Abstract Universality. It is not often that you hear this viewpoint explicitly adopted, but it underlies much of modern technological culture.

There is an extreme dualism at play here: Matter is demonized, and a confused hodgepodge of Abstraction-Transcendence-Spirit is enthroned, toward which we are morally obligated to progress. The world disappears into ecosystems or fluxes of energy, and persons disappear into information processors, cognitive processes, evolutionary processes, or historical-political processes. We may be materialists, but it is a funny materialism. We are mute about matter, about that which makes sense. Matter does not figure in our categories of truth and meaning. It appears as apocalyptic light, accompanied by the irrepressible Shadow that we cannot entomb. Or, it disappears into "information." Either scenario announces the impossibility of the existence of persons.

Dr. Cranz said thirty-five years ago that the existence of persons required transcendence, and was incompatible with what he called "public reason." It is only now that I begin to understand what he meant. But what can we mean by transcendence, with our long history of the withdrawal of participation, with the Bomb and with the World Wide Web?

THE ROCK AND THE DREAM

I've tried to suggest some of the ways in which a stark contrast between spirit and matter produces non-sense and incoherence. We are dumb about matter, and we are hopelessly muddled about things spiritual. The realm of Intellect and Spirit is abstract, distant, bloodless, and vague. Technological metaphors and technical literalisms are undermining the very possibility of experiencing ourselves as persons. We rush headlong into the oblivion of Progress.

Let me be explicit about what I intend. First: What we think of as reality is a restriction, an immense constriction of existence. Second: Scientific materialism is non-sense, and acceptance of its premises leaves us insensate. We must be willing to accept the reality of depth psychology's *psyche*, of Corbin's *mundus imaginalis*, of the Soul of the World. Or, if that seems too exotic, recall Blake and Coleridge and the Romantic claims for the primacy of the imagination.

If we want to make sense of the cosmos, of rocks and persons both, we must make moves that seem ridiculous to modern, hard-headed materialists. To recover our senses, our sense of what matters, to breathe once more the life of the world, we must move not toward Matter as we have come to conceive it, as its Masters, but, seemingly, away. We've been pushing matter around for a long time now. It pushes back apocalyptically. We should sense something wrong. We should do something else. So, let us meditate on matter by moving for a few minutes into the spaces of psyche. We need to reconsider the act of Creation.

One of the most damaging illusions of the materialist vision is the sense that the present moment is merely the necessary connection, occupied momentarily, between the causal past and the resulting future. For instance: Genesis—4004 BC for Bishop Usher, or ten billion years ago if you are Stephen Hawking. Both stories are identical in essentials. What follows Creation is the history of matter in space: furniture rearranging on a cosmic scale, punctuated for the bishop by the occasional miracle.

On the mythic view, or the psychic view, shared with many mystics, Creation is continuous. Jung writes, "The psyche creates reality every day."[10] But this psyche is not localized inside our heads. Rather, we exist in it. The present moment is pregnant with creation. The soul of this world we experience through a sense of interiority, as the availability of the world to imagination, as a kind of reciprocal imaginative interaction, a sympathy between self and world. We move here in a different space. This is not the universe of matter; it is more nearly a cosmos of qualities, presences, and harmonies. This present is not transitory. It is not going anywhere. We are close to the origin here, close to the primordial distinctions. Space itself is substantial, qualitative, generative.

In the *Timaeus* Plato speaks of that out of which all things are generated: the nurse, the receptacle "that we may liken to a mother" or a womb, "that partakes of the intelligible [but] is yet most incomprehensible." Timaeus says: "[O]f this receptacle and nurse of all creation we have only this dream-like sense, being unable to cast off sleep and determine the truth about it." It exists only as "an ever-fleeting shadow." Ivan Illich comments: "In these delightful lines Plato still speaks of the image-pregnant stuff of dreams and imagination, as one who still has the experience of living in precategorical, founded space."[11] That is, in the space of the extensive self, the pre-Cartesian, pre-Newtonian space of qualities.

Matter and space are generated together. Plato's phenomenology of creation situates us in the present of myth. As Patricia Berry has written, matter, so conceived, is both the most concrete and the most lacking.[12] We uncover here in mythic space, in psyche, the primal conjunction of the concrete and the uncertain; the fecundity of the void. It is just here, at this origin, where mystery and certainty coincide, where the waters and the earth divide, where the symmetries are broken and the metaphoric and the literal separate, where we cannot keep our balance—it is here, in the realm of the inhuman, both divine and demonic, where meaning is born. This is the *mundus imaginalis*.

And we *cannot* keep our balance. Myth gives way to Reason. Revelation to Orthodoxy. We must dance or go mad.

And here then is where empiricism must begin. This empiricism demands an attention and a sensibility for subtleties that we have largely lost. It demands a sense for qualitative spaces, not quantitative; for presences, not motions; for forms, not explanations. This participatory empiricism is based on *pathos*. It reveals the world of Corbin's Creative Imagination, Blake's Jesus the Imagination, Coleridge's Primary Imagination.

The multiple levels of attention called for are requisites for us to know where we are and who we are. But such attention is not easy. In our anesthetized, rationalized age we tend to assume that knowledge just lies out there waiting for someone to "access it." Our democratic ideals tend to become muddled with notions of knowledge as commodity or as information. But we are a long way from capitalist or digital metaphors here.

And also, this empiricism is not particularly "safe." There are mirages and illusions and demons here. Henry Corbin has said that the imaginary can be innocuous, but the imaginal never is. But materialist empiricism is if anything more dangerous, because it pretends to be safe, controlling. It is the world that is not safe. In any case, we have come to the end of materialism. We have no more places in which to dwell, only spaces in which to move.

Ivan Illich calls the modern space of highways, urban sprawl, and daily life "indiscrete, homogeneous, commercial space; bulldozed space." He says: "In this bulldozed space people can be located and given an address, but they cannot dwell. Their desire to dwell is a nightmare." He goes on to relate a tale from Italo Calvino's *Invisible Cities:*

> [Calvino] tells of Marco Polo's visit to the court of Kublai Khan. Polo tells his host about the stuff of the towns through which his imagined travels have led him. Calvino has Marco Polo describe the sickening helplessness that he experiences as a man accustomed to traveling in three dimensional space, when led through dreams of cities, each generated by a different "stuff." Polo reports to the Khan on dreams of space with a pervasive taste of "longing," on space made up of eyes, of granular space that jells into "names," of space that is made up of "the dead," space that constantly smells of "exchanges," or "innovation." Marco Polo reports on these nightmares for the benefit of the host and ends with the following entry: "Hell—if there be such a thing—is not tomorrow. Hell is right here, and today we live in it; together we make it up. There are only two ways to avoid suffering in this Hell. The first way out is easy for most people: Let Hell be, live it up, and stop noticing it. The second way is risky. It demands constant attentive curiosity to find out who and what in the midst of this Hell is not part of it, so as to make it last by giving space to it.[13]

Illich concludes: "Only those who recognize the nightmare of non-discrete space can regain the certainty of their own intimacy and thereby dwell in the presence of one another."[14]

Aristotle accused Plato of confusing space and matter.[15] I want to persist in that confusion, and engage in what Giambattista Vico called "imaginative metaphysics." In the *New Science* Vico writes, "As rational metaphysics teaches that man becomes all things by understanding them, imaginative metaphysics shows that man becomes all things by not understanding them, for when . . . he does not understand he . . . becomes them by transforming himself into them."[16]

Consider the following triad of First Principles: Mythos, Topos, Logos. Mythos: The function of myth is to open, to reveal depth, complexity, mystery, and enigma, and the connections to the nonhuman. Topos: Place. The pre-Socratics associated any kind of being with spatial existence—all being has place. Logos: This is speech, a rational account, a true account, distinguished from myth.

Myths, or mythic moves, open spaces. Rational accounts limit them. This is necessary. Both are necessary. But we live after the Enlightenment. We live amidst the wreckage of the split between the Rational and the Irrational. When Reason is your God, the repressed returns, monstrous, titanic. The wreckage of Reason, its burned-out skeleton, is the logical device: rubber bands and paper clips.

And education. We go to school to learn about the world. And we do, most of us. We learn the world we have made. The burgeoning industries based on virtual reality merely make explicit, and are the logical extensions of an education based on technique, on public reason, on orthodoxy. Virtual realities are realities without the gods, without the transhuman—realities based on illusions of human power and control. Socrates saw it coming: The rise of literacy would mean the end of education—people would stop thinking, *memoria* would fade, dialogue would wither.

It has been a long time since most of us have experienced the world. We experience instead a constriction, a selection. We step cautiously out, checking our selves at first, against What Is Allowed, What Is Known To Be True. We constantly throw a world out ahead of ourselves and move safely into it. Heidegger calls this "enframing."[17] We are weak creatures and we soon forget we are doing it. The poet Robert Duncan is strong here:

> Modern man . . . has erected an education of sensibility, class spirit or team spirit, argument and rationalization, designed to establish himself in a self-protective world of facts and problems stripped of their sympathies, in the real business of making money, serving and protecting the system of private property and capital or public property and capital, and exploiting the profitable waste, substituting his own person for soul, until the whole bag of swollen vulture's wind and meat threatens to consume our lives.[18]

Almost without exception education as we have come to know it makes this worse. "We know how things are and we will tell you." Knowledge crushes down, suffocating. To relieve the suffering and make it easy and fun, we let machines distract us and dominate the process. This is the world we are educated into. We have come to accept education not as initiation into mystery, but as training and as technique. If we learn this way, if we live this way, our lives have been lived already, and as we move we are merely occupying spaces laid out for us in advance. Merely rearranging the furniture. And living this way, we think we are empiricists, pragmatists, hard-headed realists. When in truth we completely ignore an enormous range of potential experience, to the point that most of us are insensate and numb most of the time.

The world *is* too much for us. Rationality as we have come to know it works by ignoring most of experience: laws are arrived at by selective abstraction. The optimal number of variables must be small . . . ignoring friction . . . ignoring the observer . . . under ideal conditions . . . Newtonian fluids that don't exist . . . in the absence of perturbation . . . and so on and on.

James Hillman draws our attention to an idea from Jewish mysticism: *tsim tsum,* Retreat, Withdrawal. "Since God is everywhere, the existence of the universe is made possible by a process of shrinking in God. . . . God crowds out all other kinds of existence. He must pull back for the Creation to come into being. Only by withdrawal does God allow the world."[19] Our move has been to take that creation and constrict it still further until it is almost not there at all. And we call that understanding. As Hillman suggests, the proper move for us might mean letting the creation expand, letting genesis occur by moving out of the way. Withdrawing our human control and letting the world shine forth. Creation by retreat.

It is the mythic experience, the mythic imagination that opens, reveals depth and mystery, which places the human in the context of the nonhuman, and so, *forces* retreat, humility, and awe, in the presence of spaces beyond our will.

I want to make a gesture now in the direction of that source in which lies the origin of the three categories in our imaginative metaphysics: mythos, topos, logos. Our myths and our spaces with the matter they generate, and our language, all are created together. When our connections with mythic, symbolic imagination are constricted, so are our spaces featureless, our matter dead, and our speech empty.

In trying to reimagine, to move toward a connection, a participation in the world that we have lost, being the kind of person I am, I want to talk about Thinking. Someone else might speak more easily of Dancing, or Loving, or Prayer.

Imagine that thinking, dancing, loving, and praying are primary forms of life; that each provides access to nonhuman realms by allowing openings to appear in our virtual realities, by allowing withdrawal, retreat, of the intensive self. We conceive of thinking as subjective, internal, in our heads; it depends for us on human meanings in languages that we make up. It is abstract. And too, ideas are not really real—everyone knows that intellectuals don't live in the real world. Idealism versus Realism. And as we have seen, increasingly ideas are held to be "nothing but" neurophysiology, or preferably, in a cleaner world, the logical physiology of the digital device, for which the matter doesn't matter.

Our thought, whatever else it may be, is always, also defensive. Robert Duncan again:

> Wherever life is true to what mythologically we know life to be, it comes full of awe, awe-full. . . . The shaman and the inspired poet, who take the universe to be alive, are brothers germane of the mystic and the paranoiac. We at once seek a meaningful life and dread psychosis, "the principle of life."[20]

We have found our way into a closed world and mistaken it for the infinite universe. We do not know our place, and we do not know our peril.

What manner of thinking is appropriate to our place? Imagine this: We don't "have" ideas—we do not make them up. *They* come to *us*. And we struggle with language to hold them, to make them keep still—but we manage to capture only fragments—they are from other places, not here. We are not attuned to them. We try to "think" them. We don't try to dance them, love them, befriend them, or move into the worlds they portend. Hillman says that ideas are gods. I prefer to say that ideas are openings onto other worlds, tangential to ours. They demand the attention of the whole person; they demand attention to subtleties we have almost wholly forgotten.

Henry Corbin, in his presentation of the doctrine of continuous creation in Ibn 'Arabi, writes that the divine descent into the forms of creation never ceases, nor does their simultaneous rise. There is a twofold intradivine movement of Epiphany and Return. He writes, "That is why the other world already exists in this world; it exists in every moment in relation to every being."[21] Corbin recounts a conversation with D. T. Suzuki, the Zen Buddhist: "I can still see Suzuki suddenly brandishing a spoon and saying with a smile 'This spoon *now* exists in Paradise. . . . We are *now* in Heaven."[22]

Jung tells of a conversation he had in 1925 with the chief of the Taos Pueblo in northern New Mexico. Ochwiay Biano is talking to Jung about the strange Europeans who have come west into his world. He says:

> See how cruel the whites look. Their lips are thin, their noses sharp, their faces furrowed and distorted by folds. Their eyes have a staring expression; they are always seeking something. What are they seeking? The whites always want something; they are always uneasy and restless. We do not know what they want. We do not understand them. We think that they are mad.

Jung continues:

> I asked him why they thought the whites were all mad. "They say that they think with their heads," he replied. "Why of course. What do you think with?" I asked him in surprise. "We think here," he said, indicating his heart.[23]

TWO

CONSUMING PASSIONS

The Poet, The Feast,
and the Science of the Balance

It seems to me that our three basic needs, for food, security and love, are so mixed and mingled and entwined that we cannot straightly think of one without the other.

—M. F. K. Fisher, *The Art of Eating*

A HALF-OPEN BEING

SOMETIMES WE ARE enveloped by the sudden Dark, and plunge without any warning, helpless and abandoned in a desolate space. When that dark night comes, it is almost impossible to resist walling ourselves off from the threat. But we have to do just that, because if we erect the wall we lose not only our souls but the Soul of the World as well. The darknesses of the fall must not be denied; they have to be passed through and they have to pass through us. The more adamant and unyielding the resistance, the more implacable and irresistible is the Dark. We must not petrify. We have to try to do the most difficult thing: become transparent and protean, like water. Hear these lines from the Qur'an:

> . . . among rocks are those from which rivers flow
> and there are also those which split open and water gushes forth
> as well as those that roll down for fear of God.[1]

If an entire culture hardens into dogma and fundamentalism, and persists in fending off this Dark, then it risks success: it can see only in a light of its own making. If that happens the people lose contact with the mysteries, and live impoverished, claustrophobic, and fearful in an entirely human world.

Everything human exists within the realm of the more-than-human. We are limited and bounded by it necessarily. When we no longer feel the thickness of the dark beyond, when we cannot sense the presence of something alien, vast, and Other just beyond our reach, then, just where we feel secure, we truly are cut off, lost in a universe of our own making, and the forces of the Dark take us unaware. We must manage somehow to open to the darkness, because the substance of the world, the true shape of things, can only be perceived among the shadows. But we are afraid. And yet we know that the merely human world is far too small for us. We yearn for more: more light, more space, more money, more stuff . . . more *life*.

We are caught between a rock and a hard place. Gaston Bachelard has suggested an image that captures our predicament, one that is perhaps more useful than Heidegger's intuition that we are "there" in the open. We are, Bachelard says, a half-open being.[2] We are always on a threshold; perhaps we even *are* a threshold. We are balanced between the open and the closed, the inner and the outer. This is written in our every breath, in every beat of the heart, in the stops and breathings of every word we speak. Each moment we press against immensities that press quietly back. We stand on the margin between the human and the nonhuman, always on the edge.

All our openings and closings, all the beings that we pass through and that pass through us, are gathered together in a single momentous event that is rapidly losing its essential function in our culture. The fundamental event of human-being is The Feast. Through it we daily reenact the primordial encounter of inner and outer, where the self meets the other. It is the alchemical event par excellence, in which the substance of things is internalized and transformed. It constitutes our primary engagement with the world.

THE HEARTH

A feast requires a place in which all the elements can unfold. The fire, the foods, the spices, the smells and sounds coming from the pots, the conversation, boisterous or subdued—all in their unique living intensities. A proper place allows this; a wrong one reduces it to a vapid "atmosphere." Every true hearth is unique, often ephemeral, and never reducible to physical location.

We are losing our ability to recognize or participate in the birth of such living places. Our forms of life are becoming incapable of creating them. The world is dominated by digital technologies, fantasies of frictionless markets, global villages, transnational economies: all the old boundaries are gone, the new ones demolished as soon as they appear. We are dominated it seems, by Hermes, god of boundaries and their violation, of communication, of language

and lies and the flash of inspiration. He is the god of the open road, of jour-
neys, of twisting passages, of motion. He is our disease. He eats on the run, at
Quik-stops everywhere. There is no time for slow cooking, for digestion, and
assimilation. Hermes is always grinning, always on a sugar-high.

In contrast is Hestia, goddess of the Hearth. Excerpts from several
sources gathered in a recent piece by James Hillman will help to fix her in
the imagination:[3]

> She was the first of all immortals to be honored in libations and proces-
> sions. . . . As we say "Cheers!" . . . the Romans said "Vesta!" She was the glow-
> ing, warmth-emitting hearth. That is her image, her locus, her embodi-
> ment. . . . Ovid speaks of Hestia as "nothing but a living flame."[4]

She represents sustenance, nourishment, and feeding the soul, and she is indispensable for the feast:

> [The] "only actual service performed in her honor . . . appears to have been
> a family meal." "Without her humans would have no feasts." "She presides
> over the famous progress of the raw to the cooked, transforming nature
> into food."[5]

Hestia provides the fixed point where all the forces of life can come into focus:

> She is "a potent presence, not a personal individual." "She indicates no move-
> ment" and "does not leave her place. We must go to her." "She is always seated
> on circular elements, just as the places where she is worshipped are circular."
> "To her is attributed the invention of domestic architecture."[6]

But Hestia's realm is not, as we might expect, solitary:

> "With Hestia, we are in the collective domain." She is "the center of the *oikos,*
> which does mean residence and abode, but at the same time also means set-
> tlement on urban territory and agglomeration. Hestia is represented as sitting
> on the *omphalos* or navel of the city."[7]

This connection of Hestia with *oikos,* the etymological root of both "ecology" and "economy," locates both of these together in the domain of the inter-
personal. The economy of the hearth connects us to the world through the others we encounter there. The common meal is "the primary civilizing act,"[8] and
Hestia's realm is the communal, the convivial. Hillman writes, " "[E]ating out
on the run" may do more to violate Hestia and harm the hearth of soul than
all the other proposed causes of family dysfunction. . . ."[9] The architect Christopher Alexander and his colleagues simply say, "Without communal eating, no
human group can hold together."[10] They cite Thomas Merton:

> The mere act of eating together . . . is by its very nature an act of friendship
> and of "communion." . . . To call a feast a *"convivium"* is to call it a "mystery

of the sharing of life"—a mystery . . . in which the atmosphere of friendship and gratitude expands into a sharing of thoughts and sentiments, and ends in common rejoicing.[11]

The power of Hestia creates a *social place,* but it is not a *public space,* not indiscriminately laid bare. The door is only half open. In the primordial social gathering, conversation is fundamental. One meaning of *converse* is "living or being in a place, among persons."[12] The interplay between revealing and concealing that gives life to dialogue is as much a part of the *convivium* as the enclosing and welcoming focus of the central fire. The hearth is the enclosure that shelters and enables both the Feast and the Word, and in so doing, mirrors the half-open essence of our being.

FOOD

The centerpiece is the meal itself in all its sensuous, substantial variety. Philosopher and ecologist Paul Shepard writes that throughout the course of the evolution of animals "food has been a basic generator of consciousness and qualities of mind,"[13] and that the "alimentary tract [provides] our principal encounter with the world."[14] Among the myriad animals of the world, "elaborate systems [of] teeth, tongues, stomachs . . . specialized food habits, all become . . . united in an elaborated assimilation of the world."[15] In bilaterally symmetrical animals like us, "one's brain [is] near where one's mouth is, and for us speakers, vice versa, extending the principal of nutrition to a kenning or knowing."[16]

Our eating of the world, its passage through our half-open bodies, is our fundamental act, and immerses us in a cycle of consuming and being consumed that is as archetypal and as subject to the influence of the *numinosum* as any other aspect of our being. The act of feasting is sacrifice, transformation, and encounter all in one. And this is true from the point of view of the consumed as well as the consumer. Shepard writes:

[T]he teeth of the predator may be painless for the prey because of brain-made endorphins, so that death may be euphoric, even a kind of epiphany.[17]

The sensuous richness of food connects us with the dark, unknowable source of all things. One of the epithets of Hades, god of the underworld, is "the hospitable." He too, is present at every feast.[18] But Hades is also Pluto, whose cornucopia spills over with riches and nourishment.[19]

The fruits of darkness rising from the earth provide the focus for our connection with the material and the maternal. Eating is a rite of coagulation, bringing us to earth, grounding and moistening our souls. At the same time food and all the rituals associated with it are replete with the powers of the imaginal, the sparks and flames that set the world in motion and give it life. Christopher Alexander relates the following exquisite anecdote:

I remember once, sitting in Berkeley, trying to work out a site plan on paper, for our houses in Peru. One of the . . . roads into the site was not yet properly in place . . . so I decided to take a walk around the site in my imagination.

I sat in my chair, in Berkeley, 8000 miles from the real site in Lima, closed my eyes, and began to take a walk around the market. There were many narrow lanes, covered with bamboo screens to shade them, with tiny stalls opening off them, and fruit sellers selling fruit from carts. I stopped by one old woman's cart, and bought an orange from her. As I stood there, I happened to be facing north. And then I bit into the orange. . . . And just as I bit into it, I suddenly stopped and asked myself, "Now, where is that road?" And without thinking, I knew exactly where it was, and what its relation to the market was—I knew it must be over there towards the right. . . . I knew that to be natural. . . .

It was the vividness of being there, and biting into that orange, that allowed me to know, spontaneously, the most natural place for that road to be.[20]

Food is magic and mystery. This should be obvious, but it isn't any longer for us. This is not the place to describe the multiple disasters of industrial food production, but we should note that our distance from our food is one measure of our inability to feast. Wendell Berry, always eloquent on the spirituality of food, writes:

Eating with the fullest pleasure—pleasure, that is, that does not depend on ignorance—is perhaps the profoundest enactment of our connection with the world. In this pleasure we experience and celebrate our dependence and our gratitude, for we are living from mystery, from creatures we did not make and powers we cannot comprehend. When I think of the meaning of food, I always remember these lines by the poet William Carlos Williams, which seem to me to be merely honest:

> There is nothing to eat,
>   seek it where you will,
>   but the body of the Lord.
> The blessed plants
>   and the sea, yield it
>   to the imagination
>   intact.[21]

THE SCIENCE OF THE BALANCE
AND THE MYSTIC SUPPER

The world as the body of the Lord yields itself as food to the imagination. That is how we survive. Hillman says that the *anima mundi,* the soul of the world, *is* the availability of the world to the imagination.[22] We are connected to the world in no other way. The literal, the factual, the rock bottom truth—these are all themselves modes of the imagination. We are always in psyche. Henry Corbin writes: "[T]here is no pure physics, but always the physics of some definite psychic activity."[23]

Recognizing this, we can interpret the world as we interpret dreams, words, images. This is not a step into some New Age paradise. There are requirements and demands of psyche that must be imagined as literally as the laws of physics. There are consequences; there are demons as well as angels. What we must see is that we cannot reduce the world to the literal; we live within a vastly larger universe. The literal is one necessary form of life, one form of imagination among others.

If the world yields itself to the imagination, then it is through the imagination that we are open to the body of the Lord. The world must be imaginalized, must be interpreted along with the soul. In mystical Shi'ite Islam this interpretation is called *ta'wil*—it is the Science of the Balance that is required to maintain the equilibrium between the visible and the invisible worlds. There are balances for all the kinds of beings in the world. This science is practiced by the alchemists, the astrologers, and by the hermeneuts of the Word. If the balance between the material and the spiritual worlds is not maintained, they get out of joint, and catastrophe results. For Corbin it was clear that the modern West is the result of such a catastrophe. We have lost the imaginal, and so the *anima mundi* and the animation in our souls. We think that there *is* a pure physics, and we can no longer see archetypal figures in the patterns of the stars. The science of the balance depends upon what Corbin calls the "interiorization" of the literal, material world, transforming astronomy into astrology, chemistry and metallurgy into alchemy, and the literal text of the Book into the Living Word in the human soul.[24]

In his great work on Ibn 'Arabi, Corbin writes of the cosmic sympathy that underlies and makes possible these sciences of the Balance, and the interpretation, the *ta'wil,* that is their method. The act of creation is not an act of omnipotence creating by *Fiat!* a world inferior to and external to the Creator. Rather, the Sufis cite the divine saying: "I was a Hidden Treasure and I yearned to be known. Then I created creatures in order to be known by them." "This divine passion . . . is the motive underlying . . . an eternal cosmogony."[25] And at the very heart of this is a Mystic Supper.

The unrevealed God experiences anguish in his unknownness and occultation,

> And from the inscrutable depths of the Godhead this sadness calls for a "Sigh of Compassion." This Sigh marks the release of the divine Sadness *sym-pathiz-ing* with the anguish and sadness of His divine names that have remained unknown, and in this very act of release the Breath exhales, arouses to active being, the multitude of individual concrete existences by and for which these divine names are at last actively manifested[26]

There is an eternal bond of sympathy between the creator and the creatures: the Breath gives actuality to the virtual being of the creatures, raising them from the unknown and unknowing hiddenness, and the passionate yearning of the creatures for their Lord itself gives voice to that very Breath. No creature is alone, abandoned into itself. The secret of existence is that at the heart of ourselves lies our Lord. Our actions in prayer are His passions acting through us:

> [T]he active subject is in reality not you, your autonomy is a fiction. In reality, you are the subject of a verb in the passive (you are the *ego* of a *cogitor*).[27]

But, Corbin continues, because these emancipated beings are this compassion itself,

> the Compassion does not move only in the direction from the Creator to the creature whom he feeds with his existentiating Breath; it also moves from the creature towards the Creator. . . .[28]

The emancipating Breath, which releases beings from their Hidden virtuality, initiates the *convivium* of the Eternal Feast because it is the sustenance of their being, without which they would fall back into the darkness of the *Deus absconditum* from whom they flow. And so

> to nourish all creatures with Divine Being is at the same time to nourish this [pathetic] God through and with all the determinations of being, through and with His own theophanies.[29]

The mystic task is to "preside over this mystic Supper at which all beings feed on the pre-eternal sympathy of their being." It is incumbent on the mystic to "feed God or His Angel on His creatures," which is at the same time "to feed the creatures on God."[30] This is the true meaning of the episode in Genesis that Christianity calls the Philoxeny of Abraham.[31] The interpretation of Creation that Corbin offers gives to this story the central importance that it has had in the iconography of the Eastern Orthodox Church. Abraham's spontaneous hospitality to the three mysterious angelic Strangers appearing at his door signifies this communal Supper at which all creatures must feed together in the presence of their Lord.[32]

TURNING INSIDE OUT:
CONSUMING AND BEING CONSUMED

Interiorization turns a catastrophically defaced world inside out in a process that results in the birth of the soul into its proper home. This difficult passage turns the world right side out—the soul is no longer trapped in the crypt of the literal, material world. The full immensity of Creation opens out to reveal what Ibn 'Arabi called the "ocean without a shore."

To appreciate the meaning of this, we must be quite clear about what interiorization means. We are heirs to a tradition that makes a radical distinction between the inner and the outer in a way that forces misunderstanding. Some have traced our modern sense of the isolated ego pitted against an alien and external world to Descartes and his *"cogito ergo sum."* Corbin and others prefer to see the prime moment of disjunction in the twelfth century, as we have seen. In any case it is an archetypal break—it happens in all of us sooner or later, to one degree or another. In our culture it is so much a part of us that we do not readily see it at all.

We can distinguish two kinds of interiorizing: the Devouring and the Convivial. The former is characteristic of the solitary ego regarding the world as alien and external. Its approach to the world is confrontational and defensive. This ego imagines that its imagination of what constitutes the literal is the one and only truth. It is monolithic in style because the Other is threatening and must be denied autonomy. The characteristic approach to the Other is objective Understanding—whether dogmatically nonrational (religion) or dogmatically rational (science). In either case the goal is to *know,* because what I know is no longer Other, it is part of *Me.* This drive to know, to dominate and deny the autonomy of the Other, to Devour the world, is insatiable. And this for two reasons: it is based on Fear and so can never rest; and, all this devouring gives no sustenance because there is no *sympatheia,* no connection to the source of nourishment, no possibility of feeding the soul from the soul of the world. The devouring ego drains everything it touches, and, closed in upon itself, it never empties, holding desperately onto its own waste, trying hopelessly to eat the universe. Its mode of growth is, of course, Inflation.

But there is another kind of interiorizing, and it is this to which Corbin points. A turn to the imaginal need not be experienced as a retreat inward, into the interior, to what belongs to me. Psyche is not private. But neither is it "public" in the sense of impersonal, objective, soulless. Psyche is communal. But true community transcends any boundaries between the inner and the outer, the public and the private. Community only exists among persons, and persons can only be perceived, perhaps they can only exist, when the walls dividing the inner from the outer begin to crumble. Only when we begin to hear the voices inside can we begin to listen to the voices outside. Then the boundary between what is mine and inside, and what is Other and outside grows ambiguous and unclear. We find ourselves immersed in the *convivium,* in community. We meet the Other as Other, in fear and respect. This experience is open, embodied, and mysterious. We are in company. In sympathy with the plants and the sea, and with all the persons of the world, both within and without. To receive, we must give. To be fed, we must feed. To consume we must be consumed. To live, we must die. To assimilate, we must transform—die, empty, and release—letting go of what we defend, of what we fear, of what we hide. This growth is cyclic, not inflationary. The motion of the soul is circular, says Plotinus. Death, decay, and the filth of our lowest deeds and thoughts—all passed through, and so transformed. The food of the gods comes only from ground made fertile by our own dyings.

This community of Others is the communion of the Feast and it requires the death, again and again and again, of the ever desperate ego, which can never believe that this is the only way to feed the soul. This is why no human group can survive without communal eating: only community can prevent the fission of that group into atomic, isolated egos.

WITH SYMPATHY FOR THE VOICES

How do we avoid degenerating into a mob of egos consuming, and become a *convivium,* Feasting? Is it possible to recreate the primordial union of Food, Breath, and Word, and experience that Breath that is both sustenance and voice?

One path would begin with the reimagination of the word. We can imagine words as we must our guests: as autonomous presences. Hillman writes:

> [W]ords, too, burn and become flesh as we speak. . . . A new angelology of words is needed so that we may once again have faith in them. Without the inherence of the angel in the world—and angel means originally "emissary," "message bearer"—how can we utter anything but personal opinions, things made up in our subjective minds? . . . Words, like angels, are powers which have invisible power over us. . . . For words are persons . . . [and as such they] act upon us as complexes and release complexes in us.[33]

This will seem strange, as long as we pretend to believe that the function of words is to "convey information." In literate societies words are regarded as tokens "standing for" that to which they "refer." Thus, we act as if a computer is no different from an ink pen: each is a tool for the production of Text. By extension, I suppose that the spoken word is informal Text. An arbitrary token that can be Cut, Copied, Pasted, Spoken, or Not Spoken, such a marker is hard to conceive of as a Person, let alone an Angel. On the other hand, perhaps this tells us just how we do conceive of Persons and Angels. There is no contemporary theory of meaning that can take Hillman's suggestion seriously at all. It is merely silly, at best. It is among the poets that you will find supporters of this view. And among the consciously neurotic, and among the psychotic. These are the persons who are sensitive to the feeling-toned complexes that are carried by words, who can still attend to the aura surrounding them. Text is bodiless; the written trace is an arbitrary sign. Words as persons have substance and body and presence: they must be breathed, they must be spoken, they must be heard. Oral cultures are open to this to an extent to which literate ones are not.

The world of Corbin's Islamic mystics is a profoundly oral one, as was the world of the biblical Jews. The experience of the Word and of the world that underlies the mystic Supper is wholly unlike that open to a modern reader of a Text. Seyyed Hossein Nasr writes,

> The whole experience of the Qur'an for Muslims remains to this day first of all an auditory experience and is only later associated with reading in the ordinary sense of the word. . . . [T]he oral dimension of the Qur'anic reality, combined with the traditional significance of memory in the transmission of knowledge, could not but affect the whole of the Islamic intellectual tradition. . . .[34]

In this tradition, the Word and the spiritual knowledge which it imparts are profoundly personal. Oral transmission from master to student is essential, and depends upon a vertical and nonhistorical connection to the metaphysical source of knowledge. Mere "book learning" cannot supplant the living presence of the teacher. Corbin writes, "There are living souls which, by the *energeia* of their love, communicate life to everything that comes to them."[35] This life and the knowledge that is its fruit can come only to those who have had a second birth. Traditional philosophical knowledge can only be transmitted on condition of that rebirth; "failing that it would be merely a handing over of baggage from one dead soul to another."[36]

How can we prevent our language from becoming a text that only transfers information among dead souls? By keeping alive everything in our tradition that links us to the Breath and the sustenance of the Original Convivium. We must take our stand among the poets. They say:

> The only war that matters is the war against the imagination.—Diane
> di Prima
> The universe is made of stories, not of atoms.—Muriel Rukeyser
> I don't see with my eyes. Words are my eyes.—Octavio Paz
> What can be seen is at stake.—H. D.[37]

In this quest to reestablish the primordial connection of word, breath, and body, it will be useful to consider the history of words and reading in Western culture.

Our modern kind of reading, silent, internalized and "bookish," was born along with the subjective self sometime during the twelfth century. At least this is the view of a number of scholars and historians, Ivan Illich among them. He explores the birth of this new sense of the self and of the text in his study of Hugh of St. Victor.[38] Illich says that Hugh stands at the threshold between a still largely oral and embodied "monastic" style of reading and the internalized, more abstract "scholastic" reading that followed.

What was read, the Text, was of course Scripture. Nothing else was worth reading, yet. And "study" itself, *studium,* was based upon sympathy and desire, and had as its goal not learning, but the transformation of the soul. Illich writes,

"Studies pursued in a twelfth century cloister challenged the student's heart and senses even more than his stamina and brains."[39] What the student was seeking was the illumination of wisdom: "The light of which Hugh speaks brings man to a glow."[40] "Wisdom is above all in the heart. But it is also in the object."[41] And here the object is the book:

> The translucent sheep- or goatskin was covered with manuscript and brought to life by miniatures painted with thin brushes. The form of Perfect Wisdom could shine through these skins, bring letters and symbols to light, and kindle the eye of the reader. To face a book was comparable to the experience one can relive early in the morning in those Gothic churches in which the original windows have been preserved.[42]

Reading was a spiritual discipline. Illich says, "Reading, as Hugh perceives and interprets it, is an ontologically remedial technique."[43] It engaged the entire person, not just what we have come to experience as "the mind":

Reading is experienced by Hugh as a bodily motor activity.

> In a tradition of one and a half millennia, the sounding pages are echoed by the resonance of the moving lips and tongue. . . . [T]he sequence of letters translates directly into body movements and nerve impulses. . . . By reading, the page is literally embodied, incorporated.[44]

Monastic reading was a carnal activity:

> [T]he reader understands the lines by moving to their beat, remembers them by recapturing their rhythm, and thinks of them in terms of putting them into his mouth and chewing.[45]

Illich recounts a number of characteristic instances of words experienced as food, culminating in this marvelous passage:

> Speaking about the words of the Canticle of Canticles, [St.] Bernard . . . says "Enjoying their sweetness, I chew them over and over, my internal organs are replenished, my insides are fattened up, and all my bones break out in praise."[46]

Oral reading "reverberated in all the senses," and taste and smell, which were not clearly distinguished, "were . . . vividly expressed, to describe emotions felt while thinking with affection [sympathy] or during meditative reading."[47] So carnal was the experience that "Hellenistic physicians prescribed reading as an alternative to ball playing or a walk."[48]

As we descend from an abstract textual experience of the word and the book into an embodied one, we find the person who speaks, the body that does the speaking, and also, the breath. David Abram follows Illich, Parry, Ong, and others in their analysis of the effects of alphabetic literacy on our experience of the world and of ourselves. The original Semitic alphabet shared today by both Arabic and Hebrew, had no written vowels. Only the stops. Not the breathings.

The absent vowels "are nothing other than sounded breath. And the breath, for the ancient Semites, was the very mystery of life and awareness, a mystery inseparable from the invisible . . . holy wind or spirit."[49] To read, aloud of course, requires the active physical participation of the reader, putting his breath, his spirit into the words to bring them to life. The breath of the reader is the breath of the Lord moving over the face of the deep. Reading in this sense ensures a cosmic sympathy among the reader, the Lord, and all the animate, windy world. But more than this is involved:

> [T]he reader of a traditional Hebrew text had to actively *choose* the appropriate breath sounds or vowels, yet different vowels would often vary the meaning of the written consonants. . . .
>
> The traditional Hebrew text, in other worlds, overtly demanded the reader's conscious participation. The text was never complete in itself; it had to be actively engaged by a reader who, by this engagement, gave rise to a particular reading . . . and there was no single, definitive meaning; the ambiguity entailed by lack of written vowels ensured that diverse readings, diverse shades of meaning, were always possible.[50]

This kind of reading is hermeneutic in the true sense: passionate, engaged, embodied, and personal. And it is here, in this living interpretation that the life and fundamental plurality of the Word is guaranteed. It is just this that prevents what Corbin calls the sin of metaphysical idolatry, which consists in worshipping a finite, literal being, a being without transcendence, without Breath, without Life.

In Western culture none of this was to last. We can no longer hear or speak words this way. We do not taste them or perceive their complex sensuous auras, or feel our way among the complexes that they carry. The alphabet coagulated, fixing the meaning of the literal, canonical text. The passionate, breathing reader receded, displaced by the rational mind searching for a changeless, impersonal Truth. Our soul withdrew to reside finally, Descartes tells us, in the pineal gland, for lack of suitable habitat elsewhere. The Breath of the Lord animating all things became merely air, and even that Presence withdrew into the darkness beyond the impersonal stars, retreating into the sadness from which it emerged, retreating from a lifeless universe. The Creative God known in and through the multiple theophanies of an infinite Creation, became either the literal God, constrained by the dogmas in the rigid souls of the Faithful, or the Dead God, the Hidden God, withdrawn beyond all human contact.

But all of that teeming, archaic, sensuous reality is still there, awaiting resurrection.

DESCENT OF THE GODS: STRANGERS AT THE DOOR

Our culture has been engaged for a long time in chasing after that receding Divinity. That is the source of our pathologies of motion, and emotion, our restlessness, our drive. We are always rushing somewhere else, to some other, better world. We are uncomfortable here, in this complex, confusing, plural mess. We want out. Escape. Speed. Distraction. Entertainment. Suicide. Our desire for escape gets easily confused with spirituality—the desire for Heaven, the other world. This confusion is itself archetypal: but the path to the other world must lead through this one. Our struggle is first and foremost in this world. We cannot escape by ignoring it. Corbin, and many others, say we must be born again, but I think we must be born *in the first place* into *this* world, that we may, perhaps, be born again beyond it.

And to be here, we must descend. This echoes the pattern of creation according to Islamic cosmology: Descent and Return. All beings are continuously and simultaneously ascending towards the One Source and descending into the pluralities of Creation. We have had our attention focused wrongly on only the Ascent. To regain our Balance we must descend. And during this descent the cosmos shatters into a dazzling plurality as the distance from the One increases. So in a sense, we become "pagan," polytheistic, of necessity: it is required for cosmic harmony and balance. This is a part of what Corbin called the "paradox of monotheism": the One God can be known by us only through the revelation of multiple theophanies, only in part, never as the Whole.

To be truly born to this world, we must stay descended for a long while, and resist any temptation to rise to a vision of a higher, simpler, purer state. We may perhaps, some of us, be called to that, but we cannot will it so. Viewing the world this way is a kind of mirror image of the standard Judeo-Christian habit. There are other traditions where the connection to this world is conceived entirely differently. In the tribal cultures of Indonesia, for instance, the function of the shaman-priest is to maintain the balance between the visible and invisible worlds by feeding the spirits of the ancestors, and even the gods themselves. A member of the vaudun religion of Haiti says: "The difference between Haitian gods and white man's gods is that Haitian *loas* must eat."[51] And it is the duty of humans to feed them. In an essay on black music and the blues in America, Stephen Diggs sees this influence of "voodoo" religion in a broader context:

> Where the Northern soul, from shaman to Christian priest, operates dissociatively, leaving the body to travel the spirit world, the African priest, the Hoodoo conjuror, and the bluesmen, ask the *loa* to enter bodies and possess them. It is through this possession that the *loa* is known and expressed.[52]

Diggs follows Michael Ventura in his analysis of the significance of blues, jazz, and soul music in America. Ventura says,

> The history of America is, as much as anything, the history of the American body as it sought to unite with its spirit, with its consciousness, to heal itself and to stand against the enormous forces that work to destroy a Westerner's relation to his, or her, own flesh.[53]

In the words of James Cone, the blues, and by extension, black music as whole is "an artistic rebellion against the humiliating deadness of western culture."[54]

It is not quite right then to say that it is we who must descend. We must notice, accept, and celebrate the descent of the gods, the angels, themselves. It is the descent of these spirits that wakens the dead. In Haitian vaudun, as in early Christianity, "the high gods enter by the back door and abide in the servant's lodge."[55] Jung was fond of quoting the Oracle at Delphi: Invited or not, the god will be there. But it depends upon us as to whether the Visitors are welcomed, or even noticed at all.

And so we come again to the Feast as that primary act of Welcome upon which depends our multiple births. First, into this world, and only then perhaps, beyond it, into others. We could clearly speak of music of all sorts as a primary metaphysical factor in our lives, but here I would rather include it with poetry and the arts under the heading of *poiesis*. The poetic is, in the words of George Steiner, what relates "us most directly to that in being which is not ours."[56] Steiner contends that there can be no meaning whatever, whether literal, musical, poetic or religious, without the "axiom of dialogue," the passionate imagination of connections between ourselves and those "real presences" that lie beyond the merely human world.[57]

All poetic acts open onto other worlds. All poetic acts presuppose metaphysical realities. This gets forgotten. Even some of the most radical artists don't know it. The Surrealist Andre Breton wrote:

> The poetic analogy [by which he meant the European surrealist analogy] differs functionally from the mystical analogy in that it does not presuppose, beyond the visible world, an invisible world which is striving to manifest itself. It proceeds in a completely empirical way.[58]

This is scientific empiricism applied to the random assemblages of the surrealists. The African poet, Leopold Senghor, who became president of Senegal, writes that Europeans did not understand African languages or arts because the languages are exceedingly concrete. The words are *concrete* because they "are always pregnant with images." These images themselves are inherently open, and imaginal—they lead beyond: "the African image is not an image by equation but an image by analogy, a surrealist image. . . . The object does not mean what it represents, but what it suggests, what it creates." In sharp contrast to Breton, Senghor writes: "The African surrealist analogy presupposes and manifests the hierarchized universe of life-forces."[59]

In order to avoid both the Realist leveling of the cosmos proposed by literal science or literal religion, and the Surrealist flattening of artistic images, it is necessary to reclaim the concrete by opening to the mystical—only in this way do the images have anywhere to move, any spaces to open onto.

The function of *poiesis*, whether musical, poetic, religious, or scientific, is the creation or revelation of spaces: qualitative, complex and complexified, personified spaces. But we cannot do this on our own. In our current needy condition, we are required to descend, and to welcome the Descent of the Others to allow them to complexify, multiply, and diversify these concrete, feeling-laden worlds. We are at great risk of succumbing to the Single Vision that Blake so feared—at the hands of Scientism, Fundamentalism, Capitalism, all the "-isms." And our response, our duty, is to right the Balance. This requires the democratization, the diversification, and the embodiment of *poiesis*. So, all those politically correct "movements" for the various diversities have a cosmological meaning, a metaphysical grounding: biodiversity, cultural diversity, racial, ethnic, economic, linguistic, sexual, artistic diversities—all serve to breathe life into a world that threatens to choke on Unification.

All our imaginings are necessary. But none of them should be grasped too tightly, none of them should be taken too literally. We need to keep in mind the startling words of the wandering Japanese poet Nanao Sakaki: "No *need* to survive!"[60] No need to hold *anything* too tightly! There are multiple forms of life, a myriad of forms of imagining, all necessary, and each with its own rules and structures, many perhaps more exacting and stringent than those we are accustomed to in physical science.

We must descend fully into the real, messy world, and not stop short of the real individuals who make it up. We get so constricted! So many are afraid to think about the world because only Scientists can do that. So many are afraid of their innate creativity because that is the realm of Artists. But anyone can experience the thrill that accompanies the new ways of seeing that lie at the heart of scientific discovery, anyone can write, or paint, or make music. And yet we mostly don't. Because, "I'm too busy . . . I'm not smart enough, I'm not good enough, I can't really dance, or sing, or write poetry or make pots . . . I'd be too embarrassed." We are haunted by the Canon, by the experts, by the professionals. We are afraid of our selves, afraid that we won't measure up. When great thought, art, and literature become an impediment to human life and action rather than an inspiration, then something is seriously wrong. The democratization of imagination is essential for the full descent into the world of all the virtual beings crying out in their sadness to be revealed.

LIFE ON THE MARGINS, LIFE AMONG THE STARS

The real Hermes, the one that does real work, breaks down barriers all right, but not like a bulldozer, leaving behind an empty, conquered landscape. When this Hermes is at work there is a tinge of real fear in the air, because behind the barriers He dismantles we can see the outlines of the Faces of the Others. Then we must consider the proffered opportunity: whether to accept them into our house, or whether to refuse the Feast.

These Others come to us as persons: mothers, fathers, lovers, strangers; as angels and demons, as complexes and as gods. They all embody and exemplify styles of consciousness, modes of living, ways of being. And it is only by being able to perceive the work of the real Hermes, that we can feel their presences at all. Without this, our worlds are filled with stereotypes, with typologies, with categories, with prejudices, and we never see a real person, never meet any Others at all. Until they break through in madness and misery, violence and destruction.

Jung knew this. And he knew that we harbor their presences inside us, in those innermost depths that can turn inside out, and tumble their contents out headlong into the world. For Jung, as for the alchemists, the actual structure of the psyche is plural, even though its ultimate goal may be unity. The multiple luminosities of those fragments of consciousness that are the archetypes and their associated complexes were known to the alchemists as the *scintillae* or sparks of the world soul, the natural light of the spirit of God in all things. Paracelsus says that this natural light in man comes from the *astrum* or star in man, and that *Astronomia* is the corner stone of all truth and Mother to all the other arts. Man himself is an *astrum* and all the Apostles and the saints, and heaven itself is a star.[61] And this star in man is a source of sustenance for the soul. Paracelsus writes,

> Now as in the star lieth the whole natural light, and from it man taketh the same like food from the earth into which he is born, so too must he be born into the star.[62]

The light of the stars is like the food of the earth, and we must be born into each. Jung comments on these images from the great physician:

> It strikes me as significant, particularly in regard to our hypothesis of a multiple consciousness and its phenomena, that the characteristic alchemical vision of sparks scintillating in the blackness of the arcane substance should, for Paracelsus, change into the spectacle of the "interior firmament" and its stars. He beholds the darksome psyche as a star-strewn night sky, whose planets and fixed constellations represent the archetypes in all their luminosity and numinosity. . . . In this vision astrology and alchemy, the two classical functionaries of the psychology of the collective unconscious, join hands.[63]

The luminosity and numinosity of these sparks signal their autonomy and their power. They are not there to be understood, or mapped, or investigated; they must first of all be greeted, and welcomed, and accepted. Only then can we feed ourselves upon their light, as they feed upon ours. They are not things, they are images. This does not mean they are not exacting, not real, not substantial. It means that our approach to them cannot be literal—it must be hermeneutic. Corbin says that "[t]he alchemist operates—meditates—on metals as the hermeneut practices symbolic exegesis, the *ta'wil* of a text."[64] The same applies to the *Astronomia* of Paracelsus. The interiorization of astronomy which spiritual hermeneutics requires cannot result in a system of laws telling us how the patterns of the stars affect our destinies. That is just another form of genetics, or sociology, or typology, and results in yet another set of laws applied from outside upon our lives. The true interiorization of astronomy opens us to the all too unsettling animation of the presences both within and without. For the ego finds strength in the paradoxical abolition of its own uniqueness, hiding behind the rigid boundaries of an external and literal Law. But far from giving us another set of rules devouring and annihilating our uniqueness, the interiorization that lies at the heart of the birth of the soul opens us to the unavoidable responsibilities that are the burden of our birth into this world. We must greet the bearers of those strange voices, we must be the host at the Feast, and welcome the strangers. This is a delicate business. Respect and attention, care and courtesy are required. Again we require the aid of Hermes, for the ego wants to wall itself off from the Others. We need Hermes in order to violate those boundaries. The only way we can establish the Communion that is required is by moving freely in the spaces between the stars. We can only know who we are if we know who we are not, if we experience our boundaries by experiencing where they touch those of the Others.

We must learn to live among the stars, against a background of the night. We must descend and welcome the figures that crowd around us. We can move down and in, and so, out, to find ancient roots branching into the heavens.

THREE

BLACK LIGHT

Hades, Lucifer, and the
Secret of the Secret

*The dread and resistance which every natural human being experiences
when it comes to delving too deeply into himself is at bottom, the fear of the
journey to Hades.*

— C. G. Jung

DARKNESS WITHIN

PERHAPS NO ONE can claim to know all the ways there are of going to Hell,
or attempt a phenomenology of all the kinds of Hells there are. But we do
descend, sometimes wracked with sufferings out of all proportion to any apparent external cause. We slide slowly into depressions, torn by a host of nameless
demons, or plummet with sudden silent horror into the void.

In these realms everything dissolves, emptied, unmade, withdrawn struggling into the abyss. Hillman says Hades is "the dissolver of the luminous
world."[1] The realm of the dark "extinguishes the . . . colored world . . . dissolves
meaning and the hope for meaning . . . [and] break[s] down the inner cohesion
of any fixed state."[2] This unmaking is required for all psychological change. The
indispensable descent to Hades represents the alchemical *Nigredo:*

> [T]he operations must be dark and are called in alchemical language: morti-
> ficatio, putrefactio, calcinatio, iteratio, etc. That is, the *modus operandi* is slow,
> repetitive, difficult, desiccating, severe, astringent, effortful, coagulating and/or

pulverizing. All the while the worker enters a nigredo state: depressed, confused, constricted, anguished, and subject to pessimistic even paranoid thoughts of sickness, failure, and death.[3]

We can distinguish the *processes* of dissolution from the *origin* and *cause* that is the nothingness of the void itself, destroyer of worlds, annihilator of souls. For Jung it was represented by the archetype of the Terrible Mother. Neumann writes:

> For the ego and the male, the female is synonymous with the unconsciousness and the non-ego, hence with darkness, nothingness, the void, the bottomless pit. In Jung's words: ". . . it should be remarked that *emptiness* is the great feminine secret. It is something absolutely alien to man; the chasm, the unplumbed depths, the *yin*." *Mother, womb, the pit and Hell are all identical.*[4]

The dual terrors of annihilation and meaninglessness lie at the root of the fear of turning inward. A physical origin for this fundamental angst has been sought in the "not good enough mother," in an estrangement from the physical world as represented by the mother's body. Morris Berman argues that the coupled experiences of the inner void and of the associated deadness of the outer world are based on a rupture, a "basic fault" between consciousness and the body that is fundamental to Western culture.[5] On this view it is a fundamental estrangement from our bodies and from nature that provides the basis for our characteristic style of descent into the Hell of a soulless world and the anguish of nihilism.

Hillman has analyzed this as the phenomenon of "depersonalization," in which not only is the individual's sense of self gone, but with it, the "sense of the world." In this pathology the depths of the soul are experienced in one mode only: as the void and the abyss. For Hillman the cause of the resulting psychic deadness is the loss of *anima:* both the soul of the person and the soul of the world.[6] The inner void and the deadness of the world are symptoms of the loss of interiority:

> The "within" refers to that attitude given by the anima which perceives psychic life within natural life. Natural life itself becomes the vessel the moment we recognize its having an interior significance, the moment we see that it too carries psyche. Anima makes vessels everywhere, anywhere, by going within.[7]

And, like Berman, Hillman regards this pathology as characteristic of our culture. "This loss is not merely a psychiatric condition; it is also a cosmology."[8] Work on soul is at the same time work on the *anima mundi,* and is therefore a noble, cosmogonic task. In practice, this is a work of "revivifying images" which "must constellate . . . the sense of the utter reality of the personified image."[9] The point of this psycho-cosmological labor is not to eliminate the need for the descent, but to reclaim its meaning and its efficacy, in part by learning the topographies of Hades, by differentiating among styles of descent and modes of darkness.

Loss of soul comes very readily for us, dominated as we are by the kind of rationality that we identify with intellect. The method of radical doubt led Descartes famously to assert *cogito ergo sum,* and so attempt to ground all knowledge in a rigorous inner certainty. This critical doubt loses us our world, our bodies, and even our feelings, since they cannot deliver logical precision. But perhaps worse than all this is what Descartes, as representative of this approach to the world, has done to the very meaning of subjectivity. By plunging inward to seek certainty based on universal, timeless, and abstract reason he has rooted interiority out of its last stronghold in the subject. The personal, the subjective, and the "interior" are only of interest insofar as they can be understood objectively. In anchoring public truth in the inner monologue of the solitary thinker Descartes banished the fragile, elusive *anima,* making all the worlds, inner and outer, entirely exterior, public, and objective. Radical doubt is a thoroughgoing exteriorization of everything: everything closed must be opened, everything sealed must be entered, everything secret must be revealed, everything darkened must be open to the light, every mystery must be exposed. Wherever *anima* makes vessels, critical doubt follows behind, destroying them. This is the rape of the world so ably documented by feminist thinkers.[10]

Doubt and suspicion "demythologize" the fabric of the world. Emma Brunner-Traut writes:

> In the ancient past the idea of faith in the sense of belief did not exist; for them it was a matter of "knowing." For those who "know," the unspeakable can be uttered without being misunderstood. But already when the smallest distrust creeps in and hidden meaning must be explained, then an integrity is endangered, especially so when the secret becomes a dogmatic formulation. It is placed into the light of critical doubt and demand for proof, and in this light it appears false. Myth is not definition, nor is it proof. It is self-evident. It is endowed with dignity and majesty, perfect in its inner power and validity. . . .[11]

Because the world replete with personified images requires the elusive interiority of *anima,* it cannot survive the cold light of public reason. Henry Corbin writes of the moments of doubt of even so great a mystic as Ibn 'Arabi:

> But then come the hours of weariness and lukewarmness in which the reasoning intellect, through the distinctions it introduces, through the proofs it demands, insinuates between the Lord of love and his *fedele* a doubt that seems to shatter their tie. . . . And since the spiritual visitations have ceased . . . might they [the personifications of Eternal Wisdom] not have perished, returned forever to non-being?[12]

There is "an Arabic tradition" according to which it was a doubting thought in *Ahura Mazda* the supreme Mazdean deity, that was the source and origin of *Ahriman,* the Evil One.[13]

The triumph of public reason is evident in the modern world. The absence of the fragile world of interiority, of vessels that contain the water of life, the inability of so many people to find, or even know how to seek any "inner-ness"—all this is driving us crazy. It powers the frantic compulsion of the culture as we try to transform ourselves into prosthetic gods, as Freud saw,[14] expanding our outer powers into the technological world of gadgets. In the technological landscape McLuhan found the meaning of the myth of Narcis-sus: we are victims of a self-imposed narcosis, numbed and fascinated by the extensions of ourselves with which we are surrounded.[15] With these gods, the mysteries and depths of the soul are increasingly distant and difficult of access, and the Inward shows only the Face of the Abyss that Nietzsche announced when he proclaimed the death of God. And in the mirror of the Other we see only our own reflection.

To escape these terrible alternatives, nihilism or an unfettered and Promethean humanism, we must perhaps turn inward, and as of old, make the descent to Hell, but in a way that can "constellate the sense of the utter reality of the personified image." It was Jung's genius to have provided some practical suggestions as to how this might be done.

C. G. JUNG AND THE *CONIUNCTIO*

Jung's resurrection and psychological interpretation of alchemy is perhaps his central achievement. The writings of the alchemists record the descent to Hell and the rebirth that can result from the ordeal. For Jung the Great Mother is not only the destroyer of worlds, she is also the womb and the very substance of their matter. The darknesses of the Mother are tied to the earthly, to the mortal, and to the unconsciousness of matter and of the human psyche. It is into her realm that we descend during the dark night of the soul. But after this death there may come a rebirth that signals the redemption of the soul and of the world.

Jung's account of this process as experienced in the alchemical opus cen-ters on the *coincidentia oppositorum* and the consequent attainment of wholeness in the adept. For Jung, the opus stands as a necessary complement of a male-dominated, dogmatic Christianity that ignores to its peril the realm of the Mother. As a religion of Light, of the Father, the Son and the Holy Spirit, it is dangerously one-sided, unable to see its own shadow. The alchemist's descent into matter and encounter with the shadow is an attempt to complete the work of redemption left unfinished by Christ: a redemption of matter and the *anima mundi*. In the end they were failures. Not in the sense that they failed to dis-cover the *lapis,* the Philosopher's Stone, the mysterious goal of the Work, but in that they failed to heal the rifts between matter and spirit, faith and knowledge, love and power, and so restore unity to the cosmos. Instead, the *anima mundi* retreated into the human psyche, from which it can be "projected" onto the world of inanimate matter, the lifeless world of the chemists, the physicists, and the a-gnostics of the modern world.

ALCHEMY AND THE AUTONOMOUS PSYCHE

According to Jung, Christianity and alchemy both aim ultimately at rebirth and redemption through a resolution of the "conflict between worldliness and spirituality."[16] But neither could see the true nature of the struggle because neither understood the primacy of the psyche. The problem of the union of masculine and feminine, as the prime symbol of the union of all opposites, was projected "into another medium: the one projected it into the spirit, the other into matter. But neither of them located the problem in the place where it arose—the soul of man."[17]

> Thus the Christian projection acts upon the unknown in man. . . . The pagan projection . . . goes beyond man and acts upon the unknown in the material world. . . . In the Christian projection the *decensus spiritus sancti* stops at the *living body* of the Chosen One . . . whereas in alchemy the descent goes right down into the darkness of inanimate matter. . . .[18]

All these symbolic projections have lost their foundations since the collapse of the authority of the Church and the rise of modern science. The great struggle between the opposites has lost its meaning. The symbols involved represent

> psychic contents that dropped out of their dogmatic framework at the time of the Renaissance and the Great Schism, and since then have continued in a state of secularization where they were at the mercy of the "immanentist" principles of explanation, that is, a naturalistic and personalistic interpretation.[19]

For Jung, a psychological interpretation based on the transpersonal nature of the objective psyche, which is in the end both physical and psychic, provides a means of restoring the meaning of these symbols.

From the psychological point of view the *prima materia* of alchemy "represents the unknown substance that carries the projection of the autonomous psychic content."[20] It is the unknown in their own psyche that they are in fact engaged in observing, projected onto another unknown, matter.

> Everything unknown and empty is filled with psychological projection: it is as if the investigator's own psychic background were mirrored in the darkness. What he sees in matter, or thinks he can see, is chiefly the data of his own unconscious which he is projecting into it. In other words, he encounters in matter, as apparently belonging to it, certain qualities and potential meanings of whose psychic nature he is entirely unconscious.[21]

The experiences of the adepts of alchemy must precede any conscious distinction between matter in itself and psyche in itself. They require unconsciousness of the objective reality of both the psyche and of matter. In the age of the alchemists, there was no clear distinction between the material and the spiritual realms,

> but there did exist an intermediate realm between mind and matter, i.e., a psychic realm of subtle bodies whose characteristic is to manifest themselves in a mental as well as a material form. . . . Obviously, the experience of this intermediate realm comes to a sudden stop the moment we try to investigate matter in and for itself, apart from all projection; and it remains non-existent so long as we believe we know anything conclusive about matter or the psyche.[22]

The alchemical opus must be understood as a phenomenology of the objective, autonomous psyche enacting its drama of transformation on the stage provided by the material world, the objective nature of which must remain unknown in order for the play to continue.

THE OPUS: MATTER, SPIRIT, AND INTEGRATION

The Great Work itself is "an archetypal drama of death and rebirth"[23] that requires all that the adept has to give, for the psyche is the source not only of consciousness, clarity, and reason. It is a natural phenomenon, and in the world of nature "the Heraclitean law of everlasting change, *panta rei,* prevails. . . ."[24] The psyche is "a raging torrent that flows for all eternity in the darkness. . . ."[25] The struggle between the light and the dark, the masculine and the feminine, between the principles of form and matter, is no mere intellectual problem.

> It is the moral task of alchemy to bring the feminine, maternal background of the masculine psyche, seething with passions, into harmony with the principle of spirit—truly a labor of Hercules![26]

The transformative process is a drama of integration by means of increasing consciousness, one that mysteriously redeems not only the spirit in man, but also the world itself. Jung summarized this in an interview with Mircea Eliade in 1952:

> As a matter of fact alchemy takes up and carries on the work of Christianity. In the alchemical view Christianity has saved man but not nature. The alchemist's dream was to save the world in its totality: the philosopher's stone was conceived as the *filius macrocosmi,* which saves the world, whereas Christ was the *filius microcosmi,* the savior of man alone. . . .
>
> . . . The *opus magnum* had two aims: the rescue of the human soul and the salvation of the cosmos. What the alchemists called "matter" was in reality the [unconscious] self. The "soul of the world," the *anima mundi,* which was identified with the *spiritus mercurius,* was imprisoned in matter . . . it was a question of freeing this "matter," of saving it. . . .

... [T]he alchemical opus is dangerous. Right at the beginning you meet the "dragon," the chthonic spirit, the "devil," or as the alchemists called it, the "blackness," the *nigredo,* and this encounter produces suffering. "Matter" suffers right up to the final disappearance of the blackness; in psychological terms, the soul finds itself in the throes of melancholy, locked in the struggle with the "shadow." The mystery of the *coniunctio,* the central mystery of alchemy, aims precisely at the synthesis of opposites, the assimilation of the blackness, the integration of the devil. For the "awakened" Christian this is a very serious psychic experience, for it is a confrontation with his own "shadow," with the blackness of the *nigredo,* which remains separate and can never be completely integrated with the human personality.

... In the language of the alchemists matter suffers until the *nigredo* disappears, when the "dawn" *(aurora)* will be announced by the "peacock's tail" *(cauda pavonis)* and a new day will break, the *leucosis* or *albedo.* But in this state of "whiteness" one does not *live* in the true sense of the word, it is a sort of abstract, ideal state. In order to make it come alive it must have "blood," it must have what the alchemists call the *rubedo,* the "redness" of life. Only the total experience of being can transform this ideal state of the *albedo* into a fully human mode of existence. Blood alone can reanimate a glorious state of consciousness in which the last trace of blackness is dissolved, in which the devil no longer has autonomous existence but rejoins the profound unity of the psyche. Then the *opus magnum* is finished: the human soul is completely integrated.[27]

The work begins with the *prima materia:* "[T]he serpent of Hermes or the Agathodaimon, the Nous that animates the cold part of nature—that is, the unconscious—is enclosed in the spherical vessel of diaphanous glass which ... represents the world and the soul."[28] This snake-like "damp-fiery-cold Spirit" is "the exact opposite of the Christian pneuma" and *is* the spirit of alchemy

which Christianity regarded as demonic and which therefore found no acclaim except in the realm of the magical arts and sciences.... It should not be identified outright with evil; it merely has the uncomfortable quality of being beyond good and evil.[29]

[I]t is an excellent symbol for the two aspects of the unconscious: its cold and ruthless instinctuality, and its Sophia quality or natural wisdom which is ... the maternal wisdom of the divine mother....[30]

This serpent must be sacrificed, according to certain Christian allegories, or transformed as in alchemy, and this metamorphosis "must be understood as an overcoming of unconsciousness and, at the same time, of the attitude of the son who unconsciously hangs onto his mother."[31]

Having enclosed the spirit in the vessel of the soul, the container must be sealed and the contents heated: "During this operation all relations with the outside world are broken off. . . ."[32] The requisite fire is produced by the "passionate emotionality that precedes the recognition of unconscious contents" and is symbolized by, among many other things, the dragon and the fiery lion.[33] This emotional conflict is the result of the struggle between the opposites, which both repel and attract each other:

> Although the opposites flee from one another they nevertheless strive for balance, since a state of conflict is too inimical to life to be endured indefinitely. They do this by wearing each other out: the one eats the other, like the two dragons or the other ravenous beasts of alchemical symbolism.[34]

The spirit in the vessel "corresponds to that part of the psyche which has not been assimilated to consciousness," and is "the spirit of the chaotic waters of the beginning."[35] This return to chaos is the experience of the *prima materia* in the body of the mother, a "return to the dark initial state . . . of the . . . *massa confusa*."[36] This is dangerous because it threatens the stability of consciousness, and the operations of the artifex "consisted largely of precautions whose equivalents are the rites of the Church."[37]

The transformation thus begun is a process of real-ization. The masculine spirit must be kept from flying away from the confrontation with the feminine. The "winged youth"

> will become real only if he can unite with . . . the "mother of mortal bodies." If not he is threatened with the fate of the puer aeternus in *Faust,* who goes up in smoke three times. The adept must therefore always take care to keep the Hermetic vessel well sealed, in order to prevent what is in it from flying away.[38]

The unconscious spirit must be controlled, extracted, and separated from the dissolving *prima materia*. It must be pulled out of unconsciousness, out of the darkness of matter and into the light of consciousness. This demands the attentive participation of the adept—a watchful openness to whatever emerges into the light. "The attention given to the unconscious has the effect of incubation and brooding over the slow fire needed in the initial stages of the work."[39] The analysis and interpretation of dreams performs the *solutio* of alchemy, since both open the doors of the conscious mind to affects long buried. "This loosening up of cramped and rigid attitudes corresponds to the solution and separation of the elements by the *aqua permanens* which was always present in the 'body' and is lured out by the art."[40]

Such dissolution counteracts the natural inclinations of the ego to self-defense. "Egocentricity is a necessary attribute of consciousness and is also its specific sin." But through the art, "the selfish hardness of the heart—caused by original sin—is dissolved: the heart turns to water."[41] Rigidity and the compulsions that accompany it are not of the mind only, but are deeply buried in the body:

Unconscious contents lurk somewhere in the body like so many demons of sickness, impossible to get hold of, especially when they give rise to physical symptoms the organic causes of which cannot be demonstrated.[42]

Once the opposites that were dormant in the unconscious have been activated "the body and the psychic representatives of the organs gain mastery over the conscious mind."[43] This is the journey into Hell, into the belly of the beast, when fiery affects dominate—the return to chaos in the womb of the mother.

The task of accomplishing the archetypal incest must occur "outside the ego" in the realm of symbols in order to effect the transformation.[44] Christianity elevated the conflict between matter and spirit into the mystic marriage of Christ and the Church, thus, on Jung's view, missing the central point of the struggle and effectively preventing the real-ization that the union can provide.[45] Alchemy tends to the opposite extreme, projecting the problem wholly into matter.

In this high-tension state of incestuous struggle, the labor of Hercules is at the same time the labor of the mother giving birth to the redeemed, renewed, and transformed soul. This requires a "pregnancy diet" on which the transformed and transforming substance is fed.

The underlying idea is that the material to be transformed had to be impregnated and saturated, either by imbibing the tincture, the *aqua propria* (its "own water," the soul), or by eating its "feathers" or "wings" (volatile spirit), or its own tail (uroboros), or the fruit of the philosophical tree.[46]

Or, equally, by eating the peacock's flesh or drinking the blood of the green lion.

The wild, instinctual emotionality of the lion is also "the psychic source of renewal," if it is "eaten," that is, assimilated into consciousness. The peacock's flesh alludes to the *cauda pavonis,* the peacock's tail of many colors that comes near the end of the opus. The colors represent all the feelings present in the indiscriminant chaos of the *massa confusa,* which "were brought back to unity in the *albedo* and 'all become one.'"

Morally this means that the original state of psychic disunity, the inner chaos of conflicting part souls which Origen likens to herds of animals, becomes the *"vir unus,"* the unified man. Eating the peacock's flesh is therefore equivalent to integrating the many colors (or, psychologically, the contradictory feeling values) into a single color, white.[47]

This final unity is the goal of the descent: to bring everything possible into consciousness and become as complete and whole as it is possible for a finite being to be.

[T]he aim of the mystical peregrination is to understand all parts of the world, to achieve the greatest possible extension of consciousness, as though its guiding principle were the Carpocratic idea that one is delivered from no sin which one has not committed. Not a turning away from its empirical "so-ness," but the fullest possible experience of the ego as reflected in the "ten thousand things"—that is the goal of the peregrination.[48]

The achievement of the *lapis,* the stone, the gold, is a redemptive union of psyche and matter that produces an "incorruptible body" which arises as a "lib-eration of the divine soul or pneuma from the chains of the 'flesh.'"[49]

> The psyche previously imprisoned in the elements and the divine spirit hid-den in the flesh overcome their physical imperfection and clothe themselves in the noblest of all bodies, the royal gold. Thus the "philosophic gold" is an embodiment of psyche and pneuma, both of which signify "life-spirit." It is in fact ... a living being with a body, soul, and spirit, and it is easily personi-fied as a divine being or a superior person like a king, who in olden times was considered to be God incarnate.[50]

Flesh itself "is a synonym for the *prima materia* and hence for Mercurius,"[51] which is the Agathodaimon, the spirit of the cold part of nature. So Mercurius, as the arcane substance, "stands at the beginning and the end of the work"[52] and "was believed to contain the opposites in uncombined form as the *prima materia,* and to amalgamate them as the *lapis philosophorum.*"[53] In the crude form of the *prima materia* Mercurius is "in very truth the Original Man dis-seminated through the physical world, and in his sublimated form he is that reconstituted totality."[54]

The uroboric feasting, the self-enclosed feeding of the soul upon itself is the *opus circulatorum* which mimics the circling of the sun and the Zodiac in the heavens, and the cycles of birth, death, and renewal on earth, as well as the mystery of God in the whirlwind. It aims at the production of the "Original Man who was a sphere."[55] "The transforming substance is an analogy of the revolving universe, of the macrocosm, or a reflection of it, imprinted in the heart of matter."[56]

THE LIGHT AND THE DARK OF NATURE

Jung writes "We may safely call the light the central mystery of philosophical alchemy."[57] The fiery sparks, or scintillae, of the light of nature, "of the 'World Soul' were already in the chaos, the prima materia, at the beginning of the world."[58] It is these "tiny spirit-sparks from which the shining figure of the *fil-ius* is put together. They correspond to the particles of light imprisoned in the dark Physis. . . ."[59] They are symbols of consciousness, and their psychological significance is that they represent the autonomous complexes "which may pos-sess, as splinter psyches, a certain luminosity of their own."[60]

Of this light in matter Jung says: "Almost always it is personified as the *fil-ius* ... it is a *daimonion* pure and simple."[61] This figure is the Son of the Macro-cosm and is God and creature both. It has numerous parallels in the "pagan,"

Christian, Jewish, and Arabic traditions. He is as we have seen, the alchemical Mercurius. He is the "man of light" in Zosimos, Adam Kadmon of the Cabala, *homo maximus* of Paracelsus, Metatron of the Zohar, and the Persian Gayomart. He is for Jung the archetypal image of the Self.

As the light of nature this arcane substance "was in the inner man," and was for the alchemists

> a ubiquitous and all-pervading essence, an *anima mundi* and "the greatest trea-
> sure," the innermost and most secret numinosum of man. There is probably
> no more suitable psychological concept for this than the collective uncon-
> scious, whose nucleus and ordering principle is the self (the "monad" of the
> alchemists and the Gnostics).[62]

By finding the Self in matter, the alchemists found God there as well. "The *anima mundi* was conceived as that part of God which formed the quintessence and substance of Physis."[63] Thus, "the alchemists came to project even the high-est value—God—into matter."[64]

Mercurius is a hermaphrodite and contains "both the feminine element, Sapi-entia and matter, and the masculine, the Holy Ghost and the devil."[65] Here we encounter that difficult relationship among matter, the feminine, and evil that continues to haunt our culture. Mercurius "is not only spiritual and physical but unites in himself the morally highest and lowest."[66] On Jung's account, the alchemists sought not only the redemption of the *anima mundi* who must be "freed from the shackles of matter" but also the inclusion of the "prince of this world," the devil. "He is the metaphysical figure who is excluded from the Trin-ity, but who, as the counterpart of Christ, is the *sine qua non* of the drama of redemption."[67]

From the point of view of Jung's psychology, the conjunction of opposites at which alchemy aims requires understanding that good and evil both are pro-jections. The "moral problem of opposites" is a psychic problem. Christianity partially recognizes evil as a human "projection" and alchemy was in part suc-cessful in recognizing the psychic origin of good. For dogmatic Christianity God is wholly Good. Evil is "laid at man's door."

> This idea together with that of original sin formed the foundation of a moral
> consciousness which was a novel development in human history: one half of
> the polarity, till then essentially metaphysical, was reduced to a psychic fac-
> tor, which meant that the devil had lost the game if he could not pick on
> some moral weakness in man. Good however remained a metaphysical sub-
> stance that originated with God and not with man. Original sin had cor-
> rupted a creature originally good. As interpreted by dogma therefore, good
> is still wholly projected but evil only partly so, since the passions of men are
> its main source. Alchemical speculation continued this process of integrating

metaphysical projections in so far as it began to dawn on the adept that both opposites were of a psychic nature. . . . This development was extremely important, because it was an attempt to integrate opposites that were previously projected.[68]

All the darknesses thus tend to gather together. All are projections of the psyche: the daemonic spirit of nature, the dark unconsciousness of matter, sin, woman, and the devil.

ALCHEMY, SCIENCE, AND THE WILL TO POWER

It is our modern consciousness that cannot conceive of the unity of the physical and the mystical, of the material and the psychic components of the alchemical procedures. Jung quotes Julius Evola:

> The spiritual constitution of man in the premodern cycles of culture was such that each physical perception had simultaneously a psychic component which "animated" it, adding a "significance" to the bare image, and at the same time a special and potent emotional tone. Thus ancient physics was both a theology and a transcendental psychology, by reason of the illuminating flashes from metaphysical essences which penetrated through the matter of the bodily senses. Natural science was at once a spiritual science, and the many meanings of the symbols united the various aspects of a single knowledge.[69]

Jung writes, "The process of fission which separated the *physika* from the *mystika* set in at the end of the sixteenth century. . . ."[70] We can now see this animate cosmos as a result of projection, and can regard matter in itself from an objective standpoint. Jung regards alchemy as the precursor of modern science, not because it prefigured the empirical methods of chemistry, or inadvertently discovered certain chemical compounds, but for several, deeper, and interrelated reasons.

To begin with, it embodied a certain "questing religious spirit" which came to animate natural science and Protestantism alike,[71] and which served to "emancipate natural science from the authority of tradition."[72] Yet the equation of Christ with the *lapis* "had the effect of channeling the religious numen into physical nature and ultimately into matter itself. . . ."[73] Then, because "the highest value was safely embedded in matter, a starting point was given for the development of genuine chemistry . . . and . . . the more recent philosophical materialism. . . ."[74] Because of the schism between the light of nature embedded in matter and the light of revelation accessible only through grace, there arose "that conflict between knowledge and faith which poisoned the spiritual atmosphere of the nineteenth century in particular."[75] The alchemists tended to "put their art on the level of divine revelation and regarded it as at least an essential complement to the work of redemption."[76] As Christ saved the soul of man, so man would save the soul of the world. Thus, the alchemists "were the unwitting instigators of the schism between faith and knowledge, and it was they who made the world conscious that the revelation was neither complete nor final."[77]

This conflict Jung saw most clearly in Paracelsus, who wrote:

> There are . . . two kinds of knowledge in this world: an eternal and a temporal. The eternal springs directly from the light of the Holy Spirit, but the other directly from the light of Nature.[78]

The goal of alchemy is the unification of the *homo totus* through the gathering together of the light in nature that is "the star in man." Paracelsus, like all the alchemists of his time, understood his "art" as complement to his religion. All were unaware of what Jung regards as an essential incompatibility, which amounts even to blasphemy. He writes,

> [T]he "star in man" sounds harmless enough. . . . And yet that light or *filius philosophorum* was openly named the greatest and most victorious of all lights and set alongside Christ as the Savior and Preserver of the world! Whereas in Christ God himself became man, the *filius philosophorum* was extracted from matter by human art, and by means of the opus, made into a new light bringer. . . . [T]he salvation or transfiguration of the universe is brought about by the mind of man—"Deo concedente," as the authors never fail to add. In the one case man confesses "I under God," in the other he asserts "God under me." Man takes the place of the Creator.[79]

> Paracelsus did not see that the Truth of the Church and the Christian standpoint could never get along with the thought implicit in all alchemy: "God under me."[80]

> Not for nothing was Paracelsus the prototype of Faust. . . . From Faust the line leads direct to Nietzsche. . . . What still maintained the balance in the case of Paracelsus . . .—"I under God and God under me"—was lost in the twentieth century, and the scale sinks lower and lower under the weight of an ego that fancies itself more and more god-like.[81]

And so it is that

> Medieval alchemy prepared the way for the greatest intervention in the divine world order that man has ever attempted: alchemy was the dawn of the scientific age, when the daemon of the scientific spirit compelled the forces of nature to serve man to an extent that had never been known before. It was from the spirit of alchemy that Goethe wrought the figure of the "superman" Faust, and this superman led Nietzsche's Zarathustra to declare that God was dead and to proclaim the will to give birth to the superman, to "create a god for yourself out of your seven devils." *Here we find the true roots, the preparatory processes deep in the psyche, which unleashed the forces at work in the world today.* Science and technology have indeed conquered the world, but whether the psyche has gained anything is another matter.[82]

So Nietzsche and modern science are siblings. Their compulsions and delusions of grandeur and mastery are born of the schism between Nature and God, knowledge and revelation, and are the results of the imbalances and fatal inflations that were inherent in alchemy. "The inner driving force behind the aspirations of alchemy was a presumption whose daemonic grandeur on the one hand, and psychic danger on the other should not be underestimated."[83] The means of maintaining equilibrium between God and man were lost when the light of Nature was understood to be autonomous, and man a wholly natural being. Equilibrium requires the "circular distillation" of the opus. The psychic contents must be contained in the opposites so that the tension between them "gradually changes into the bilateral activity of the point in the center."[84] "Ascent and descent, above and below, up and down, represent an emotional realization of the opposites, and this realization gradually leads, or should lead, to their equilibrium."[85] An autonomous Nature, a natural ego, with no possibility of balance from above, is doomed to the identifications and inflations of dementia.

FREEDOM, COMPULSION, AND THE ANTHROPOS

One of the chief psychic benefits that results from attaining some degree of "wholeness" is freedom from *compulsion*: "[M]aximum consciousness . . . amounts to maximal freedom of the will."[86] And yet this freedom cannot in itself be the goal of the *opus*. The will "can best be regarded as a dynamism subordinated to consciousness,"[87] and thus is a function of the ego, which is necessarily subordinate to the wholeness represented by the Original Man. The goal is not liberty for the ego to act as it pleases, but to free it *for* its conscious submission to the larger whole that is "the greater man within, the *Anthropos*."

As with all things psychic, compulsion has a dual nature. It is an unconscious dynamism and is

> the great mystery of human life. It is the thwarting of our conscious will and
> of our reason by an inflammable element within us, appearing now as a con-
> suming fire and now as life-giving warmth.[88]

This fiery substance is the sulfur of alchemy, which is *sulphur duplex,* the active masculine substance of the moon and the sun. Its combustion can be both a blackening and a whitening; it is the dragon and the lion, Christ and the devil, and in it "the highest and the lowest are close together."[89] It is a symbol for all unconscious dynamism.

Jung says that there are two origins of this unconscious dynamism that causes our lack of freedom, and this explains the paradoxical nature of sulfur. "Compulsion . . . has two sources: the shadow and the Anthropos."[90]

The shadow is "inconvenient and repellent because it stands for something that demonstrates quite plainly our secret inferiority."[91] This shadow extends from the merely embarrassing and inconvenient all the way down into the truly evil and "has affinities with the devil." The compulsions originating here we are best rid of, and freedom from these would be a worthy goal of any great work. With regard to these causes for our lack of freedom, any gain of consciousness that denies them autonomy expands the power and scope of reason over darkness and evil. This is the goal of the withdrawal of projections.

But what of the other source of compulsion, the Anthropos? The cause of our lack of freedom is unconscious compulsion. Notice what Jung says:

> The *causa efficiens et finalis* of this lack of freedom lies in the unconscious and forms that part of the personality which still has to be added to the conscious man in order to make him whole.[92]

Although it is not spelled out clearly, Jung intends to assign only the *efficient* cause of our lack of freedom to the shadow—that is the source of our cramps and rigidities, our egocentricities, and worse. All of these thwart our attempts to act in accordance with reason and block our ability to see clearly and act freely, and limit our abilities to truly relate to other people.

But Jung assigns a *causa finalis* as well. A final cause is a telos, an end and a goal. Our lack of freedom *points toward* something. This can only be the Anthropos:

> [T]here is in the unconscious an already existing wholeness, the "homo totus" of the Western and the Chen-yen (true man) of Chinese alchemy, the round primordial being who represents the greater man within, the Anthropos, who is akin to God.[93]

There is in us a compulsion, an inner dynamism, propelling us toward divine wholeness. It must remain unconscious, and so, compelling, "because consciousness is only part of a man, and cannot comprehend the whole."[94] With regard to *this* cause of our lack of freedom, increasing consciousness, increasing wholeness, would not reduce the autonomy of this divine totality, but rather serve to humble the ego that can only exist as a shadow in the face of this greater light. This compulsion may take the form of a need for a secret.[95] Paradoxically perhaps, this final wholeness necessarily remains unconscious, dark and hidden.

But what, one might well ask, prevents Jung's conception of the Self from being nothing other than that wholly Natural perversion of the *homo totus* that is the Superman? Are Jung's critics right in accusing him of psychologizing God and so, of making gods of us, as Jung accuses the alchemists of doing? If good and evil are both projections, as he has said quite clearly at times that they are, then why isn't the Self merely autonomous Natural Man, Master of the Ten Thousand Things, seeker after knowledge and ever-increasing consciousness? Jung was personally motivated by an imperious compulsion for knowledge. He was driven to a frenzy by "not understanding," and the whole of his life work is an attempt to understand the psyche. Barbara Hannah writes,

> This understanding "why" was always the most important thing to Jung. I
> have often heard him say that the only unbearable torture is the torture of
> not understanding. [At the university] . . . he learned that understanding fol-
> lows only if you always face this "unbearable torture" and never turn your
> back on it.[96]

Surely this explains some of his insistence on the autonomy and comprehen-
siveness of the psyche, which so often characterizes his writings.

But the question about the nature of the Self cannot be answered by ana-
lyzing Jung. The question centers on the meaning of projection. Jung is almost
never consistently clear about the nature and meaning of projection, and the
natural scientist in him was always a Kantian, after the thing-in-itself, trying to
strip away all that is coming "from us," to reveal what is "really there." In the
end, therapeutically speaking, our projections must be withdrawn; at least
those that cloud our view of the worlds of man and nature and of God. And
yet there are "projections," psychic contents, which we cannot withdraw
because they are the very substance of the world. They are our connections to
the world. Jung has no very clear metaphysics, no overarching theory to help
him differentiate these psychic or psychoid contents, and he vacillates among
various accounts.

One of the best (if not the clearest) of his statements of his ultimate intuitive position on the transcendence of the archetypes and of the figure of the
Anthropos comes at the end of "The Spirit Mercurius."[97] Christ and Mercurius as archetypal images are beyond our control and "were never invented
but experienced." They cannot be withdrawn as projections. Christ is the
archetype of consciousness, Mercurius of the unconscious. Mercurius, for all
his connections with darkness and the underworld, "is by no means the Christian devil." The latter is rather a "diabolization" of him. Mercurius is Lucifer,
"an adumbration of the primordial light bringer, who is never himself the
light, but a *phosphoros* who brings the light of nature, the light of the moon
and of the stars. . . ."[98]

Jung then offers an interpretation of passages in Augustine concerning
the morning knowledge, the *cognitio matutina,* and the evening knowledge,
cognitio vespertina. His account is this: The morning knowledge of the first day
of Creation is knowledge of the self, and is the *Scientia Creatoris,* the light of
God, of the Creation, of the coming of consciousness out of the darkness of
the unconscious.

> Then, following the order of the days of Creation in Genesis, comes knowl-
> edge of the firmament, of the earth, the sea, the plants, the stars, the animals
> of the water and air, and finally, on the sixth day, knowledge of the land ani-
> mals and of . . . man himself. . . . As Augustine describes it, the *cognitio matutina*
> gradually grows old as it loses itself in the "ten thousand things" and finally
> comes to man. . . .[99]

The knowledge of the first day of creation "finally and inevitably becomes the *scientia hominis,* the knowledge of man, who asks himself: 'Who is it that knows and understands everything? Why, it is myself.' *That marks the coming of darkness. . . .*"[100] But this need not be the end. It was the end for Nietzsche. It is the end for a secular, literalist humanity, for whom all projections must be withdrawn, leaving the impersonal universe of matter in-itself. But out of the darkness arises the seventh day: "The Sabbath is therefore the day on which man returns to God and receives anew the light of the *cognitio matutina.*" The darkness of greatest intensity is Good Friday. On Saturn's day Mercurius is *senex,* but heralds the light to come: "And this day has no evening."

Jung ends with this warning against a knowledge that is only human:

> It seems to me that Augustine apprehended a great truth, namely that every spiritual truth gradually turns into something material, becoming no more than a tool in the hand of man. In consequence, man can hardly avoid seeing himself as a knower, yes, even a creator, with boundless opportunities at his command. . . . The alchemist could still pray: "Purge the horrible darknesses of our mind," but modern man is already so darkened that nothing beyond the light of his own intellect illumines the world.[101]

HENRY CORBIN AND THE ORIENT OF LIGHT

There is considerable obscurity in Jung's writings on alchemy. Much of this is inescapable and derives from the alchemical texts and the workings of the psyche that they reflect. Alchemy is a rationalist's nightmare. It is also to some extent the result of Jung's failings as a writer, his emotional identification with the adepts, and his intuitive, associational approach to alchemical symbolism.

But there may be other reasons. Henry Corbin, Jung's friend and colleague at Eranos, would have argued, I think, that much of the trouble stems from philosophical confusions that are themselves the result of a cultural and metaphysical calamity that has profoundly affected Jung, many of the alchemists he studied, and indeed all of Western Christendom and the modern world that is its outcome.

The schism between faith and knowledge, between the *mystika* and the *physika* that Jung associates with the alchemists of the sixteenth and seventeenth centuries, Corbin places much earlier, as we have seen.[102] It is a result of the loss of the individual's direct connection with the transcendent world of symbols and symbolic knowledge that is *gnosis.* This bond, explained in Islamic doctrines by the hierarchical Neoplatonic cosmology of Avicenna, was ruptured in the West by the triumph of the doctrines of Averroes and the Aristotelians. For them, the principle of individuation was matter, not Gabriel, the Angel of Revelation.[103]

It is this prior rupture that makes possible the Paracelsan distinction between the Light of Nature and the Light of Revelation. But more is involved.

The central doctrine of dogmatic Christianity, the Incarnation, is deeply flawed on Corbin's view, and expresses in symbolic form a disastrous misperception of the relations among Spirit, Matter, and Soul, which has resulted in all the various dualisms that have split the consciousness of Western man. Partly as a consequence of this failure the Christian tradition lost contact with its roots in *gnosis* as an effective spiritual practice. The path for us is not well trodden, and where tradition is lacking there is great room for error, with disastrous results for the individual and for the culture as a whole.

I want to focus on two closely related aspects of Corbin's critique of Jung and the Western tradition. The first is Jung's failure to differentiate clearly between levels of being in the "unconscious." The second is the failure in the West to distinguish the darkness of the abyss from the luminous Black Light at the approach to the Pole.

A COSMOLOGY FOR THE SOUL

In order to make sense of Corbin's work it is necessary to sketch briefly some relevant characteristics of the cosmology that his writings presume. The mystics of Islam whom he takes as his guides all share certain fundamental assumptions about the nature of reality that have long since been discarded in the Western world.

Islamic thought does not distinguish between "things that belong to God" and "things that belong to Caesar." Cosmology and theology are inseparable. Natural science is the study of Nature as the Primordial Revelation, as a Book written by God. The world of material objects lies on an unbroken continuum, a Great Chain of Being, with a much greater realm that extends forever into the heavens: an "ocean without a shore." In this hierarchical cosmos, all beings are in perpetual descent from God as aspects of Revelation, and simultaneously all beings are in perpetual ascent toward God, in longing and love, aiming at their final resurrection in the Absolute.

Only God is the True reality, and there is an infinite hierarchy of degrees of being leading up to Him. For the human soul this means that different modes of knowledge correspond to different degrees of reality. Spiritual transformation requires attaining higher modes of being, states that are closer to God. The focus of spiritual life is always to change one's being by means of Ascent.

This ascension does involve increasing wholeness, since one does become more complete, more real, closer to God. To attain the full possibilities of human perfection human beings have to experience to some degree all the attributes of God.[104] But the journey toward the Divine consists in overcoming that which is lower, not in integrating it to become whole. The lower is the less real; one includes it only by surpassing it. The wholeness to be attained is a wholeness of perfection, not a wholeness of inclusion. The Carpocratic ideal could not be farther from the ideal of the Sufi. The method of alchemy is to extract "the organism of light from beneath the mountains under which it lies imprisoned,"[105] but this involves freeing it from the lower soul. Both the collective shadow and the individual shadow must be overcome.[106] Humans are potential demons and angels both, not prospective unions of the two. The goal is not a totality of the less real and the more real; it is ascent toward the truly Real. Where Jung and the alchemists are ambivalent and speak both of wholeness and of freeing the spirit in matter, there is little such ambiguity in the forms of Islamic mysticism that Corbin represents.

In a sense, Islam combines the God of the Old Testament with that of the New. He is both Vengeful and Loving, and so *is* in fact, a *coincidentia oppositorum*. The relationship of God to the cosmos is expressed in two radically different ways. Sachiko Murata writes,

> In one respect, God is infinitely beyond the cosmos. Here, the theological term is *tanzih,* which means "to declare God incomparable" with everything that exists. From this point of view, God is completely inaccessible to His creatures and beyond their understanding. . . . "Nothing is like Him" (Qur'an 42:11). In this respect, God is an impersonal reality far beyond human concerns. He is the God of a certain form of negative theology.[107]

This is the God of the dogmatic and legalistic aspect of Islam. "God's incomparability calls to mind such names as Mighty, Inaccessible, Great, Majestic, Compeller, Creator, Proud, High, King, Wrathful, Avenger, Slayer, Depriver and Harmer."[108] These are the names of Majesty *(Jalal).* And yet the Qur'an is equally clear about the other aspect of Divinity:

> Popular Islam, the philosophical tradition, and the spiritual tradition represented by the great Sufis stressed or at least found room for a second point of view. . . . God's love for creation brings about love for God in the creatures. This God of compassion and love can be grasped and understood. To use the theological term, He must be "declared similar" *(tashbih)* in some fashion to His creation. . . . This is the point of view of God's immanence in all things. . . . "We are nearer to the human being than the jugular vein (50:16)." In this respect God is a personal God. . . .
>
> God's similarity calls to mind such names as Beautiful, Near, Merciful, Compassionate, Loving, Gentle, Forgiving, Pardoner, Life-giver, Enricher, and Bestower. These are known as the names of beauty *(jamal).* . . .[109]

The contrasts between the names of Majesty and the names of Beauty may be conceived as expressing a dualism that is characteristic of abstract rationality and the "legalistic" side of Islam. But they may also be seen as expressing not *duality* but *polarity,* and this is characteristic of the spiritual, gnostic teachings of Islam represented by Corbin. Roger Ames describes the difference between these senses of opposition:

> The separateness implicit in dualistic explanations of relationships conduces to an essentialistic interpretation of the world, a world of "things" characterized by discreteness, finality, closedness, determinateness, independence, a world in which one thing is related to the "other" extrinsically. By contrast, a polar explanation of relationships gives rise to a holographic interpretation of the world, a world of "foci" characterized by interconnectedness, interdependence, openness, mutuality, indeterminateness, complementarity, correlativity, coextensiveness, a world in which continuous foci are intrinsically related to each other.[110]

The world of the alchemists is characterized by polar relationships. The world of the empirical science that replaced it was a world of dualisms.[111] Jung's own work shows the tension between these two perspectives, and he did not benefit from a philosophical position that clearly demarcated them.

In comparing this cosmology with Jung's understanding of alchemy it is crucial to see that none of the names of Majesty suggest that God is in any way evil. We surely may not understand Him[112]—he is the Inaccessible—but God is never the source of evil. God has no shadow. He cannot be a *coincidentia oppositorum* where the opposites are Good and Evil. Corbin comments: "[C]omplementary elements can be integrated, but not contradictory ones."[113] Jung suggests as much: the unconscious is *compensatory*. But because Jung's focus is wholeness, and because the empiricist in him wants to find the source of everything psychic in the soul of man, he tends to see wholeness as including everything, even contradictories.

In the Islamic view, sin and evil are always a result of a falling away from God. This God is not the simple, kind and loving God of an insipid Good News New Testament. He is also Terrible, as Jung well knew. But not Evil.

A few words about the cosmological status of matter will help clarify Corbin's position. The material "sublunary" world is that part of Creation that is most distant from God. But it remains the result of the Breath of the Compassionate, Who said according to tradition, "I was a Hidden Treasure and I desired to be known, and so I created the world." Matter is in itself not sinful, and there is in Islam no doctrine of Original Sin. The common Christian identification of flesh, sex, woman, and sin is largely absent in those traditions of Islamic thought represented by Corbin.[114] Mohammad, as a fully human being, albeit the best of men, is a figure wholly unlike the androgynous and celibate Christ. When Corbin asked about the doctrines of the Fall and of original sin in Islamic thought, Shaykh Mohammad Hossayn Tabatabai said: "The fall is neither a lack, nor a defect, even less a sin; if it had not been for the forbidden fruit of the tree, the inexhaustible possibilities of Being would never have been manifested."[115]

Matter itself, the "clay" from which God made Adam, is neutral. Murata and Chittick write:

> There is nothing evil about clay. It is a good substance for making pots (if you are a potter) or bodily things in general (if you are a god). Clay has its draw-

backs. It is dark and dense, so when you pour liquid light into the pot, the light is hidden, and some people might imagine the pot is empty. But without pots you would have no containers for the light. Clay is not devious and deceptive, it is simply dull.[116]

Jung tends to share the conflation of matter, evil, and the Feminine that characterizes much Christian theology. Corbin represents, for the most part, a theology that does not commit this error.[117] Matter can be separated from the principle of evil, writes Schuon,

> if one distinguishes in the Cosmos two poles, the one existential, blind and passive and the other intellectual, therefore conscious and active: matter is [the extreme limit in the process of manifestation] in relation to the existential pole only, while the intellectual pole gives rise, at the extreme limit of the flight from God, to the "personifiable force," or that perverted consciousness, who is Satan or Mara. In other words, Matter is the existence most remote from pure Being, and the Devil is the consciousness most remote from pure Intelligence.[118]

Satan (the Iblis of the Qur'an, Ahriman of the Zoroastrians) can never be integrated into the perfected soul, but his association with matter is accidental, not essential.

ORIENTATION AND THE MAN OF LIGHT

Corbin's spiritual itinerary is a "quest for the Orient" that determines the orientation of man in the world. This quest is to find the vertical dimension symbolized by the Pole Star, which makes possible the ascent of the soul toward the threshold of the worlds beyond. This is a cosmology in which alchemy, astrology, and a geocentric cosmos still have sense. If we try to discover how we in the West lost the cosmological basis for the irreducible reality of the individual,

> [t]hen it may happen, just as we have learned to understand alchemy as signifying something quite different from a chapter in the history or prehistory of our sciences, that a geocentric cosmology will also be revealed in its true sense, having likewise no connection with the history of our sciences. Considering the perception of the world and the feeling of the universe on which it is based, it may be that geocentrism should be meditated upon and evaluated essentially after the manner of the construction of a *mandala*.
>
> It is this *mandala* upon which we should meditate in order to find again the northern dimension with its symbolic power, capable of opening the threshold of the beyond.[119]

This North, the centralizing power of the universe, was lost with the Copernican revolution which was a revolution of the human presence, a revolution of the mode of presence in the world [by which] the Earth was "lost in the heavens." "To lose sight of the North" means no longer to be able to distinguish between heaven and hell, angel and devil, light and shadow, unconsciousness and transconsciousness.[120]

The quest for the Orient

> is the ascent out of cartographical dimensions, the discovery of the inner world which secretes its own light, which *is* the world of light; it is an inner- ness of light as opposed to the spatiality of the outer world which, by con- trast, will appear as Darkness.[121]

This inward turn is no "narcissism." It is just the opposite of such self- absorption. It can seem like a withdrawal into solipsism and subjectivity only to those whose capacities for suprasensory perception have been so neglected or disparaged that they no longer function at all. This is because each individual person as such, irrespective of anything collective, virtually has a transcendent dimension at his disposal. Its growth is concomitant with a visionary apperception, giving shape to the supersensory perceptions and constituting that totality of ways of knowing that can be grouped under the term *hierognosis*.[122]

Now, to make our way in this, for us, uncharted territory, we need to know more than merely that plunging "inward" will lead us North to the Light. It is not so simple. There are dangers. To free oneself from the "unconsciousness of ignorance" the soul

> must pass through the Darkness; this is a terrifying and painful experience, for it ruins and destroys all the patencies and norms on which the natural man lived and depended—a true "descent into hell," the hell of the unconscious.[123]

Only a true Orientation, an understanding of the structure of the worlds of hierognosis, can guard the soul during the descent to the depths. There are three dimensions in this psychospiritual realm,

> which the ordinary two-dimensional view cannot account for, since it is restricted to contrasting *consciousness* and *unconsciousness*. To put it more pre- cisely, it has to do with two Darknesses: there is one Darkness which is only Darkness; it can intercept light, conceal it, and hold it captive. When the light escapes from it . . . this darkness is left to itself, falls back upon itself; it does not become light. But there is another Darkness, called by our mystics the Night of light, luminous Blackness, black Light.
>
> . . . That is why *orientation* requires here a threefold arrangement of planes: the day of *consciousness* is on a plane intermediate between the lumi- nous Night of *superconsciousness* and the dark Night of *unconsciousness*. . . . Ori- entation by the Pole, the cosmic north, determines what is below and what is above; to confuse one with the other would merely indicate *disorientation*.[124]

The divine and the satanic remain ambiguous so long as consciousness is unable to distinguish between what is its Day and what is its Night. . . . The ending of this ambiguity is the harbinger of the "midnight sun" with its horizons upon horizons: it may be the divine Night of superconsciousness irradiating the field of light of consciousness, and it may be the light of consciousness overcoming the Darkness of the subconscious, of the unconsciousness which was hemming it in.[125]

We are not alone on this journey. There is a Figure, a Guide, who leads the soul onward out of the well of darkness. This heavenly partner is

the Figure of light, the Image and the mirror in which the mystic contemplates—and without which he could not contemplate—the theophany . . . *in the form corresponding to his being.*[126]

The mystic transformation consists in the growth and development of the resurrection body of the man of light that is hidden in the physical body. The science of mysticism, of alchemy, of astrology, is the science of the physiology of the man of light. This is the same figure we have encountered before: Hermes/Mercurius, Adam Kadmon, the Anthropos, and *homo totus.*

With this scheme in place, Corbin engages in a fairly explicit critique of Jung's conception of the shadow. Jung's refusal to engage in "metaphysics" and his attempted insistence on "empiricism" is what, on Corbin's view, prevents him from seeing clearly the true nature of things. For Jung, unconscious contents are indistinguished; every content is contaminated with every other, in what must seem to Corbin a spurious wholeness.[127] Corbin writes:

Is not the sense of all myths of *reintegration* henceforth affected by this orientation? For the totality of man's being, the transcendent personal dimension he discerns in the northern light, in the "midnight sun," is not merely the sum total of orient and occident, of left and right, of conscious and unconscious. The man of light's ascent causes the shades of the *well* where he was held captive to fall back into themselves. Hermes does not carry his *shadow* with him. . . . And it is difficult, we must confess, to read with equanimity certain interpretations of the *coincidentia oppositorum* where complementaries and contradictories are apparently indiscriminately lumped together under the head of *opposita.* To deplore that Christianity is centered on a figure of goodness and light and entirely overlooks the dark side of the soul would be no less valid an evaluation if applied to Zoroastrianism. But how could reintegration consist in a complicity between, a "totalization" of Christ and Satan, Ohrmazd and Ahriman? Even to suggest such a possibility is to overlook the fact that even under the reign of a figure of light the satanic forces remain in operation. . . . And it is exactly for this reason that one has to affirm that the relationship of Christ to Satan, Ohrmazd to Ahriman, is not complementary but contradictory. Complementary elements can be integrated, but not contradictory ones.[128]

At the beginning of the journey, there will indeed be darkness, but it is the darkness of Ahriman: "[T]he Black figure sometimes visualized by the Spiritual at the beginning of his mystical journey, is *not* the celestial Guide, the Witness in Heaven. The blackness, or darkness, is precisely the absence of the Witness of light," and is the "active negativity which prevents him from being seen."[129] At the beginning there is shadow, but it is cast by the opacity of the soul trapped in both the dullness of matter distant from the light and the negativity of the satanic, and is a measure of the soul's own being. As always for Corbin, the mode of knowledge reflects the mode of being of the knower. Here he writes: "Your contemplation is worth whatever your being is worth; your God is the God you deserve; He bears witness to your being of light or to your darkness."[130] In the beginning it is your own shadow that you see.

This initial darkness can only be distinguished from the Luminous Night if one acknowledges the triadic diagram of the soul. Corbin asks:

> [C]an the phenomenon of shadow and light . . . really be translated simply by speaking of consciousness as the region of light and the unconscious as the region of shadow? The soul-consciousness is placed between the two: between the lower soul and the higher soul. . . . How could one possibly say that the "two souls" between which the soul-consciousness is placed both belong equally to the same region of *shadow*?[131]

Without this cosmology of the soul it will be impossible to understand the moral situation and the cosmic orientation of man. Man is not a summation, but an intermediary:

> [A]n anthropogony in which antithetic forces (murderer and victim, for example) objectively represent one divine primordial reality is one thing; an anthropogony situating man between two worlds is quite a different thing. Man according to Ismaelian gnosis is an intermediary—potential angel or demon; his complete eschatological reality is not the sum of these two antithetical virtualities. Man in Ibn 'Arabi's anthropogony is likewise intermediate: situated between being and non-being, between Light and Darkness, at the same time responsible and respondent to both sides; he is responsible for the Darkness to the extent that he intercepts Light, but he is responsible for the Light to the extent that he prevents the Darkness from invading and governing it.[132]

It is of central importance for Corbin that the orientation provided by this cosmology also avoids what he sees as the failure of Jung's scheme to accommodate his own notion of individuation. Supraconsciousness is essentially individual, and it is the very existence of the Pole that guarantees the ontological individuality of the Self. An undifferentiated unconscious of the sort that Jung suggests, must, from Corbin's point of view, be "collective," and so incapable of freeing the soul from the domination of the laws of history, mass society, and the impersonal laws of the natural world.[133]

LUMINOUS NIGHT

The approach to the realm of supraconsciousness is signaled by the Black Light. This higher consciousness is *sirr* in Arabic, and can also be translated as *secret,* as Corbin does in his book on Ibn 'Arabi, or as *mystery* or *inmost consciousness.*[134] It is a world of the suprasensory and the interior, but is in no way *subjective.* It can only be approached if we abandon our habit of confounding the subjective and the interior. In this cosmology, the most real *is* the *inner.* From Corbin's point of view it is to Jung's credit that he understood the reality of the inner world, but he did not understand the structure of the world he opened up.

The Black Light of supraconsciousness is not an absence of light. It is a luminous, dazzling darkness that "marks the most perilous initiatic step, the stage immediately preceding the ultimate theophany, which is heralded by the green light."[135] It signals the presence of the Hidden Treasure which is the source and origin of all being, yet which is itself unknown and unknowable—that side of divinity which makes one see and yet cannot itself be seen, that which makes all things *be* and yet cannot itself be an object—it is the *Deus absconditus.* In the works of Najm Razi (d. 1256), a Sufi master from Central Asia[136] the Black Light refers to the Names of Majesty, and the lights of all the worlds refer to the Names of Beauty. Corbin writes: "[W]ithout the blossoming of Beauty as theophany man could not approach the sublimity of the *Deus absconditus.*"[137] The Black Light "brings about vision, but is itself invisible."[138] All the colors of the worlds are thus mixtures of light with this existentiating darkness and must be "understood as the relation of the act of light with the infinite potentiality which aspires to reveal itself ('I was a Hidden Treasure, I wanted to be known'), that is, as the epiphanic act in the night of the *Absconditum.*"[139]

All the lights and colors of the worlds, insofar as they are darkened by matter, are held captive, and it is the struggle of the mystic to develop the capacity to perceive these lights in their higher states where the pure colors are the acts of light which preexist and make possible the appearances of objects in the "sublunary world." The aetheric, subtle matter in which these lights are actualized is more real than the matter that science knows, and which is clouded by the obscurity of its distance from God. All of the characteristics of this world derive from above: "[M]aterial bodies are never the sufficient reasons for the properties they manifest."[140] The darkness of this material world "is not what makes the light manifest; it releases it when forced to do so."[141]

The subtle matter that causes the suprasensory phenomena of colored lights represents the act of light itself, not the darkness that is its antagonist. "The Divine Night *(Deus absconditus),* as the source and origin of all light *(Deus revelatus),* is not a compound of the demonic and the divine."[142] During the mystic journey through the world of lights this Divine Night must be distinguished from the shadow that obscures it. The demonic shadow of the lower soul is not the light, itself invisible, which *causes seeing,* but it is the Darkness that prevents seeing, as the darkness of the subconscious prevents seeing. The black light, on the other hand, is that which cannot itself be seen, because it is the cause of seeing, since it is Absolute Subject. It dazzles, as the light of supraconsciousness dazzles.[143]

Light without matter

is the incandescence of the *mundus imaginalis.* . . . To see things [there] . . . is to see them in that state which can only be perceived by the "supersensory senses." This perception is not a passively received impression of a natural object, but the activity of the subject, that is, conditioned by the physiology of the man of light.[144]

To perceive these lights of Beauty one must approach the Black Light of the Pole wherein lies the Absolute Subject that is precisely what "makes one see," and is itself invisible. This recalls Jung's intuition that "our consciousness issues from a dark body, the ego"[145] but the metaphysical scheme is totally different.

As intermediary beings, we are flanked by dangers both below and above. Satanic demons below threaten to turn us away from our true end, our essential self. And the darkness above too is dangerous:

The "black light" is that of the attribute of Majesty which sets the mystic's being on fire; it is not contemplated; it attacks, invades, annihilates, then annihilates annihilation. It shatters the "supreme theurgy," that is, the apparatus of the human organism. . . .[146]

It is therefore not for everyone to attempt this encounter. Corbin's account centers in large part on the mystical philosophy of the great thirteenth-century Iranian Sufi Alaoddawleh Semnani.

The black light is the light of the pure Essence in its ipseity, in its abscondity; the ability to perceive it depends upon a spiritual state described as "reabsorption in God . . . the state in which Semnani perceives the danger of a supreme ordeal. . . .[147]

At the heart of the experience lies the realization of the *mystical poverty* of all of creation, which is "the very secret of being, it can only *be,* as *made-to-be.*" Mir Damad[148] perceived this as the "great occult clamour of beings, the 'silent clamour of their metaphysical distress.'"[149] What the Absconditum does for all beings is to turn them to water—it is the origin of the *solutio* of alchemy, of the mercurial fluidity and endless mysteriousness of *anima.* It is the source of that openness which Rilke longs for in the Eighth Elegy:

> . . . the beast is free
> and has its death always behind it and God before it,
> and when it walks it goes toward eternity,

as springs flow. Never, not for a single day
do we have pure space before us in which the flowers
are always unfolding. . . .[150]

This distress at their essential insufficiency, at the impossibility of autonomy, is
indispensable for the transcendence of all beings—humans, animals, even flowers. Corbin writes, "[T]he flowers of earth form a train behind the Angel who
is the leader of the 'divine series' to which they belong."[151]

The luminous night is the night of supraconsciousness that is an "unknowingness which, as such, is knowing." To attain this luminous night is to have
attained the mystical poverty of the "Dervish," (darwish) or "poor in spirit." The
supreme test for the human soul lies in the confrontation with the *Deus absconditus*—to face not the Shadow of Ahrimanian darkness, but the Black Face of
inaccessible Majesty within which is the Water of Life.[152]

This "*fana fi'llah,* the test of reabsorption into God,"

comprising an experience of death and annihilation, is for man alone to
attempt, and marks his hour of greatest peril. Either he will be swallowed up
in dementia or he will rise again from it, initiated in the meaning of theophanies and revelations. . . . By passing thus through the annihilation of annihilation . . . the recognition of the Guide is authenticated, of the "witness in
Heaven," the reddening sun against the background of divine Darkness. For
this recognition implies recognition of the Unknowable, which is to say metaphysical renunciation and mystical poverty.[153]

Shamsoddin Lahiji[154] writes:

The perfection of contingent being is to regress to its basic negativity, and to
come to know through its own unknowingness. It means to know with the
certainty of experience that the *summum* of knowledge is unknowingness, for
here there is infinite disproportion. The mystical station is that of bedazzle-
ment, of immersion of the object in the subject. . . .[155]

To be non-being through one's own efforts is the very same as *to be* through God.[156]

This mystic station "is indeed Night . . . the night of unknowingness and of
unknowableness, and yet *luminous* night, since it is at the same time the theophany of the *absconditum* in the infinite multitude of its theophanic forms."[157]

After having attained to the supreme poverty and made the crossing
beyond the black light, which is "perilous in the extreme," "comes the resur-
gence from the danger of dementia, from metaphysical and moral nihilism, and
from collective imprisonment in ready-made forms."[158]

A FAILED INITIATION

In the metaphysical anthropology and physiology of Semnani there is described
a "series of subtle organs . . . each of which . . . is the typification of a prophet . . .

whose role and action it assumes. . . . [E]ach of these . . . is marked by a colored light . . . [which] informs the mystic as to his spiritual state."[159] The penultimate stage of ascent through these "seven prophets of your being" is Jesus. His color is luminous black. In the Qur'an "it is said that Jesus, as the prophet before the last of the prophets of our cycle, was the herald of *the last prophet,* i.e., of the advent of the Paraclete."[160] Jesus thus presages the "stage of the divine center (Mohammad) which is brilliant *green.*"[161] This is the emerald splendor of the complete fulfillment of personal initiation.

For Semnani, the Jesus of your being marks "exactly the perilous distracting stage whereat Christians in general and certain Sufis in Islam have been misled."[162] Corbin says of Semnani's critique that "everything takes place as though this Sufi Master's aim were to perfect the Christian *ta'wil* [hermeneutic], that is, to 'lead it back,' to open the way at last to its ultimate truth."[163]

Corbin now draws together all the threads of his mystical, metaphysical, and psychological themes to declare a pivot point for the mystical seeker, and for the history of the Western world. In order to avoid the catastrophes of dementia, nihilism, idolatry, and the annihilation of the person in social and collective anonymity, the soul must achieve the "mystical poverty, mystical nakedness" that completely eliminates "intoxication," or, in Jung's terminology, the dangers of inflation. One must overcome the lower modes of perception—the allurements of the lower states of the soul must be overcome and transcended. A profound misunderstanding of the true situation is common to dogmatic Christianity, to certain Sufis, and to Nietzsche, who stands as the representative of nihilistic modern man. Corbin writes:

> By a striking comparison, Semnani establishes a connection between the trap into which the Christian dogma of the Incarnation falls by proclaiming *homoousia*[164] and by affirming that 'Isa ibn Maryam [Jesus, son of Mary] is God, and the mystical intoxication in which such as Hallaj cry out: "I am God."[165] These dangers are symmetrical. On the one hand the Sufi, on experiencing the *fana fi'llah,* mistakes it for the actual and material resorption of human reality in the godhead; on the other, the Christian sees a *fana* of God into human reality. This is why Semnani perceives on the one side and other the same imminent threat of an irregularity in the development of consciousness. The Sufi would need an experienced shaykh to help him avoid the abyss and to lead him to the degree that is in truth the divine center of his being . . . where his higher, spiritual Ego opens. If not, the spiritual energy being wholly concentrated on this opening, it can happen that the lower ego is left a prey to extravagant thoughts and delirium. The "scales" are then completely unbalanced; in a fatal moment of looking back, the newborn higher Ego succumbs to what had been overcome and perishes in the moment of triumph. And this is just as true in the moral domain as in respect to the metaphysical perception of the divine and of being. It is a pre-

mature rupture in the process of growth, a "failed initiation." One could say that the mortal danger described by Semnani on both sides is the very same situation with which the West came face to face when Nietzsche cried out: "God is dead."[166]

Corbin sums up Semnani's conclusion:

> If in the course of spiritual growth "intoxication" has not been eliminated, that is, the subconscious allurements [of the lower levels which are the seats of the drives and the passions], then a lower mode of perception continues to function. . . . This is why the mystery of the theophany, the manifestation of the Holy Ghost in the visible form of the Angel Gabriel appearing in Maryam, his "breathing into" Maryam by which Jesus is made *Ruh Allah (Spiritus Dei)*—all of this—was not perceived by the Christians in their dogma of the Incarnation on the level of the *arcanum*. . . . Their dogma would have the birth of the one God take place materially "on earth," whereas "the Jesus of your being" is the mystery of spiritual birth.[167]

Thus, they cannot see the theophanic nature of beings: that all beings are mirrors, places of theophany. "If one thinks in terms of theophany . . . not in terms of hypostatic union, one is speaking only of a corporeal receptacle . . . which fills the role and function of a *mirror*."[168] The Christian dogma of the Incarnation on the other hand proposes "the *fana* of the divine into human reality." This amounts to a "historicization, secularization, socialization" of the divine.[169] *It is this fall of the divine into the historical, material world, which provides the necessary condition for the projection of God into matter in which Jung found the seeds of modern science.* It is the dogma of the Incarnation that underlies the alchemist's inabilities to distinguish spiritual birth and material transformation. The identification of God with man, of the divine with the material, confounds the levels of being, and causes the disappearance of that intermediate realm that stretches forever between creatures and their Creator. This identification led to the eventual deification of the human, and the demythologization of the divine. The realm of the *anima,* of the elusive, symbolic soul is eliminated.

Hallaj and Nietzsche both err because of a failed initiation: in Jungian terms, they both identify with the archetype of the Self, and perish in dementia. They fail to make that perilous journey beyond the *ego* and so the true Self escapes them—they discover "an ego with the godhead as predicate" rather than understanding and experiencing it as the organ and place of a theophany. They fail to see what Corbin elsewhere refers to as *sirr sirr,* the "secret of the secret." And the secret consists in this: "your autonomy is a fiction. In reality you are the subject of a verb in the passive (you are the *ego* of a *cogitor*)."[170] This is what prevents the inward turn from collapsing into narcissism. At the heart of the innermost consciousness is the Anthropos, Hermes, guide of souls, who for Islam is Gabriel the Angel of Revelation appearing to each individual in a form which is secret, absolutely unique, and Objective in the true sense. This secret was inaccessible to Descartes whose doubt decimated the inner world and left it ravaged, impersonal, and empty, a mere abstract scheme whose logical entities represent, as Corbin is fond of saying, "only the dead bodies of Angels."

The result of all of these failures is the same: idolatry. Idols on either side: the worship of a God who is an Object, or of an autonomous Self who is such a God. The experience of Western man is for Corbin defined by two symmetrical events. On the one hand, by the annihilation of God into matter, and so into history, and in the end into the realm of natural science, and of objects which cannot then be symbols, theophanies, revelations. And on the other hand, by the birth of Faustian man, represented most purely by Nietzsche, whose failure to attain the mystical poverty required in order to prevent the demonic inflation of the Superman defines our own present predicament. The problem is, in one sense, rooted in a failure of masculinity to come to terms with the femininity of matter at several levels. The Puer and the Narcissist both fail to relate to the potentialities for the experience of otherness and of transcendence inherent in the material world. The Puer refuses to be born, and tries to engage in a premature escape from the world. The Narcissist can see only his own face—this is the vision characteristic of modern humanity.

Corbin's account of the turn inward toward the Darkness within reveals a dual challenge which can only be met if we are oriented initially in such a way that we cannot confuse the blackness of the abyss of evil and Ahrimanian Darkness with the terrors of annihilation stemming from the encounter with the Hidden God. Without such orientation, without guidance, without an adequate psycho-cosmology and the help of a Guide, the individual seeker faces long odds indeed.

In the modern world we are heirs to a materialistic agnosticism for which the very category of the person has nearly disappeared in favor of biological and historical descriptions of the human being. At the same time we face a truly demonic dementia of inflation as we fancy ourselves Masters of the Earth in a final, fatal narcissistic frenzy of attempted control. On both counts Jung was right—we are the heirs of the alchemy that gave rise to both modern technology and to Nietzsche.

Jung's drive toward wholeness, and his claims for of the autonomy of the psyche conflict inevitably with the open-endedness of the transcendence that derives from the mystical poverty of being. Jung himself could never quite escape from the world of the human. At the end of his life he could still say, "[W]e are hopelessly cooped up in an exclusively psychic world."[171] And yet he did see the way out, sometimes very clearly. He relates the following tale:

There is a fine old story about a student who came to a rabbi and said, "In the olden days there were men who saw the face of God. Why don't they any more?" The rabbi replied, "Because nowadays no one can stoop so low." One must stoop a little in order to fetch water from the stream.[172]

For Corbin too our salvation must be sought in *islam,* which means submission. It can only be found in that poverty of the *darwish* that opens onto the immense spaces at the heart of the secret of the secret of the inner man.

FOUR

WITHIN THIS DARKNESS

─────────────────────────

Incarnation, Theophany, and the Primordial Revelation

The black color, if you follow me, is light of pure Ipseity;
within this Darkness is the Water of Life.
—Shabestari's *Rose Garden of the Mystery*

FACES OF DARKNESS, FACES OF LIGHT:
MYSTICAL POVERTY AND THE
SILENT CLAMOR OF BEINGS

LISTEN TO THESE EXCERPTS from a haunting meditation, written by Henry Corbin in 1932 at the edge of Lake Siljan in Sweden when he was twenty-nine years old. He called it *Theology by the Lakeside:*

Everything is but revelation; there can only be re-velation. But revelation comes from the Spirit, and there is no knowledge of the Spirit.

It will soon be dusk, but for now the clouds are still clear, the pines are not yet darkened, for the lake brightens them into transparency. And everything is green with a green that would be richer than if pulling all the organ stops in recital. It must be heard seated, very close to the Earth, arms crossed, eyes closed, pretending to sleep.

For it is not necessary to strut about like a conqueror and want to give a name to things, to everything; it is they who will tell you who they are, if you listen, yielding like a lover; for suddenly for you, in the untroubled peace of this forest of the North, the Earth has come to Thou, visible as an Angel

63

that would perhaps be a woman, and in this apparition, this greatly green and thronging solitude, yes, the Angel too is robed in green, the green of dusk, of silence and of truth. Then there is in you all the sweetness that is present in the surrender to an embrace that triumphs over you.

Earth, Angel, Woman, all of this is one thing that I adore and that is present in this forest. Dusk on the lake: my Annunciation. . . .

The Mystery of Holy Communion where you will be ushered in, where all the beings will be present, yes, you can only say it in the future. Because at each moment where you read *in truth* as now what is there before you, where you hear the Angel, and the Earth and Woman, then you receive Everything, Everything, in your absolute poverty. But as soon as you have read and have received, as soon as you consider, as you want to understand, as you want to possess, to give a name and restrain, to explain and recover, ah! there is only a cipher, and your judgment is pronounced. . . .

. . . you are the poor one, you are man; and he is God, and you cannot know God, or the Angel, or the Earth, or Woman. You must be encountered, taken, known, that they may speak, otherwise you are alone. . . .[1]

With these extraordinary words Corbin presents the vision that ruled his life. They were written when he was in Sweden to visit the philologist and historian of religions Georges Dumézil and the orientalist H. S. Nyberg. Earlier that year he'd traveled to Germany to meet Karl Barth. The previous year he had gone to Freiburg to speak with Martin Heidegger, whose *What is Metaphysics?* he was translating. Three years before, in Paris, Louis Massignon had given him a copy of *The Philosophy of Illumination* by the twelfth-century Persian mystic and philosopher Suhrawardi. Corbin wrote many years later, "[T]hrough my meeting with Suhrawardi, my spiritual destiny for the passage through this world was sealed. Platonism, expressed in terms of the Zoroastrian angelology of ancient Persia, illuminated the path that I was seeking."[2]

In the imagination of this remarkable man, just beginning his long life's work, we find an astonishing variety of influences: Christian theology, Heideggerian phenomenology, and Islamic mysticism fused with Zoroastrian angelology; all united by a deep reverence for what in Islam is called the Primordial Revelation: the book of nature.

As participants in the catastrophically destructive modern world we need to understand what makes possible this vision of the earth and its creatures. In the attempt, we will find ourselves at the heart of difficult questions regarding Gods, both hidden and revealed, language, imagination, sensation, and matter. We begin with an outline of Corbin's understanding of the gnostic quest and the cosmology underlying it. Then we turn to an examination of the dominant tradition in Christian theology to see why he saw it as the result of a failed initiation that has had disastrous consequences for Western culture. Finally I will take some liberties with Corbin's vision and with the Islamic perspective as he represents it, to suggest a view of the place of humanity in the natural world that is, I hope, in keeping with the spirit of Corbin's passionate personal quest.

Corbin reveals to us a phenomenology of the Earth of the Primordial Revelation, an earth where beings announce themselves and tell us who they are in the twilight of the setting sun. In accordance with his vision, we look to Heaven as it was conceived in the imagination of the Zoroastrians of ancient Persia.

In the cosmology of the Avesta the supreme being Ohrmazd is surrounded by six celestial Persons of Light whose holiness takes the form of "an activating Energy that communicates being, establishes it, and causes it to superabound in all beings."[3] These seven Presences provide for the existence and the salvation of the world of creatures, and by cooperating with them all creatures can participate in the ascent toward the heaven from which they originally descended. There is reason to struggle for this return because the world of creation is a world of mixture and conflict, where the powers of Darkness, ruled by Ahriman, battle with the powers of Light. But in this battle the creatures are not abandoned. Between them and the Archangels of Light there are arrayed countless intermediary celestial beings. Among them is the feminine Angel of the Earth whose image is Sophia, the feminine figure of Wisdom. And there are the Fravartis, whose name means "those who have chosen," chosen, that is, to fight against the powers of Darkness. Every being belonging to the world of Light has a Fravarti, a celestial counterpart, in the world of Light. And so every being has a dual structure that defines its orientation in the struggle toward the Light. The quest to unveil this heavenly twin defines the moral and spiritual destiny of the soul of every human being, and of the soul of the world itself. The task is to actualize, on this earth, the "Energy of sacral Light" that transforms, transfigures, and glorifies the souls of all beings. This transformation is an alchemical process: the very substance of things is the locus of the work, both container and content, and the goal is the transmutation of each being into a more subtle, more definite, more real state.

Corbin discovered this ancient cosmology imagined anew in a context fundamentally in harmony with it, in the work of the twelfth-century Persian mystic and Master of Illumination, Shihab al-Din Yahya al-Suhrawardi. Suhrawardi's project was to fuse Zoroastrian angelology with Platonic and Neoplatonic cosmology and with the prophetic revelation of Islam. It was Suhrawardi who first articulated a clear grasp of the world of the Imagination, the world intermediary between sensation and intellect that Corbin was to call the *imaginal* world. It is by means of imaginal perception that the Zoroastrian Light of Glory can be perceived. It is in the imaginal world that the alchemical transformation takes place. It is the place of the visions of the prophets. The Presence of God in the Burning Bush, the apparitions of Gabriel to Mary and to Mohammad, all the events of sacred history are perceived by means of organs of perception that open onto this world and its myriad beings of light.

In order to experience the Earth as an Angel, to hear the voices of beings calling to us in the twilight, to encounter another *person* in any sense at all, we have to be able to perceive at least the vestiges of the light of Glory, of the Presence at the summit from which they all descend. All of us, however dimly, perceive events in the imaginal world, and the task of transformation requires the development of the senses that open us into that world.

In order to understand the critique of Western civilization that Corbin proposes, we have to outline the process of approach to the Light of Glory that illuminates the Earth. Our being derives from the Light of Heaven. In Zoroastrianism this is *Xvarnah*. In Islam it is the light of Allah, who is "light upon light." The supreme human science is the physiology of the "body of light" that derives from Him. And it is this physiology that is the chief concern of the Central Asian Sufism of the order known as the *Kubrawiyyah*.[4] Suhrawardi himself refers to the lights that a mystic sees in the imaginal world, but it is in the work of Najm Kubra[5] that a detailed phenomenology of lights and colors is first developed. Among his followers two stand out, as we have seen above: Najm Razi[6] and Alaoddawleh Semnani.[7]

The details of this physiology of light are complex and beautiful. We can barely present its skeleton here. It describes a process of transformation in the body and soul of the gnostic during the journey toward God. The fundamental doctrine is that "like can only be known by like." What is known corresponds to the mode of being of the knower. You can only know what you *are*. There are different modes of being for both the soul and the worlds it inhabits. These worlds are arranged in a hierarchical series ascending toward the divine. But to speak of the soul and the world as if they were two things can be misleading because it emphasizes a sharp distinction between them. But this is just what must be discarded. We never have knowledge of an "objective" reality. The soul can only know what it *is*. Corbin writes,

> [U]ltimately what we call *physis* and the physical is but the reflection of the world of the Soul; there is no pure physics, but always the physics of some definite psychic activity.[8]

It only seems to us that the soul and the world are distinct. That is because we are not sufficiently conscious. Najm Razi tells us this:

> Know that the soul, the devil, the angel are not realities outside you: you *are* they. Likewise Heaven, Earth and the Throne are not outside you, nor paradise nor hell, nor death nor life. They exist in you; when you have accomplished the mystical journey and have become pure you will become conscious of that.[9]

The gnostic journey is a process of becoming conscious. It accomplishes the interiorization of the world. This does not mean swallowing it, taking it into the ego. That is what modern culture is trying to do. It is instead a "coming out toward oneself," an *exodus* out of the narrow and constricting world of literal, public materiality and a resurrection of the psychocosmic unity that is the soul and its world.

This epistemology is founded on a doctrine of participation. We can only know by virtue of our participation in the being of the thing known. In Najm Kubra's words,

> You can only see or witness an object by means of some part of that same object . . . it is only the mine whence it came which a precious stone sees, desires, and yearns for. So when you have vision of a sky, an earth, a sun, stars or a moon, you should know that the particle in you which has its origin in that same mine has become pure. The more pure you become, the purer and more radiant will be the sky that appears to you, until in the last stages of the journey you travel within the Divine Purity. But Divine Purity is limitless, so never think that there is not something more exalted still ahead.[10]

The principle that like can only be known by like is the fundamental principle of alchemy. Coming to consciousness, coming to *know* is an alchemical procedure because it can only occur by means of a transformation of the body and of the world. It requires the development of a subtle, imaginal body, a resurrection body, as a refinement, not a rejection, of the literal, material body perceptible by the common senses. This can only take place in and through the imaginal world. For Najm Kubra and his followers the achievement of the subtle body can be recognized and accomplished by means of the imaginal perception of "photisms," of colored lights. They mark the stages on the path. They occur *in* and *to* the traveler and are realizations of the mode of being attained. They are interior, but not subjective. They occur in the *mundus imaginalis* and are perfectly real, just as the Burning Bush is real, but are not thereby visible to all: they are *too real* to be visible to everyone. What we call objective reality isn't precisely *false*, it is merely the lowest form of reality.

Alchemy requires a method. Every Sufi Order specifies a particular method. The rules of the *Kubrawiyyah* include the Eight Principles of Junayd of Bagdad: ritual purity, fasting, silence, seclusion, invocation *(dhikr)*, absolute devotion to the shaykh, repression of all thoughts, emotions, and impulses as they occur, and surrender to the will of God. The disciple must at all costs avoid the impulse to desire visionary experience—this comes directly from the lower soul.[11] But the method par excellence in Sufism is the *dhikr,* the "remembrance" of God. *Dhikr* is "meditative recitation of the Qur'an, ritual prayer, the names of God."[12] Islam is based upon the Revelation of the Word of God. The Qur'an was and is experienced first and foremost as an oral phenomenon.[13] It is the spoken word that is primordial, and the written text is spoken and memorized for recitation. The embodiment of the Word of God is fundamental to Islamic spirituality. God has spoken through the prophets, but He also sings, speaks, and bodies forth his signs in the Heavens and in the souls of the believers. Thus the meditative, interiorizing recitation of the Word can bring forth tremendous energies for drawing creation toward the divine. But this is too abstract. The energies released by *dhikr* don't merely raise the soul: they transform it by enabling it to attain a new mode of being. And this includes the transformation of the organs of perception that give form and body to the soul and its world, and the growth of a subtle body in harmony with the attributes that characterize the state of the soul and the world it now inhabits. Among the *Kubrawiyyah* the *dhikr* embraces an array of techniques of posture and breathing that serve to emphasize that this remembrance is grounded in the body.

The gnostic journey is not without risk: it is easy to get lost in an infinite world. It is no sojourn into a vague Paradise of disembodied forms. The closer to divinity, the more real and more individual the soul becomes. Infinite because God is the All-Encompassing. More definite because God is the Unifier, and it is His Oneness that grounds the uniqueness of every being. As William Blake knew well, things in the world of imagination are *more* detailed, *more* definite than anything in the public world. The ascent through the modes of being is the ascent of the self toward the Angel that defines its individuality. The status of personhood is not given: it must be *won*. We are born with the freedom to become demons or angels or anything in between. Our task is to travel toward the Light that emanates from our celestial counterpart, our Fravarti, our Angel, through whom the Light of the Divine is transmitted to us.

The stakes are very high and the opportunities for losing one's way are great. That is why a guide is required. You *cannot* raise yourself: that is the reason for Revelation. That is why there are prophets. Islam is not a religion of salvation as is Christianity. It is a religion of guidance. There is no doctrine of original sin in Islam. Though we are surely free to descend to the level of demons, and are prey to the temptations of Iblis (Satan), our fundamental trouble is ignorance, and we need constant reminders of who we are and where we should be heading. The Qur'an says that for every people there have been sent messengers. The lineage of their followers provides for guidance after they are gone. For the Peoples of the Book, there is of course the sacred text. For everyone there is the Primordial Revelation of Nature, though we forget, and lose sight of the signs placed there. Corbin was himself suspicious of human masters. He gave preeminence in his writings to the role of the Paraclete in both Christian and Islamic eschatology as the Figure who ushers in the reign of the Spirit, the true religion of the eternal gospel. The goal for Corbin is to be able to seek freely the teachings of all the masters, but to be bound as no one's slave. The gravity of this work must be acknowledged. One does not trifle with the alchemy of the soul. Corbin writes:

> The seriousness of the role of the Imagination is stressed by our philosophers when they state that it can be "the Tree of Blessedness" or on the con-

trary "the Accursed Tree" of which the Qur'an speaks, that which means Angel or Demon in power. The imaginary can be innocuous, the *imaginal* can never be so.[14]

The pilgrim must trust in the Guide, the Word, and the method. Suhrawardi has said, "only the heart that holds fast to the cable of the Qur'an and the train of the robe of the *dhikr*" can escape from the snares of darkness and evil.[15]

For an account of the stages of the quest we turn again to the doctrines of Semnani. It is in his work that the correspondence between prophetic religion and luminous physiology is most clearly outlined, and as we have detailed above, it is his insight into the significance of Christ that provides a pivot point for Corbin's critique of Christian civilization.

For Semnani the stages correspond to the modes of being of the major prophets in the lineage of Abraham as it is known in Islamic tradition. To each prophet, each stage, there corresponds a light of a characteristic color that appears to the mystic, as well as specific moral and psychological attributes. The correspondences occur because the soul's mode of being *is* its mode of understanding and its mode of perception. The soul's self-knowledge is its knowledge of its world. But since the Word of God takes the form of the signs in the world and in the soul as well as the Revealed Text, the soul "reads" itself and the world in accordance with its stage in the process of coming to consciousness. This means that the depths of meaning that can be discerned in the exegesis of the Qur'an must correspond to the spiritual hermeneutics that the soul is able to perform upon itself and on the world of Nature. Recall Corbin's lakeside meditation. He says there that one may "read *in truth* . . . what is there before you." When we read Nature in this way we perceive her as a person, an Angel. There are profound correspondences among spiritual alchemy, the hermeneutics of the Sacred Text and of the Book of Nature, and the structure of prophetic religion as it takes form in the physiology of the body of light. There is a perfect correspondence between the birth, initiation, and growth of the soul on its journey to God and the cycle of prophecy in the Abrahamic tradition. It is because of this that the Imam Jafar could say: "Alchemy is the sister of prophecy."[16]

In the mystical physiology of Semnani introduced above, there are seven levels on the path toward the divine and they are homologous to the seven "prophets of your being."[17] First there is Adam. The color that dominates this stage is a smoky grey-black. The physical organ or center with which this resonates is the "subtle bodily organ" or the "mold." This derives directly from the *anima mundi* and is "the embryonic mold" providing the basis for the growth of the resurrection body.

The second level is that of Noah—the Noah of your being. Its color is blue, and to it corresponds the *nafs ammara,* the extravagant lower soul or *ego* of the natural human. It is passionate and prone to evil, and must be overcome through self-consciousness.

The third level is that of Abraham. The organ is the heart *(qalb)*. This is the embryonic form of the celestial Self, the eternal Individual. Its color is red. This is the "pacified soul" and is the organ of perception of the imaginal world.

Fourth is the Moses of your being. The organ is the mystery, secret, or threshold of supraconsciousness *(sirr)*. It is the place of intimate conversation between Persons. The color is white.

Fifth is the noble spirit *(ruh)*. Yellow is the color of the David of your being.

The sixth level marks the stage of Jesus. It is what in the Latin west was called the *Arcanum,* through which help and inspiration from the Holy Spirit, the Paraclete, may come. Its color is black.

The final level is of course that of Mohammad. It is the stage of the truth, the reality of your being, the true Self whose embryo is found at the origin, at the stage of Abraham. The journey, Corbin writes,

> ends by actualizing, in the human microcosm, the truth of the meaning according to which the religion of Mohammad originates in the religion of Abraham, for "Abraham was neither Jew nor Christian, but a pure believer, a *Moslem . . .*" (Qur'an 3: 60).[18]

In accordance with Islamic iconography, the color of the final stage is emerald green. For Corbin this stage marks the meeting with the heaven Guide, the perfectly individuated and individual Angel of Humanity and Angel of Knowledge that is the biblical Angel of the Face. This is the Figure of whom Mohammad could say: "I have seen my Lord in the most beautiful of forms." It announces the truth that beauty is the supreme theophany. The Qur'anic source for this Person is Sura XVIII. The figure that came to be interpreted as *Khidr* in Islamic tradition appears here in an enigmatic episode. Moses and his servant travel to "the meeting place of the two seas." There they meet an unnamed messenger, a personal guide who initiates Moses into "the science of predestination. . . . He reveals to Moses the secret mystic truth . . . that transcends the *shari'a,* and this explains why the spirituality inaugurated by Khidr is free from the servitude of literal religion."[19] The seeker is born into his true self through the encounter with Khidr, the interpreter of a law beyond the Law, the divine hermeneut.

Now we come to the crux of the matter. The penultimate stage, that of Jesus the herald of the Paraclete, is known by the appearance of the color Black. The experience of this Darkness is common to all the Sufis of the Central Asian school and to others as well.[20] To understand the significance of this "darkness at the approach to the pole" we must be oriented in the scheme of the tripartite psychocosmology that we have outlined earlier.[21] There is first of all the realm of consciousness, the daylight of the normal human being and the world of common, public, and objective things. This is the clear and distinct world of literalists of all kinds: scientists, religious dogmatists, anyone who relies on the "plain and simple facts" that all can see. But this world is in reality a world of mixture, of chiaroscuro, of colors shading off into the shadows. Pervading all things, penetrating every truth, every *ego,* every "object" there is a shifting infinitude of half-known or unknown powers, presences and correspondences that prevent our knowing anything with precision and certainty. But remember. As Semnani has made clear, there are two kinds of darkness, two sources of bewilderment. There is the Darkness that is only Darkness, a darkness that refuses Light and is demonic in the extremity of its distance from the Light. This is the darkness of un-consciousness emanating from the counterpower, the darkness of Ahriman, of Iblis, of Satan. It is easy to confuse this active Darkness that is evil, with the passive and unconscious darkness of matter as unformed potential. The material state per se is neither evil nor even in a sense inherently dark, since the darkness of matter is a measure of its distance from the Divinity.[22]

Corbin's view of the essential purity and goodness of the bodily state is in accord with ancient Zoroastrian beliefs. It is only by admixture with Ahrimanian darkness that the boundaries are breached and the body is defiled. In its original state, to which it can return, the body is a source of intelligent life and good action. Williams writes that "purity is felt to be an intensely fecund state: the higher the state of purity, the more intense may be the impregnation by the creative forces of the divine beings. . . ."[23] The Zoroastrians held it to be a duty to make the body an abode for the gods.

The active darkness of evil is the darkness and confusion to which the *nafs ammara,* the lower soul, is susceptible. It is a realm marked by contamination and confusion and lack of discrimination of qualities and of one thing from another. It is the task of the alchemical hermeneutic to put each thing in its proper place. We are filled with the undiscriminated darknesses of Earth, Air, Water, and Fire, and we are thus buried underneath them. Najm Kubra has written:

> The only way to separate yourself from [these darknesses] is to act in such a way that every rightful part in you comes together with that to which it rightfully belongs, that is, by acting in such a way that each part comes together with its counterpart: Earth receives the earthly part, Water the watery part, Air the etheric part, Fire the fiery part. When each has received its share, you will finally be delivered of these burdens.[24]

And then the soul and its world, this *psychocosmos,* is freed not merely *from* the Darkness, but *for* the Darkness. Because there is another Darkness, one that is not merely black, but is a luminous Night, a dazzling Blackness, a Darkness at the approach to the Pole. This is the Black Light of what Corbin calls supraconsciousness. If we do not recognize the existence of this second Darkness pervading all things, this Black Light of Divine Night, we will be forever disoriented among the shadows, unable to distinguish one darkness from another, incapable of that transmutation of the soul that has as its goal the meeting with the celestial Self and the genesis of the celestial Earth.

The appearance of Black Light marks the moment of supreme danger. We are surrounded by dangers: God and the Devil both. This dazzling Black Light heralds the annihilation of the *ego* in the Divine Presence. It reveals the unknowable origin of the divine power, glory and beauty. It announces the Nothing that exists beyond all being, beyond all the subtle matter that mirrors its uncanny light. The Black Light marks the region of the Absolute, the *Deus absconditus,* the unknown and unknowable God.

Corbin tells us that one of the paramount differences between the philosopher and the gnostic lies in the way this absent God is encountered and experienced. He writes, "[W]hat to a philosopher is doubt, the impossibility of proof, is to [the gnostics] absence and trial."[25] The experience of emptiness and of human abandonment in a meaningless universe is conceived entirely differently by the philosophers and the gnostics. He continues,

> What we experience as an obsession with nothingness or as acquiescence in
> a nonbeing over which we have no power, was to them a manifestation of
> divine anger, the anger of the mystic Beloved. But even that was a real Pres-
> ence, the presence of that Image which never forsook our Sufis.[26]

One of the ways in which Divinity appears is by withdrawing, even into nothingness.

Najm Razi relates the supersensory lights of the mystical journey to one of the most fundamental doctrines of Islamic theology, the doctrine of the Names of God. The Names or Attributes of God fall into two great categories: the Names of Majesty and the Names of Beauty. The Names of Majesty express God's wrath, rigor, inaccessibility, and sublimity, the Names of Beauty His gentleness, mercy, and nearness. For Najm Razi the theophanies of the divine lights are also so divided: Lights of Majesty and Lights of Beauty. The colored lights are the Lights of Beauty. The Black Light is the Light of Majesty. Unlike the Ahrimanian Darkness that can be conquered and banished by the spiritual pilgrim, the Black Light of Majesty is inseparable from the Lights of Beauty. Corbin writes that Majesty and Beauty

> are the two great categories of attributes which refer respectively to the divine
> Being as *Deus absconditus* and as *Deus revelatus,* Beauty being the supreme
> theophany, divine self-revelation. In fact they are inseparable and there is a
> constant interplay between the inaccessible Majesty of Beauty and the fasci-
> nating Beauty of inaccessible Majesty.[27]

This duality is the central feature of all Creation: "[W]ithout the blossoming of Beauty as theophany man could not approach the sublimity of the *Deus absconditus.*"[28] And without the *Deus absconditus* there would be no world at all. This hidden deity is the beyond-being of negative or *apophatic* theology. Corbin writes,

> Any metaphysical doctrine which attempts a total explanation of the universe,
> finds it necessary to make something out about *nothing,* or rather, to make

everything out about *nothing,* since the initial principle from which the world derived, and which it must explain, must never be something contained in this world, and simultaneously it is necessary for this initial principle to possess all that is necessary to explain at once the being and the essence of the world and that which it contains. . . . It is necessary . . . that this initial principle be at once "all" and "nothing." . . .

. . . [This] is a *nihil a quo omnia fiunt,* a nothing from which all things are derived. This is the Nothing of the Absolute Divine, superior to being and thought.[29]

The absolute Divine from which everything proceeds provides the energy for the existence of all Creation. It is the source from which everything emanates, and corresponds for Corbin to the Light of Glory, the *Xvarnah* of Zoroastrianism, the power that brings all things into being. The Divinity beyond-being is absolute and absolutely annihilating. Come too close and the human subject disappears.

The archetype of the mystic journey in Islam is the *miraj* of Mohammad, his ascent to the Absolute, mediated by Gabriel, the Angel of Humanity, of Knowledge, and of Revelation. In this *miraj* the moment of greatest danger is the penetration beyond what the Qur'an calls the Lotus of the Limit where there occurs the *fana fi'llah,* the annihilation of the soul and its resorption into God. This ordeal is the experience of death to which the Prophet refers in the saying "You must die before you die!" This moment of the mystic's greatest challenge signifies the recognition of the Unknowable in a supreme act of metaphysical renunciation. This is the real meaning of poverty, of the Persian word *darwish.*

Metaphysical poverty is the true state of all beings: everything in creation *has* nothing in itself, *is* nothing in itself. Mir Damad heard "the great occult clamor of beings," the "silent clamor of their metaphysical distress" that appeared to him as a music of cosmic anguish and as a sudden black light invading the entire universe.[30] This is a direct perception of what rational philosophy calls the contingency of being. It is the experience behind the great question of metaphysics: "Why is there something rather than nothing?" For the gnostic it takes the form of a shattering experience of annihilation and terror, undoing all the solid foundations upon which the *ego* and the literal world is built. In Corbin's words,

The black light reveals the very secret of being, which can only *be* as *made-to-be;* all beings have a twofold face, a face of light and a black face. The luminous face, the face of day, is the only one that . . . the common run of men perceive. . . . Their black face, the one the mystic perceives, is their poverty. . . . The totality of their being is their daylight face and their night face. . . .[31]

And at the same time, this Absolute beyond-being is also, in the Abrahamic tradition, the Absolute Subject. This giver of being can never be an object, a thing, a being. In its infinite fecundity and mystery, its forever-receding depth and absolute Unity, it is the unifier and archetype of the Person, and of that personhood and interiority that infuses all the beings of the Earth perceived and experienced as an Angel.

The dual face of every being explains the necessity for two kinds of theology: affirmative *(kataphatic)* and negative *(apophatic)*. Both are indispensable. They interpenetrate in the same way as the attributes of Majesty and Beauty. Positive theology in isolation becomes Positivism. Dogmas and idols spring up everywhere. Negative theology unaided can disclose no beauties, no Treasures longing to be known. Without the balancing perceptions provided by the Names of Beauty, apophatic theology cannot distinguish between the *Deus absconditus* and the abyss of nihilism. It must collapse into blindness, denial, and bitterness and end as nihilism pure and simple. Only through the perception of the indissoluble unity of the two faces of being in creation, the poverty of the soul of humanity and of the world, can we perceive the beauty and the animation and the personification of the things of the world. It is only by the continual perception of this beauty-in-poverty that our certainties, our graspings, our hardnesses of heart can be perpetually undone.

IN VAGABONDAGE AND PERDITION

FAILURES OF INITIATION, FAILURES OF IMAGINATION

Corbin said that the philosophical tradition of the Christian West has been the theater for the "battle for the Soul of the World."[32] It is a battle that we have largely lost. For Corbin the pivotal events in this history concern the interpretation of the doctrine of the Incarnation, what theologians call Christology: the attempt to answer the question, "Who was Jesus?" On this crucial question he accepts Semnani's reading of Christianity. Corbin says:

> It is worth our while to listen attentively to this evaluation of Christianity as formulated by a Sufi. . . . Semnani's critique is made in the name of spiritual experience; everything takes place as though this Sufi Master's aim were to perfect the Christian *ta'wil* [hermeneutic], that is, to "lead it back," to open the way at last to its ultimate truth.[33]

We have seen that for Semnani the Black Light erupts at the level of the Jesus of your being, and that this is the most perilous stage on the initiatic path. The pilgrim is threatened here most of all with madness and with metaphysical and moral nihilism.[34] Corbin follows Semnani in affirming a homology between the ecstatic cry of Sufis such as al-Hallaj, "I am God!" and the proclamation that Jesus is God Incarnate. He writes,

These dangers are symmetrical. On the one hand the Sufi, on experiencing the *fana fi'llah,* mistakes it for the actual and material reabsorption of human reality in the Godhead; on the other, the Christian sees a *fana* of God into human reality.[35]

This is the result of a failed initiation. It signals a failure to avoid the abyss that opens up at just that precarious point where the *ego* gives way to the higher Self. If the divine center is not attained, if the poverty of the soul is not complete, then the lower modes of perception remain operative, the higher realities cannot be attained and the lower soul is subject to dementia, intoxication, and a compensating inflation, which grows Promethean and unbounded in response to the vision of the Abyss. Corbin writes, "In a fatal moment of looking back the newborn higher [Self] . . . perishes in the moment of triumph." On the one hand the *ego* mistakes itself for God. On the other, God collapses into history. And seeing all of Western history encapsulated in this momentous event, Corbin argues that this "is the very same situation with which the West came face to face when Nietzsche cried out: 'God is dead.'"[36] In this momentous failure, the West finally lost its celestial Pole, for we are only persons "by virtue of this celestial dimension, archetypal, angelic, which is the celestial pole without which the terrestrial pole of [our] human dimension is completely *depolarized* in vagabondage and perdition."[37]

The encounter of the unprepared *ego* with the *Deus absconditum* results in the experience of the Abyss, the *nihil* of radical nihilism. If God is dead then man is master. The human subject claims the vertiginous freedom to be the source of all values. At the same time this marks the brutal violation of the Hidden Treasure who created the world out of the depths of an eternal loneliness and longing to be known. It signals the end of mystery, the rending of the veils, the destruction of the cosmic Temple, the death of the Soul. What is an experience of the Abyss from the point of view of the human soul, is, from the point of view of the Divinity, so to speak, the collapse of God into history. To say that Christ *is* God incarnate, is equivalent to saying that God is dead. The entry of God materially, wholly, and substantially into historical, material, and public time and space is the archetypal act of secularization. A *fana* of the divine into human reality can only result in the secularization, historicization, and socialization of all religious phenomena, which must then be defined in terms that are public, general, universal, and abstract. If the Incarnation is a historical event that has occurred once and for all, then sacred history is closed and access of the individual soul to God is made problematic at best and impossible at worst, since it must rely on the common dogmas of the Church as the bearer of the collective memory of this unique, definitive Event. A God who is only Public, a God who is only Visible, a God in History, is no God at all. A God not balanced by the overwhelming *absconditum* is an Idol and a Holy Terror.

It is vital for orthodox Christian dogma that God became human *in the flesh* and was both fully God and fully human, since it is only through this union that a sinful humanity can be saved. Christianity is a religion of salvation, and doctrines of how that salvation or Atonement can come about are central to its teachings. We cannot save ourselves, but must be saved through the descent of Christ. For Corbin it is this idea that God must descend and live here among the fallen creatures in order for salvation to be possible that is the root of the problem. His contention is that because of an emphasis on sin and human helplessness with respect to salvation, Christian theologians have felt the need to unite the divine and the human at the level of fallen humanity. But this shattering violation of the Mystery turns the world inside out. It collapses the celestial hierarchies, and reduces being to a single level. God is demythologized, the world is abandoned to secular history, and the possibility of a personal relation to the Divine is eliminated.

The connection between the Violation of the Hidden Treasure and the terrible Void of the Abyss is intimated in the Gospel's narration of that most horrible moment in Christian history:

> There was darkness over the whole land . . . and at the ninth hour Jesus cried with a loud voice . . . "My God, My God, why hast Thou forsaken me?"[38]

> and behold, the curtain of the temple was torn in two, from top to bottom; and the earth shook, and the rocks were split.[39]

Truly this is the hour of darkness. The encounter with the Hidden God is the moment of greatest danger. All of Creation teeters on the brink: "Either he will be swallowed up in dementia or he will rise again from it, initiated in the meaning of theophanies and revelations."

Two paths lead out from this pivotal moment. On one there is the Death of God and the birth of a Promethean, rapacious, and monstrous Humanity. On the other, Resurrection and the poverty of a life in sympathy with beings.

Read now these words from the Qur'an:

> . . . but they neither killed nor crucified him,
> though so it appeared to them . . . but God raised him up. . . .[40]

They did not kill him. They could never kill him, because the meaning of Christ does not lie in a body or in a moment in time. Christ was never a man. Christ was, Christ is, and Christ will ever be a *theophany*, "a forever inexhaustible event of the soul."[41] Everything is at stake here. The whole cosmos depends upon the interpretation of this moment. Remember Corbin's words: "There is only Revelation." There are *only* theophanies. This is the truth that we are called to see. Our knowledge, our vision, our hearing, all of this is worth what we *are*. Our world is a measure of our being. The event of the Transfiguration as told in the apocryphal *Acts of Thomas* makes this quite clear. The form of the Lord was visible only to some, and among these each saw something different, some a boy, some a youth, some an old man. But each could say: "I saw him as I was able to receive him."[42]

The alternative to the catastrophe of the death of God is the theophanic cosmology of the gnostics in the Abrahamic tradition. Corbin devoted his life to articulating this vision of the essential harmony at the root of all of the religions of the Book, the vision of what he was to call in his late work the *Harmonia Abrahamica*.[43] It is based on a Christology radically different from the one that became dogma. It requires a return to the Christology of the Ebionites, who had no doctrine of the Trinity, or of the substantial union of the divine and human in Jesus. For these Jewish-Christians, Jesus was a manifestation of the celestial Son of Man, the *Christos Angelos,* who was consecrated as Christ at his baptism. Jesus then takes his place in the lineage of the True Prophets. Corbin writes,

> [F]or Ebionite Christianity . . . sacred history, the hierology of humanity, is constituted by the successive manifestations . . . of the celestial *Anthropos,* of the eternal *Adam-Christos* who is the prophet of Truth, the True Prophet. We count seven of these manifestations, eight if we include the terrestrial person of Adam himself. They are Adam, Noah, Enoch, Abraham, Isaac, Jacob, Moses, Jesus. . . . The fundamental basis of this prophetology is therefore the idea of the True Prophet who is the celestial *Anthropos,* the *Christus aeternus,* hastening from christophany to christophany "toward the place of his repose." Now, this is the same structure that Islamic prophetology presents, with this difference, that the succession of christophanies is no longer completed with the prophet Jesus of Nazareth, but with the prophet of Islam, the "Seal of the Prophets" whose coming Jesus himself announced, and who is the "recapitulation" of all the prophets. . . .[44]

Thus, Mohammad is identified with the figure of the Paraclete in the Gospel of John. Among the Shi'ites, the Twelfth Imam, the Hidden Imam, is sometimes identified with this final manifestation of the True Prophet, the central figure of the Eternal Gospel.

The death of Christ signifies something utterly different from what we have come to accept. Corbin relates with evident approval the story of Christ's death told in the Medieval Gospel of Barnabas. Jesus is taken up by the Angels, *before* Good Friday. Judas Iscariot, transformed to resemble Jesus, is arrested and killed upon the Cross. And so His followers believe that He has died. It must be this way, since, as Corbin writes,

> in making of him the "Son of God" it is Man himself that humanity has equated with God, and it was only possible to expiate this blasphemy through succumbing to the belief that his God was dead. Everything occurs as if the Ebionite-Islamic prophetology here went ahead to denounce and refute the false news of the "death of God."

It is undeniable that this vision overturns from top to bottom some eigh-
teen centuries of the Christian theology of History.[45]

Without any illusions about the magnitude of the transformation he is sug-
gesting, this vision is Corbin's answer to those who wonder whether Christianity itself is capable of surviving. It is only by being open to a radically
reformed Christianity in harmony with the mystical traditions of the rest of the
Abrahamic tradition, that the religion of Christ can find its fulfillment. Only a
Christianity based on theophany can survive.

There is a balance, an "essential community being visible and invisible things"[46]
and it is the function of theophanic perception to reveal this community as it
is within the power of each being to perceive. To train our senses to recognize
this community even dimly, is to begin to realize the "cognitive function of
sympathy"[47] and to sense in the presence of the beings of this world the harmonies that resonate through all the worlds beyond. To live in sensate sympathy with the beings of the world requires that we experience the spaces that
extend singing between the Terrible Majesty of the Unattainable *Deus absconditus* and the Beauty and Glory of the *Deus revelatus*. It is the dissolving power
of the Hidden God that guarantees the freedom from dogma and from idolatry. Idolatry "immobilizes us before an object without transcendence."[48] A theophanic perception knows that there are no such objects. Likewise, since the
Face of Darkness must have a Face of Light, a Face of Beauty that reveals it,
there *is* no unbridgeable chasm between the Absolute Subject who is the Thou
of the soul's love and longing and the soul itself. And so there is no gulf
between love of a creature and love of the divine—their union is achieved
through theophanic perception. We are saved not just from idolatry, but from
the "furies and rejections" of world-denying asceticisms.[49] The identity of being
and perceiving that theophanic vision implies is beautifully expressed by
Corbin when he refers to "a God unknown and unknowable, God of Gods, of
whom all the universes and all the galaxies are the *sensorium*."[50]

On the Islamic view the reason we do not understand any of this, that we
don't experience ourselves as *organs* in this grand sensorium is not because of
an Original Sin, "sinned before us." We are not so much inherently sinful as we
are *forgetful*. We need more or less constant reminders. And the word for
remembrance is *dhikr*.

Corbin's passionate vision derives not only from Islamic theosophy. The
doctrine of the power of the Hidden God is central to the apophatic tradition
both in the Abrahamic religions, and in the history of Neoplatonism that is so
intimately connected with them. Michael Sells has shown that the Neoplatonic
hierarchy in Plotinus, Dionysius the Areopagite, John Scotus Eriugena, and others in the Christian tradition was never the static system that its detractors have
scorned. It can only be read that way if the apophatic component is ignored, if

the power of the Dark Face of the deity is not understood. The effect of A. O. Lovejoy's *The Great Chain of Being* on scholarly interpretations of the hierarchic cosmology was immense and one of the very few scholars to appreciate the apophatic component in Neoplatonism was Emile Bréhier.[51] In the 1920s while he studied with both Etiénne Gilson and Louis Massignon, Corbin attended Bréhier's lectures on the relation between Plotinus and the Upanishads. He wrote later of this experience, "How could a young philosopher avid for metaphysical adventure resist this appeal: to study deeply the influences or traces of Indian philosophy in the work of the founder of Neoplatonism?"[52]

Speaking of the element of negative theology in Plotinus, Sells writes, "Apophasis demands a moment of nothingness."[53] It is this nothingness that is the fount of all being. Corbin has told us that for the gnostics the encounter with nothingness is seen as only withdrawal, absence, and trial. He writes elsewhere of the *numinosity* of Sophia, the Angel of Wisdom, Angel of the Earth, and theophany of Beauty:

> In her pure numinosity, Sophia is forbidding. . . . Because she is a guide who always leads [the gnostic] towards the beyond, preserving him from metaphysical idolatry, Sophia appears to him sometimes as compassionate and comforting, sometimes as severe and silent, because only Silence can "speak," can indicate transcendences.[54]

Voice and Silence, Beauty and Majesty, All and Nothing, Presence and Absence: these opposites coincide in the unknowable deity.

That Corbin's vision is rooted in Christian as well as Islamic mysticism is made abundantly clear in this description of the theophanic concept of creation given by John Scotus Eriugena:

> For everything that is understood and sensed is nothing other than the apparition of the non-apparent, the manifestation of the hidden, the affirmation of the negated, the comprehension of the incomprehensible, the utterance of the unutterable, the access to the inaccessible, the intellection of the unintelligible, the body of the bodiless, the essence of the beyond-essence, the form of the formless, the measure of the immeasurable, the number of the unnumbered, the weight of the weightless, the materialization of the spiritual, the visibility of the invisible, the place of the placeless, the time of the timeless, the definition of the infinite, the circumscription of the uncircumscribed, and the other things which are both conceived and perceived by the intellect alone and cannot be retained within the recesses of memory and which escape the blade of the mind.[55]

Everything proceeds from this God in whom the opposites coincide. The *Deus absconditus* is the *coincidentia oppositorum*. Out of the God beyond-being comes everything. Dionysius speaks of the divine Word as "undiminished even as superceding and overflowing all things in itself in a single and incessant bounty that is overfull and cannot be diminished."[56]

One way of understanding this view of the world and the forms of life that it entails is to see that what makes it different from modern materialism is the experience of the relation between the *thing* and the *thought* of the thing. If I look at a rock, there is the object, the rock, and the subject, me. Just what it is about me that is the subjective part is a bit problematic, and increasingly over the course of the history of modern science there has been the growing sense that there really is no subject at all. But at least for several hundred years we've been able to assume that there is something like a subject. This subject perceives the object and has ideas about it, that exist somewhere, and they either apply to, map onto, or are true of the thing, or are not. It doesn't matter how I'm feeling or what mood the rock is in. There is no question of sympathy. No questions arise about whether I am more intensely myself today than I was yesterday when I looked at this rock—there are no "modes of being" involved: there's just me and the rock. Therein lies the problem: only one mode of being. If your cosmology doesn't include a plurality of modes of being, then there can be only one. Then everything "flattens out" as Heidegger and Corbin both say, and pretty soon you can't tell the difference between me and the rock—we're both just quantifiable "standing reserve" (Heidegger's term), equally subject to commodification in the universal economy of objects. Just two bits of matter present in a uni-modal world. But of course if you lose the subject, if you lose hold of the notion of a Person, then the rock can no more be present to me than I can be to the rock and what you have is really *Absence* and everything falls away into the Abyss, the darkness from which nothing comes. We will have more to say about this Absence later.

The theophanic experience is not this. As we have seen, there is ample precedent for the theophanic vision in Christianity, but it has not been in the mainstream. It is linked to a doctrine that has all but disappeared in Christian theology, the heresy of Docetism. This is the belief that Christ was not God Incarnate but was instead an Image.

The fusion of the Divine and the human in the person of Jesus Christ has implications for the meaning of the person, the nature of salvation and the relation of the material creation to the transcendent Creator. Schleiermacher identified the four central "heresies" that help define these relations. Docetism is the claim that Christ is not human, but only an apparition of the Divine. Ebionitism is the opposing belief that Christ was fully human, with no true divinity, thus merely another Prophet. Pelagianism is the claim that man can redeem himself by means of his own efforts and that the grace of God through Jesus Christ is unnecessary, which suggests that there is nothing inherently evil or unredeemable in human nature. The contrary heresy is an understanding of Manicheanism that contends that matter is inherently evil and unredeemable, thus that the natural world and its creatures are creatures of the Devil. Corbin's theophanic theology links the "Ebionite" view and the docetic. It denies the split between the divine and the merely human that is the basis of Schliermacher's scheme. Christ was human, but as the Anointed One, was the locus of manifestation of the *Christos Angelos,* whose appearance is dependent upon the mode of being of the individual who sees Him. To those who cannot see, he is a man. To those who can, he is a Figure of Light.

There is a tradition of angel Christology in the early Church that is perfectly consistent with the theophanic vision.[57] Corbin says that the figure of the *Christus juvenis,* the *Christos Angelos,* "translates the idea that God can only come into contact with humanity by transfiguring the latter."[58] Theophanic psychocosmology is based upon this transfiguration. In it ontology and epistemology are united in a cosmogenesis of the individual.

We have to look carefully at what *Docetism* means, for on it hinges the entire epistemology of the theophanic consciousness. Corbin says that the dogmas of positivist theology are "propositions demonstrated, established one time for all and consequently imposing a uniform authority on each and every one."[59] What the theophanic vision manifests is

> the relation, each time unique, between God manifested as a person (biblically the Angel of the Face) and the person that he promotes to the rank of person in revealing himself to him, this relation is fundamentally an existential relation, never a dogmatic one. It cannot be expressed as a *dogma* but as a *dokhema.* The two terms derive from the same Greek word *dokeo,* signifying all at once to appear, to show itself as, and also, believe, think, admit. The *dokhema* marks the line of interdependence between the form of that which manifests itself, and that to whom it manifests. It is this same correlation that can be called *dokesis.* Unfortunately it is from this that the routine accumulated over the centuries of history of Occidental dogmas has derived the term *docetism,* synonym of the phantasmic, the irreal, the apparent. So it is necessary to reinvigorate the primary sense: that which is called *docetism* is in fact the theological critique, or rather the theosophical critique, of religious consciousness.[60]

The *dokhema* expresses a relation between the knower and the known that is not sundered into object and subject because it is based on an experience of participation. The figure of Christ is the Heavenly Twin who is the source of personhood, the figure who in other guises is the very Soul of the World and the source of all Presence, all personifications in all the worlds. The *Christos Angelos* is the transfiguring presence visible by means of the Light of Glory that is the soul itself. The *Imago animae* is the Image that "the soul projects into beings and things, raising them to the incandescence of that victorial Fire with which the Mazdean soul has set the whole of creation ablaze. . . ."[61] The transfiguration of the *anima mundi* and of the body of light are inseparable. This dual eschatology achieved in the present is the centerpiece of the theophanic vision.

With the *dokhema* we enter the strange imaginal interworld where *thought* and *thing* mingle, where bodies give up their literal heaviness and where thoughts have body. It is the realm of subtle bodies and of embodied thoughts. Here we experience what Jung once called the "thing-like-ness of thought."[62] It represents what to a rationalist consciousness seems confusion and nonsense, but it is the foundation of theophanic consciousness. And it is not foreign to the ancient Greeks. Even Aristotle assumed a kind of relation between thought and being that is nearly incomprehensible to the modern mind. He says that "the soul is somehow, all things."[63] And Plotinus says: "When we know (the intelligibles) we do not have images or impressions of them . . . but we are them."[64]

As we have seen, the apophatic dynamic in Plotinus makes possible the continual undoing of definitive, "dogmatic" statements and perceptions. Access to this boundary-breaking experience requires a special kind of "in-sight" that he calls *theoria*. This seeing, or *theasthai* requires the ability to "let go of being" in the moment of nothingness that the *coincidentia oppositorum* entails. Such letting go results in wonderment, *thauma,* and the transformation of discursive reason into an open-ended process.[65] The Greek *thauma* means "a wonder, a thing compelling to the gaze."[66] The gaze that is turned upon this wonder is the *theoria,* an inward-turning contemplation of the theophanic apparition. We again are in the interworld where thought and thing mingle. It is the meeting place of the two seas, of the divine and the earthly, where Moses meets Khidr. The *dokeo* unites thought and being by bringing together appearance, thought, and belief. Likewise, *thauma* is the source of both *theory* and *theater;* both speculation and spectacle, seeing with the mind and seeing with the eye. John Deck writes, " 'Theoria,' with its cognate verb, θεορειν, seems to have evolved in meaning from 'sending an official see-er to the games,' to 'being a spectator at the games,' to 'being a spectator generally,' (i.e., simply 'seeing, viewing'), to 'contemplating, contemplation.' "[67]

In his essay *Emblematic Cities* Corbin discusses Proclus's *Commentary* on the *Parmenides* of Plato. He suggests there another use of the term. The philosophers have come to Athens for the festival of the Goddess of Wisdom whose splendidly embroidered robe "was carried like the sail of a galley"[68] in the procession, or *theoria* "in celebration of victory over the Titans who unloose chaos."[69] For Proclus the colorful, spectacular Athenian *theoria* is symbolic of the return of the soul to the One. Corbin compares this procession with the pilgrimage to another symbolic center. Compostella too is an emblematic city, and the goal of pilgrims for hundreds of years. Among them was Nicolas Flamel the great alchemist, "because," Corbin writes, "in reality the pilgrimage to Compostella is the symbolic description of the preparation of the Stone."[70]

The alchemists too have their *theoria.* The endless profusion of symbolic images is central to the method of alchemy. It is the *amplificatio,* which is, as Jung writes, "understood by the alchemist as *theoria,*" and is "a *theoria* in the true sense of a *visio* (spectacle, watching scenes in a theater . . .)."[71] The *opus* itself consists in "the extraction of thought from matter,"[72] the *extractio animae*[73] by means of Imagination which is the "star in man," the spark that is the "concentrated extract of life, both psychic and physical" that gives rise to the subtle body in the intermediate, imaginal world where the *physika* and the *mystika* unite.[74]

For Najm Kubra the seeker himself is a particle of light imprisoned in the darkness, and the alchemical opus frees him to perceive the figures and the lights that "shine in the Skies of the soul, the Sky of the Earth of Light." These lights reveal the Figure "dominating the *Imago mundi*: the Imam who is the *pole, just* as in terms of spiritual alchemy he is the 'Stone' or 'Elixer.'"[75] In the West, Christ is the miraculous Stone,[76] and the aura surrounding the subtle body of the transfigured Christ is that same *Xvarnah* and Light of Glory that flies upward as particles of light reclaiming their home in Byzantine, Manichean, and Persian painting.[77]

The whole difference between dogmatic, literal consciousness, and theophanic, imaginal consciousness lies in the mode of perception. The soul that can perceive these lights can do so because it is able to open to the spectacle which the *theoria* presents. Corbin writes,

> Dogma corresponds to dogmatic perception, simple and unidimensional, to a rational evidence, demonstrated, established and stabilized. The *dokêma* corresponds to a theophanic mode of perception, to a multiple and multiform vision of figures manifesting themselves on many levels. . . . Dogma is formulated and formulable *ne varietur*. Theophanic perception remains open to all metamorphoses, and perceives the forms through their very metamorphoses. . . . Theophanic perception presupposes that the soul that perceives the theophany—or all hierophany—is entirely a mirror, a *speculum*. . . . It was necessarily a complete a degradation for the word "speculative" to end by signifying the contrary of what the visionary realism intended to announce in the etymology of the word: *speculum*, mirror. A degradation concomitant to that of the status of the Imagination.[78]

The *imaginal* world is the realm of the symbolic, the alchemical, the visionary, the wonder-ful. The imagination is a mediating function, an organ of the subtle body. Through the *theoria* that "pours forth a vast power," it overflows the limited discursive meaning of words, and dissolves the idolatry inherent in the experience of beings without transcendence. We have lost touch with this imagination and with the concrete reality of beings, with their openness, their animation. We stand disoriented in a world of distant objects. In accordance with the literal way in which the Incarnation has been interpreted we have become so far removed from reality that it seems paradoxical to say that it is the realities of the objective, public world that that are abstract and the subtle realities of the *imaginatio vera* that are concrete. The nihilism and the death of God that is the heritage of the West is for Corbin a direct result of the destruction of the functions of the imagination, of the shattering of the speculum. It is this that made it possible for Christ to be seen by the eyes of dogma as God Incarnate. It is to an examination of the doctrine of the Incarnation that we now turn.

THE EMPTYING GOD IN CHRISTIAN THEOLOGY

In the Christian West, Docetism was all but entirely eclipsed by the doctrine of the Incarnation: God and Man in one substance, Christ in time on earth. Singular, unique, factual. This, Corbin and Semnani say, marks a failure of initiation, the *fana* of God into the world. As Corbin notes, the descent of God into the world is the subject of the Christian doctrine of *kenosis,* the self-emptying, or self-limiting of God. The idea has its source in Paul's *Epistle to the Philippians:*

> Have this mind among yourselves, which you have in Christ Jesus, who, though he was in the form of God, did not count equality with God a thing to be grasped, but emptied himself, taking the form of a servant, being born in the likeness of men. And being found in human form he humbled himself and became obedient unto death, even death on a cross. Therefore God has highly exalted him and bestowed on him the name which is above every name, that at the name of Jesus every knee should bow, in heaven and on earth and under the earth, and every tongue confess that Jesus Christ is Lord, to the glory of God the Father.[79]

Exaltation through emptying lies at the heart of Incarnationist doctrine. How is such an emptying possible and what does it mean?

In a footnote to *The Man of Light in Iranian Sufism* Corbin suggests a comparative study of the *kenosis* of God into human reality and the *fana* of the erring mystic who claims, "I am God!"[80] This leads into a dense thicket of historical and theological complexity. Such an effort would require the work of years. For our purposes it will be enough to provide a brief review of the manifold meanings of *kenosis* in Christian theology. We are indebted to Sarah Coakley for introducing some order into the *massa confusa* of the theological controversies.[81]

At issue in the debate is the nature of the relation between the man Jesus and God the Father. The passage in Paul's *Epistle* was probably a hymn already in use before Paul appropriated it in his exhortation to his audience to "have the mind among yourselves which you have in Christ Jesus." The first question is how this "mind of Christ" was understood in the early Christian community. Corbin points out that there has been a docetic strain in Christianity from the very beginning, which continues to the present day. As we will see, the discussion of *kenosis* and incarnation always wavers between one extreme, arguably docetic, emphasizing Christ's divinity, and another that emphasizes his humanity.

There is a wide range of views on how Paul and his predecessors and contemporaries would have understood the "emptying." At one end of the spectrum are those who argue that Paul modified pre-Christian gnostic doctrines of the descent of the *Anthropos* who delivers a salvational *gnosis* to his disciples. The emptying then refers simply to his appearance on earth.[82] This gnostic mythology is docetic in the sense that Christ only appeared to take on "the form of man" in order to accomplish his mission of salvation.[83] This is the kind of position that Corbin is defending. On the other hand, a purely ethical read-ing asserts that the emptying refers to the example of humility set by Jesus, whose earthly life provides the standard for humanity. This would be "Ebion-ite" in Schleiermacher's sense, but not in Corbin's or in that of the original Ebionites, for whom the Prophets are special bearers of the Spirit, and there-fore rather more than "mere" human exemplars. New Testament scholars nearly all agree that Paul is focused on the ritual enactment of the salvational story of Christ's example, not on theological claims about the relation of Father and Son that were to arise later on. The nature of Jesus' relation to God *before* the Incarnation was not at issue. In the earliest history of the religion *kenosis* meant either relinquishing or pretending to relinquish divine powers while acting as redeemer, or choosing never to have worldly powers that are wrongly assumed by erring humans to be the ends of ethical action.[84] Neither of these options is the Incarnationist doctrine attacked by Corbin.

The period between the composition of Paul's *Epistle* in the first century and the Council of Chalcedon in 451 was rife with theological controversy, but by its end the doctrines of the Incarnation and the Trinity had been given their dogmatic form. The encounter between Christian faith and Greek philosophy made the following question inevitable: Is the Supreme Being, the One of the Platonists, the same as the God of the Christians? And if so, Who is Jesus Christ? That is: How can this Supreme Being have a personal relation to his creatures? The doctrine of the *Logos* as presaged in the Gospel of John developed in response. There is the Immutable Father, to be sure, but there is another com-ponent in the divinity, the *Logos,* the Word who became flesh. This incarnate Word is the human face of God. Then the theological issue is the relation between the Father and the Word. This came to a head in the Arian Controversy, resolved as far as official doctrine is concerned, at the Council of Nicea in 325. Arius, a presbyter of Alexandria, argued that the Word, though divine and exist-ing with God before the Incarnation, was not coeternal with the Father, but was rather first among creatures. He tried in this way to maintain a strict monothe-ism, rather than claim a duality in the One God. Alexander, Bishop of Alexan-dria, argued that the Word was divine and *therefore* coeternal with the Father, and sought to defend the total divinity of Jesus who could only thereby be worthy of worship. The Council of Nicea agreed on a formula rejecting Arius and affirming that Father and Son are of one substance, *homoousios.*

Between Paul's time and the Council of Nicea and during the ensuing debates leading up to the Council of Chalcedon a significant change took place. Coakley writes: "[T]he formative christological discussion of the fourth and fifth centuries . . . takes Christ's substantial pre-existence and divinity *for granted*."[85] The contrast between the human and the divine aspects of Jesus has been sharpened. For a docetic doctrine there is no problem of incarnation since only an appearance is at issue. Neither is there a problem for a purely ethical reading since there is no true divinity at stake. But when Jesus must be thought as both man and God, the paradoxes force themselves forward. The discussion of *kenosis* becomes far more problematic. What can "emptying" mean if it is assumed to be essential for the incarnation and if divine attributes such as omnipotence and omniscience are understood to be unchanging elements of God?[86] How can the perfections and powers associated with the Father as immutable divinity be in any way compatible with the human frailties and sufferings of the man Jesus? On the one hand he must be fully God to be worthy of worship, and yet to be Savior he must share our fallen humanity. The paradoxes were brought into sharp relief by Cyril of Alexandria (d. 444). In his Christology the eternal divine Logos was also paradoxically the personal subject of Christ's human states but in some incomprehensible way such that there is no change or impairment in the perfections of the divinity. This leads to another meaning of *kenosis,* one that incorporates the idea that Christ must be actually God and actually human, for here *kenosis* refers to the *taking on* of human flesh by the divine Logos, without diminishing the divine powers in any way.[87]

In order to resolve these tensions, a statement of orthodoxy was agreed upon at the Council of Chalcedon in 451 that affirmed again that the Son is consubstantial with the Father, but is at the same time "of two natures in one person" in such a way that the divine and the human are united and yet distinct. This formulation leaves the issue as difficult as ever. Coakley notes that the paradoxes of the Council hardly resolved questions about the form of Christ's earthly life "and certainly left many points of christological detail unanswered."[88] As Jung says, "Even the most tortuous explanations of theology have never improved upon the lapidary paradox of St. Hilary: 'Deus homo, immortalis mortuus, aeternus sepultus' (God-man, immortal-dead, eternal-buried)."[89]

The argument continues today, between those who tend to emphasize Christ's divinity (the "Alexandrian school") and those who emphasize his humanity (the "Antiochenes"). Cyril's solution is in some sense docetic since he said that Christ at times "permitted his own flesh to experience its proper affection" and this suggests that Christ's humanity was in truth an appearance.[90] In the Eastern Church an even more one-sided view was developed by John of Damascus in the eighth century. For John the communication of the two natures ran "only one way (from the divine to the human), the divine fully permeated the human nature of Christ by an act of 'coinherence'"or *perichoresis.*[91] This leaves no room for human weakness, and *kenosis* is hardly an emptying at all, but is more like an obliteration of the human by the divine. If this is a kind of docetism, it is not that defended by Corbin where the human must be raised to meet the divine. Here it is merely crushed.

These issues were stirred to life again during the Reformation. Luther's Christology was based simultaneously on Christ's extreme vulnerability on the cross and on his "real presence" in the Eucharist. But how is it possible for Christ's divinity to be active in his cry of despair at death?[92] In 1577 the Lutherans sided with John of Damascus in saying that the divine attributes fully permeated Christ. But this denied the human helplessness with which Luther began. In the seventeenth century a group of Lutherans from Giessen proposed a novel resolution: the *kenosis* operated only on Christ's *human* nature, not on his divine. This is a post-Chalcedonian version, that is, one that recognizes the two-nature doctrine, of one of the early possible interpretations, Christ's "choosing never to have certain forms of power in his incarnate life."[93]

In the late nineteenth century another Lutheran, Gottfried Thomasius, proposed the radical idea that the Logos itself is "emptied" in the incarnation. He says, "The Logos reserved to Himself neither a special existence nor a special knowledge outside his humanity. He truly became man."[94] Thus, the incarnation marks the abandonment of all attributes of divinity and a Christology based upon human attributes alone is entirely justified.[95]

There is yet one more important part to this story, involving a development of the ethical reading of *kenosis*. Among twentieth-century theologians there are those who see Jesus' "emptying" "not just as a blueprint for a perfect human moral response, but as revelatory of the humility of the *divine* nature."[96] On this view *kenosis* reveals divine power to be intrinsically "humble" rather than "grasping."[97] For John Robinson there is "a radical seepage of the *human* characteristics into the *divine,* such, indeed, as to collapse the apparatus of the two natures doctrine altogether."[98] John MacQuarrie says that Christ "has made known to us the final reality as likewise self-emptying, self-giving and self-limiting." To what extent these ideas are compatible with the traditional Christian doctrines of the nature of God is open to question. Surely for Corbin they would represent at best a rearguard action against the nihilism of the contemporary world.

Based on this brief review of the idea of *kenosis* we can make two observations. First, the paradoxes involved are insoluble. This may not be a criticism, since theology is not necessarily bounded by the rules of human logic. There is a dynamism in Christology that mitigates the rigidity of dogma, and which would perhaps disappear if the contradictions were not right on the surface as they clearly are. Second, it is evident that all but the most "docetic" of these doctrinal options are deeply suspect from Corbin's point of view. Any direct contact, any substantial union of the divine and the human taking place in the time of history and in the material, public world has the same effect in the end, however subtly one tries to arrange it. There can be no *kenosis* of any sort in the Christology that Corbin is defending. He is hostile to any historicizing of the Christian message that would compromise the universality of the figure of Christ, or a figure "like Christ" available to anyone, anywhere at any time, in accordance with the individual's capacity to "see." He defends with passion the *Harmonia Abrahamica* wherein the lineage of the prophets since Adam represents successive appearances of the one True Prophet. There can be no fundamental incompatibilities among the religions of the Book when thus understood. He defends a viewpoint that is extremely ecumenical and cross-cultural, as is the case with traditional Islam.[99] In this, Corbin is in the camp of Justin Martyr who, in the second century saw the Logos as the common source of all human knowledge, and too, of Origen's "illuminationism" that accepts both truth and salvation outside of Christianity.[100]

We have seen some of the ways in which the descent of God into the world has been understood within the theological tradition. We are now in a position to see how the results of the descent have been judged by a few of those who, like Corbin, see it as the definitive event in Christian consciousness.

KENOSIS AND THE DESTINY OF THE WEST

Amidst all the complexities of the Christian theological debate there is a common theme: that the birth, life, and death of Jesus as a man among us represents a descent of God into creation and so in one degree or another an "incarnation" and "enfleshment" of God and in some sense an "emptying" of God into this world. Christ's life is the central fact of Christianity, and Christianity is the religion of the Western tradition. So incarnation and *kenosis* are part of the basic fabric of our history, and of the culture that is coming to dominate the world. There are others besides Henry Corbin who see these doctrines as essential components of our history, of our psychology, and of contemporary culture. A review of their positions may help clarify Corbin's perspective and the critique of the West that he offers.

Silence and Communion: A Power Made Perfect in Weakness

A central part of the attack on the assumptions of modernism is the critical examination of gender issues in every area of life. Theology is no exception.[101] That the Abrahamic religions have been dominated by male power structures is undeniable. Whether this is integral to the doctrines of these faiths is an open question. The relevance of the kenotic moral example of Christ for women has been vigorously debated in Christian feminist literature. At issue is whether Christ's example of humility and self-sacrifice, however necessary for men, is not for women merely another means of oppression and domination. Elizabeth Cady Stanton famously said that after so many years of depersonalization and repression "self development is a higher duty than self-sacrifice."[102]

Daphne Hampson has pointed out that Luther's theological anthropology, to take one characteristic example, is based essentially on masculine psychology. It depends for its force on an experience of the self as isolated and insecure, as *incurvare in se,* "curved in upon itself," not at-home-in-the-world, and able to find freedom finally only in a binding relation to God or to the devil.[103] Women, Hampson argues, tend to experience the self in terms of connectedness, openness, and community, that is, as a relational entity. Whereas for men the problem is finding a way out of isolation and into community, and whose sin is therefore *hubris,* for women the problem is lack of center, and the "sin," so to speak, lies in having no autonomy. If this is generally true, then *kenosis* as self-denial can be no moral guide for women. And if that is true then it is hard to see how there can be a feminist Christianity, and there would be, in Coakley's words, "little point in continuing the tortured battle to bring feminism and Christianity together."[104]

Coakley argues that there is one meaning of *kenosis* that holds promise for feminist Christians. Recall that the Lutherans of Geissen saw *kenosis* applying only to Christ's human nature. In this way human vulnerability and weakness can be united with divine power so that a special form of self-effacement can occur "which is not a negation of the self, but the place of the self's transformation and expansion into God."[105] She finds this special form of making space for waiting on and responding to the divine in the *ascesis* of wordless prayer or contemplation. Opening to the divine is both perilous and subversive. The self is in a posture of truly Christ-like vulnerability and doubt. She writes:

> [E]ngaging in any such regular and repeated "waiting on the divine" will involve great personal commitment and great personal risk; to put it in psychological terms, the dangers of a too-sudden uprush of material from the unconscious, too immediate a contact of the thus-disarmed self with God, are not inconsiderable. To this extent the careful driving of wedges—which began to appear in the western church from the twelfth century on—between "meditation" (discursive reflection on Scripture) and "contemplation" (this more vulnerable activity of space-making), were not all cynical in their attempts to keep contemplation "special."[106]

Her appeal is to just that apophatic moment beyond speech that we have already encountered:

> The "mystics" of the church have often been from surprising backgrounds, and their messages rightly construed as subversive; their insights have regularly chafed at the edges of doctrinal "orthodoxy," and they have rejoiced in the coining of startling (sometimes erotically startling) new metaphors to describe their experiences of God. Those who have appealed to a "dark" knowing beyond speech have thus challenged the smugness of accepted anthropomorphisms for God, have probed . . . to the subversive place of the "semiotic."[107]

This vulnerability is required by both men and women, and is not incompatible with the development of a centered self. It is only by this special kind of vulnerability that the self can both find its true center and be able to connect with others in an authentic way.

However "mystical" the contemplation of wordess prayer may be, Coakley says that she must "avoid the lurking 'docetism' of the Alexandrian tradition." This can be done she feels, by recognizing that what Christ "instantiates is the very 'mind' that we ourselves enact, or enter into, in prayer: the unique intersection of vulnerable, 'non-grasping' humanity and authentic divine power." In the *Second Epistle to the Corinthians* Christ says, "My grace is sufficient for you, for my power is made perfect in weakness."[108] Here is something that surely is akin to the mystical poverty of Sufism. And whether this is "docetic" or not, it suggests a relation of the individual to the divinity in Christ that Corbin would have found congenial.

The idea that such a power in vulnerability is the fundamental meaning of *kenosis* is common to Coakley and the Catholic theologian Hans Urs von Balthasar.[109] In Balthasar's theology there is an explicit attempt to present *kenosis* and the Incarnation as linked to a conception of relational personhood and to a theology of Beauty that in respects parallels some of Corbin's key themes.

Balthasar's theology is emphatically Trinitarian. And this for a reason that echoes Corbin's warnings. O'Hanlon puts it succinctly: "If God were simply one he would become ensnared in the world process through the incarnation and the cross."[110] Any simple monism is incompatible with the fact of divine-human interaction. In order to explain any such communion there must be a dynamic within the divinity that makes it possible. God must be both immanent and transcendent. The incarnation must signal a real event in God, and this real dynamic is "the eternal event of the divine processions." The trinity is "an event of the communion of persons," and is an event of kenotic self-giving love.[111] This love of the Father, out of whose "abyss-like" depths it arises, is returned eternally by the reciprocal self-giving of the Son. The movement of this love requires otherness and distance and is the archetype of all love of the other whether human or divine. We know the divine kenotic love only through the incarnate Christ who, says Balthasar, "*is* the Person, in an absolute sense, because in him self-consciousness . . . coincides with the mission he has received from God."[112] Papanikolaou writes, "One becomes a true person, for Balthasar, when one is able to relate to the Father in the way the incarnate Son relates to the Father, and that relation takes the form of obedient response to the Father's call to a unique, personal mission."[113]

It is far beyond the scope of this chapter to contrast Balthsar and Corbin in any detail. Such a vast project would shed considerable light on these central theological disputes. It is clear that there are some revealing common themes. Balthsar's Trinitarian procession serves a function similar to the Neoplatonic emanation for Corbin, and the insistence that God must be somehow both immanent and transcendent is the basis for Corbin's theophanic theology. The abyss of God's giving expresses that same apophatic moment we have encountered before. And Balthasar's account of the accession to true personality, that Christ is the exemplar for a unique and personal mission, recalls Corbin's concern with individuation.

Corbin's docetic theology, grounded as it is in Islamic mysticism, has little place for Trinitarian doctrines. Almost the only important reference to the Triune God in his work occurs in his discussion of the *unio sympathetica* in the mystical theology of Ibn 'Arabi. The Breath of the Compassionate grants existence to all the beings in Creation, and thus all these creatures *are* this very breath itself. The Compassion thus moves in both directions: from Creator to creature and back again. This "existentiating Breath" is *food* for both the creature and his God. Ibn 'Arabi writes,

> Feed then God's Creation on Him, for thy being is a breeze that rises, a perfume which He exhales; We have given Him the power to manifest himself through us, Whereas He gave us (the power to exist through Him). Thus the role is shared between Him and us.[114]

This continuous mystic Supper, consisting of the giving and receiving of substantiating sympathy, of the interpenetration of Creator and creature in primordial beauty and mutual love, is represented for Corbin by the Biblical and Qur'anic event of the *philoxeny* of Abraham.[115] This story is depicted in Andre Rublev's fifteenth-century masterpiece, sometimes known as *The Old Testament Trinity*.[116] Some Islamic commentators have interpreted the three mysterious strangers as the angels Gabriel, Michael, and Seraphiel.[117] In the Eastern Orthodox tradition they represent the three persons of the Trinity.[118] Corbin tells us that Ibn 'Arabi has given a most magnificent mystical exegesis of this icon. This mystical Supper is the Feast at the heart of Creation:

> [T]o feed God's creatures on Him is to reinvest them with God, is therefore to make their theophanic radiance flower within them; it is, one might say, to make oneself capable of apprehending the "angelic function" of beings, to invest them with, and perhaps awaken them to, the angelic dimension of their being.[119]

This continuous cosmic Feast, which ensures the substantiation, individuation, and continual existence of all the beings in Creation, and which is always visible to those who have the eyes to see, takes the place in Corbin's theology of the sacrament of Holy Communion.

Balthasar's Trinitarian theology is in some ways in fundamental resonance with Corbin's vision despite, indeed because of the absolute centrality of the Incarnation. This is because at root the doctrine of *kenosis* as love presupposes the ever-present availability of the spirit of Christ, and so avoids the historicism that Corbin rejects. The doctrine of the Holy Spirit permits Balthasar to provide a transformational doctrine of perception that is in some respects strikingly like that which Corbin outlines. Nichols writes,

> Balthasar has made it clear that, in all authentic perception of the divine glory of Jesus Christ, seeing goes hand in hand with transformation. . . . [H]e sees that here perceiving is impossible without a being caught up in love. A theory of perception cannot be had in this context without a doctrine of conversion, and so ultimately of sanctification.[120]

This could easily have been written about Corbin himself. In Balthasar's vision, *kenosis* signifies the Glory and Beauty of the Lord made manifest. Significantly, he shares Corbin's respect for Jakob Georg Hamann's theology of Beauty.[121] It is perhaps true that Balthasar and Corbin share a common Catholic sacramental attitude toward the beauty of the earth. David Tracy has suggested that Catholic theologians and artists "tend to emphasize the presence of God in the world, while the classic works of Protestant theologians tend to emphasize the absence of God from the world."[122] If something like this is true, then we might say that Corbin, while vehemently rejecting the hierarchy of the Catholic Church as an institution, in favor of a more "Protestant," indeed Lutheran emphasis on the freedom of the individual, nonetheless displays a deep and pervasive sacramental sensibility that perceives the world as "haunted by a sense that the objects, events and persons of daily life are revelations of grace."[123] As Greeley points out, the danger in this is idolatry—but Balthasar guards against this in a way that recalls Corbin: The Father is the Abyss of Giving, He is the Unknown and Unknowable Gift—the very fullness of Being of apophasis. Father and Son are correlative: Majesty and Beauty.

Balthasar is also not unaware of the very dangers inherent in the doctrine of the Incarnation that Corbin warns against. Nichols writes: "Balthasar is keenly aware of how easily an incarnational attitude to living . . . can collapse into either a dualism of matter and spirit as only incidentally related or a mere materialism where spirit is but an epiphenomenon of matter."[124] His solution to this tension rests upon metaphors that are strikingly reminiscent of those Corbin depends upon throughout his own work. Balthasar says: "As a totality of spirit and body, man must make himself into God's mirror and seek to attain to that transcendence and radiance that must be found in the world's substance if it is indeed God's image and likeness—his word and gesture, action and drama."[125]

That being said, there is at least one central issue where Balthasar and Corbin must part company, and it involves, as one might expect, issues of authority, personal freedom, and the meaning of the Incarnation. For Balthasar Christ is the absolute guarantor of objectivity. Upon Him rests the indestructibly solid support for supernatural revelation. Nichols writes,

> Even the scholastic axiom that "whatever is received is received according to the mode of the receiver" is to be brushed aside in this context. . . . Here hermeneutics, whether cultural or philosophical are sent packing, on the grounds that One who is both God and man cannot but draw what is universally valid in human life and thought to himself. . . . In the last analysis, Christ is the all-important form because he is the all-sufficient content, the only Son of the Father.[126]

The critique of individual hermeneutics distinguishes Balthasar's position from Corbin's irrevocably, and illustrates quite clearly the reason Corbin was so vehement in his attacks on the incarnational attitude. It is because of his unwavering emphasis on the freedom of the individual that Docetism and hermeneutics must be linked for Corbin.

In the end it seems clear that there are ways of interpreting *kenosis* that are compatible with a "theophanic cosmology" of some kind. An incarnational Christology can be articulated that is not a result of a failure of initiation, and does not end in nihilism and catastrophe, but it must be one that addresses Corbin's central worries about the secularizing effects of historicism and about ambiguities concerning the relation of matter and spirit. For a very different analysis we will step outside the confines of theology to encounter another reading of what the weakness of *kenosis* entails. We begin by returning to that crucial moment when, according to Corbin, the West came face to face with its failed initiation.

A Hermeneutics of Absence: Adrift in the Sea of Technics

The Italian philosopher Gianni Vattimo works in the tradition defined by Nietzsche, Heidegger, and Derrida.[127] He can be counted among those who are, often unhelpfully, labeled "postmodernists." In our context, what is important and "postmodern" about Vattimo is his attack on dogma, on any attempt to impose a single truth on the plurality and variety of human lives.

For Vattimo, Nietzsche's radical nihilism, expressed in Zarathustra's cry "God is dead!"[128] is the prelude to a freedom that is only now coming within our reach, and that is in fact the culmination and final destiny of the Christian tradition. It is significant that both Nietzsche and Corbin look back to the Zoroastrian roots of the eschatological religions of the West. Norman Cohn has argued that it was Zoroaster who shattered the vision of a cyclic, timeless cosmos, and initiated a view of a world moving inexorably forward toward a final consummation in history. The origins of the eschatological worldview can be traced back to Zoroaster's proclamation of the Final Battle at the end of time that will usher in the paradise that is the goal of history.[129] Nietzsche reaches back to the *Avesta* and reads there the desperate, ultimate fate of this history in the death of the God who promised so much and gave, in the end, Nothing. For Corbin, the mythic and the transhistorical have never in truth been fully suppressed. We still live in that mythic present. Our insertion in history is only partial. The timelessness of the eternal present is always available, and eschatological hopes apply here and now.

For Nietzsche himself this "greatest recent event,"[130] the death of God, was an occasion for joy and freedom:

> [O]ur heart overflows with gratitude, amazement, anticipation, expectation. At last the horizon appears free again to us, even granted that it is not bright; at last our ships may venture out again, venture out to face any danger; all the daring of the lover of knowledge is permitted again; the sea, *our* sea, lies open again; perhaps there has never yet been such an "open sea."[131]

Nietzsche's sensation of looking out over a horizon, free if not "bright," is a fair description of Vattimo's assessment of our situation. We live at the end of the era of metaphysics, of grand architectonics of thought claiming to uncover the final truth. For Vattimo as for Nietzsche "there are no facts, only interpretations." That is the meaning of the death of God. The idea of Truth has collapsed in upon itself. There is no Reality behind the appearance; there *is* only the appearance. This is what the process of secularization comes to in the end: there is no other, higher, transcendent world that can justify or ground our thoughts and actions. There is only this secular realm of things, reduced, as Heidegger has said, to the calculable, the manipulable, where everything is reduced to "exchange value" and treated as "standing reserve." This is the technological worldview.[132]

Technology is often understood as the triumph of positivism, as the triumph of fact over interpretation. But if *everything* is subject to interpretation, then the dominance of scientific objectivity is itself subverted.[133] Natural scientists have no sympathy with the claims of postmodernists who claim "there is nothing outside the text."[134] But one does not have to understand "text" in a literal way to hold that there is nothing but interpretation, and the attempt to understand the contextual aspects of natural science is a major feature of modern epistemologies. But even this less obviously "literary" position is nonsensical, or at best entirely irrelevant, to most practicing scientists who are very happy to ignore hermeneutics and get on with discovering facts. Yet Vattimo's point, and Heidegger's too, is, I think, that when everything has become "objective," when all things are reduced to objects for manipulation, then anything goes. There are no more natural boundaries to be respected, nothing has an inside or an outside, no individual can have more than an evanescent coherence, every thing is understood as cobbled together from parts that are subject to recombination by nature or by technology. Permanence and stability have been replaced by perpetual metamorphoses. The radical position of the feminist thinker Donna Harraway gives a hint of the possibilities here. For Harraway modern technology merely makes obvious what has been true all along: the boundaries between our tools and ourselves are really not boundaries at all. We are already *cyborgs,* amalgamations of machine and organism. Modern medicine will only continue to make this clear. What this suggests is that all boundaries are in some sense arbitrary, capable of dissolution and restructuring. This includes gender boundaries, racial boundaries, as well as boundaries between species, between animal and human, as Charles Darwin clearly saw. This situation, says Harraway, provides the possibility for envisioning the ultimate liberation from social constructions of class, race, and gender, from the dominations of all essentialisms, all social and political powers.[135]

Nihilism as the ungrounding of all facts and the dissolution of all boundaries is expressed through the corrosive dissolving power of technology and of modern economics as its inevitable extension. It cannot be avoided, overcome, or denied. Nihilism is, says Vattimo, "our sole opportunity." Any attempt to institute something new in reaction to it, either a return to some prior primordial "foundations" or a leap into a new order, would only be a reenactment of old violence, the same sad old story of repression and domination. Our only option is to abandon ourselves to this fluid, rootless, insecure position—to a radical acceptance of "not knowing" that Vattimo calls "weak thought."

Vattimo argues that we are able to see the truth of nihilism only when we have been engulfed by the contemporary "society of generalized communication." It is only by living in the fluid and ever-changing flux of modern secular technology where nothing is sacred and nothing secure that we have been finally freed to enact the truth of Nietzsche's vision. And this, as Frascati-Lochhead points out, recalls to us again the words of Christ: "My grace is sufficient for you, for my power is made perfect in weakness." But the dissolving power of nihilism has to be turned upon the claims of the very technology that gives rise to it. Even the domination of technology must be dis-located in a continuous process of undoing. This is an active, "accomplished" nihilism, one that recognizes the implausibility of *any* dominating structures in thought or society.

For Vattimo it is paradoxically this secularization and the dissolution of certainty that is the destiny of Christianity. Just the situation that seems to have resulted in the eclipse and repudiation of the Christian tradition is the only authentic outcome of that tradition itself. The way that Vattimo understands this strange twist is full of striking echoes of Corbin's work. On Vattimo's account what the flux of the modern world reveals is that facts must give way to interpretation. And what is the science of these interpretations? Hermeneutics. Here Vattimo turns directly to the Incarnation and *kenosis* as the central doctrines of the Christian tradition, and therefore vital for the destiny of the West. Vattimo says that the Incarnation has mostly been read in a "Hegelian" way, so that

> God and Jesus Christ are thought . . . in the light of an idea of truth as the objective articulation of evidence that, as it becomes definitive, renders interpretation superfluous. . . . [T]he revelation somehow concluded with the coming of Jesus, the scriptural canon was fulfilled, and the interpretation of the sacred texts became ultimately the concern only of the Pope and the cardinals.[136]

This is of course precisely Corbin's point. That is how the Incarnation *has* in fact been read by the official Church. The doctrine of God's entry into human history freezes the mystery of Christ into time and into the hierarchical structures of those in power. We have seen Balthasar reject any application of hermeneutics to the revelation of Christ. Corbin vehemently rejects a "Hegelian" reading in favor of individual hermeneutics, of *gnosis*. But Vattimo rejects it because he says the metaphysics of Truth is no longer an option for us. We have, thanks to Nietzsche and Heidegger, finally been freed from the violence that is the inevitable outcome of metaphysical thought.

What dissolves the dogmatic vision of the Incarnation for Vattimo is a hermeneutic philosophy that gives equal rights to story, myth, and philosophy—to all the forms of thought and meaning, and so explodes the single vision that dogma imposes. Hermeneutics in the modern sense began, Vattimo notes, with the Enlightenment project of biblical exegesis, and represents the culmination of Christianity in a post-Christian form as a secular philosophy. This extends its power far beyond the analysis of readings of the sacred text. And because hermeneutics "ungrounds" all claims to Truth and Transcendence, it is the heart of that nihilism in which we live.

This "freedom" that nihilism imposes is where the true meaning of *kenosis* lies. The emptying of God into the world results in "secularization" and the irreducible plurality of interpretations, of visions, of forms of life that this entails. Vattimo writes,

> [M]odern philosophical hermeneutics is born in Europe not only because here there is a religion of the book that focuses attention on the phenomenon of interpretation, but because this religion has at its base the idea of the incarnation of God, which it conceives as *kenosis,* as abasement, and, in our translation, as weakening.[137]

This weakening in the form of the rejection of dogma and the celebration of a plurality of voices has precursors in the Christian tradition. Vattimo points to Joachim of Fiore's doctrine of the Third Age of the Holy Spirit, in which the inner, spiritual sense of the scriptures takes precedence over the legal, disciplinarian interpretation. It is, he says, a matter of taking the doctrine of *kenosis* seriously. We can look to those pages where Schleiermacher

> dreams of a religion in which everyone can be the author of their own Bible; or those of Novalis, in which a re-evaluation of the "aesthetic" aspects of religiosity (the images, the Madonna, the rituals) runs alongside the same dream of a Christianity that is no longer dogmatic or disciplinarian.[138]

Everyone the author of their own Bible. This is the culmination of the general philosophy of hermeneutics born from Biblical interpretation.

> If one discovers that hermeneutics is closely related to dogmatic Christianity, neither the meaning of hermeneutics nor that of dogmatics will be left intact. As regards the latter . . . the relation with hermeneutics produces a critical rethinking of its disciplinary character: the nihilistic "dissolution" that hermeneutics reads in the "myth" of the incarnation and crucifixion does not cease with the conclusion of Jesus' time on earth, but continues with the descent of the Holy Spirit and with the interpretation of revelation by the community of believers. According to the line that . . . I propose to call Joachimist, the meaning of Scripture, in the age opened by the descent of the Holy Spirit, becomes increasingly "spiritual," and thereby less bound to the rigor of dogmatic definitions and of strict disciplinarian observance.[139]

Joachim of Fiore is for Corbin too a representative of the religion of the Spirit, of the Paraclete, the Figure who alone can inaugurate the True Church. Corbin compares Joachim and his disciples in the twelfth and thirteenth centuries with the Shi'ite theosophers who

> speak of the "eternal religion" and of the "Paraclete." The Joachimites, centered in the tradition of prophetic Christianity, invoke the "Eternal Gospel" and the "reign of the Paraclete." For the Shi'ites the coming of the Imam-Paraclete will inaugurate the reign of the pure spiritual meaning of the divine revelations: it is this that they mean by "Eternal Religion." . . . For the Joachimites, the reign of the Holy Spirit, of the Paraclete, will be the time where the spiritual comprehension *(intelligentia spiritualis)* of the Scriptures will dominate; and this is what they mean by "Eternal Gospel." The consonance is striking. It is possible to speak of a common "hermeneutical situation," that is to say, of a "mode of comprehension" common to one side and the other, notwithstanding the difference issuing from the Qur'anic Revelation and all the more rich in its instruction.[140]

But in a complete reversal of Corbin's view, the appearance and triumph of the spiritual Church beyond all dogma is for Vattimo only possible through the secularization that the *kenosis* of the Incarnation brings about. Vattimo writes,

> The idea of secularization, if considered in relation to hermeneutics, seems to be less univocally definable than is generally believed: rather paradoxically, in fact, hermeneutics which, in its Enlightenment origins, shows a demythologizing and rationalist trend, leads in contemporary thought to the dissolution of the same myth of objectivity . . . and to the rehabilitation of myth and of religion. This is a paradox that . . . focuses on the intrinsic relation of hermeneutics to the Christian tradition: nihilism "resembles" *kenosis* too much for this similarity to be but a coincidence, an association of ideas. The hypothesis to which we are led is that hermeneutics itself . . . is the outcome of secularization as . . . an "application," an interpretation of the contents of Christian revelation, first of all of the dogma of the incarnation of God.[141]

This, from Corbin's perspective is precisely right: *kenosis* and nihilism are connected in just this way. But for him as for Semnani they represent a metaphysical failure, the catastrophe that is destroying the West, and making the Spiritual Church an impossibility. Hermeneutics, far from being the culmination of secularization, is the royal road to the sacred.

The active "accomplished nihilism" that Vattimo describes is not completely without content. It is not merely a dissolving power, but carries with it the central core of the Christian tradition: Love. For *kenosis* is God's self-emptying love. Frascati-Lochhead writes,

The principle of *caritas,* love, knows no limitation. This is Vattimo's answer to the criticism that secularization, instead of developing the Christian tradition, often places itself explicitly outside of it. The core of Christianity is love, *kenosis,* and hence, no doctrinal conclusion, no "truth," is guaranteed as ultimately and eternally valid. Augustine's word, "Love God and do as you please!" is as applicable to the interpretation of Scripture and dogma as to anything else.[142]

Here again, as with Coakley and Balthasar, we find a point of contact with Corbin's theology. Vattimo's ethics includes an almost sacramental sense of attention to the particulars of the world that he calls *pietas.*[143] Vattimo says that he uses the term

> in the modern sense of piety as devoted attention to that which, however, has only a limited value and that deserves attention because this value, even though limited is the only one we know. *Pietas* is love for the living and its traces— those lived and those carried insofar as they are received from the past.[144]

But for Corbin this love finds its source in the transcendent figure of the Beloved who is infinitely renewed and renewable through that very transcendence and so can never become an idol. As we have heard, "Theophanic perception remains open to all metamorphoses, and perceives the forms through their very metamorphoses. . . ." But the metamorphoses of which Corbin speaks presuppose the vertical hierarchies of being that are implicit in all Islamic thought. For Vattimo and the modern world, all metamorphoses can only be horizontal, Darwinian, temporal. All that prevents idolatry and dogma for Vattimo is the knowledge that one's idols will always melt away into another, merely different form. There can be no orientation in a world with no boundaries, and our sole opportunity is acceptance of the transience of this mortal world of ceaseless flux.

Vattimo's work is part of the project of post-Nietzschean philosophy to destroy what Derrida calls the metaphysics of Presence. That is, metaphysics understood as the attempt to get a grip on the structure and eternal Truth of Being. If we follow Nietzsche, Heidegger, and Derrida we realize that having come to the end of metaphysics we no longer have the option of believing in structures of permanence and domination, whether metaphysical or moral or scientific. We are left with the play of signifiers, the play of interpretations, or the flux of boundary-less entities that modern technology and economics provides. Being must be understood as *event.* We are freed for an active nihilism that holds itself open in self-giving love and *pietas* and can acknowledge the rights of *no* powers of violence or violation, because *no* dogmas, *no* interpretations are true, all stories, all myths, all religions, all powers and authorities are evanescent and groundless and infirm.

Everything becomes hermeneutics. No facts. Only interpretations. The hidden god that is the abyss of nihilism is dominant, but is given a positive twist: if there is no truth, there can at least be no rationale for domination and control.

There may of course be such domination without any rationale. Corbin indeed argues for what he calls a "permanent hermeneutics."[145] But there are subtle, significant, and yet immense differences. The "open sea" that Nietzsche celebrates is not the "ocean without a shore" that Ibn 'Arabi finds at the end of the mystic quest. There is a world of difference between *hubris* and mystical poverty, between the *übermensch* and the *darwish*. For Nietzsche and Vattimo there is nothing underlying the individual. Nothing gives structure or direction to the metamorphoses of personality. Nothing prevents the plurality of Bibles from becoming a Babel of chaos. And for Nietzsche, for Vattimo, there can be no ascent. Corbin's freedom from dogma always moves upward toward the Angel of your being. Corbin's vision is based upon a primary orientation that precedes all human acts. It is founded upon a metaphysics that Vattimo must reject: the perception that like can only be known by like, and that, as for Balthasar, being, that is, moral existence, is intimately connected with perception. Speculative thought can only approach the truth when it serves to polish the mirror, the *speculum* in which the images of transcendence can be apprehended. Corbin's hermeneutic is always gnostic, it is always an uncovering, a revelation of something given as presence and as Gift. And it can never be the world of Promethean man, of technology, that frees us for this uncovering: the Revelation has always been there in the more-than-human world, and there it remains.

On Vattimo's account God's descent into history dissolves the world, unmakes its structures, and reveals Being as *event*. The *fana* of God into the world annihilates God Himself. The Incarnation removes the Reality behind the appearances and plunges us all into the endless world of story telling and interpretation. The metaphysics of Presence devolves into a metaphysics of Absence, of continual undoing, in a cosmos where there are no Names. Positive knowledge is vaporized into a perpetual unknowing through the encounter with the Absent God. We are left with weak thought, *pietas,* and love.

Vattimo's interpretation allows an uncompromising stand against tyranny and oppression. It privileges freedom over domination by removing any possible grounds for the justification of any Master. But clearly from a viewpoint such a Corbin's or that of the Sufi masters he represents we are on very dangerous ground indeed—truly standing on the edge of the Abyss. Where is the individual in all this? Where does the human person stand? And how are we to understand the primordial facts of nature, and the miracle of language itself? It is not clear that this "accomplished nihilism" can give an account of the world that can do justice to the body, and to the place of humans in the natural world. And practically speaking we must ask what the consequences may be of trying to make openness to the *nihil* a public program. How far can people live without Presence to balance Absence? We have seen already that the Great Chain of Being was not the static structure of Presence that its critics claim. Surely it is true that when Being *is* regarded as Presence alone, not balanced by that moment of nothingness that the *Deus absconditum* initiates, then idolatry and violence and violation are ensured. But it is far from clear that we can live with Absence alone. The encounter with the Darkness is the most perilous stage, but Semnani tells us that it must result in dementia, or in Resurrection. The encounter cannot be maintained forever.

Finally, it is not at all clear that science and technology and the engines of capitalist economics are in any real sense subverted by hermeneutics as Vattimo hopes. Technicians, capitalists, and scientists don't behave as if they are: from within the modernist worldview, facts *are* real, interpretations are only means to an end, and therein lies their power and their drive to domination.

But as we shall see technology can be interpreted in a radically different way and still be understood as the final destiny of the Incarnation and *kenosis* at the heart of the Christian myth.

The Word Made Flesh: I Am Become Death, Destroyer of Worlds

Like Vattimo, Wolfgang Giegerich regards modern technology as the logical culmination of Christianity.[146] His perspective is that of a practicing psychologist and he presents his case as a description of the psychological and mythical dominants of our time—as the unconscious working out of Christian history. But for all that he borrows his terminology from the philosophers and presents a story that he says reveals the essence and the underlying truth of the modern world. Like Vattimo, he sees the global reach of technology as the defining characteristic of modern Western culture. Yet listening to his description of that technology is like hearing a voice from a world radically different from the one Vattimo inhabits. If Vattimo attempts to read technology in the manner of Joachim of Fiore, then Giegerich provides an account of the "Hegelian" way that technology has, he argues, *in fact* developed, no matter how much we may wish that it hadn't. Giegerich focuses his attention on that most horrific display of technological domination, the nuclear bomb. His question is: How is it that only in the West such an instrument of annihilation has become possible? While other civilizations have had the means to develop a scientific technology, only the West has done so, and we have done it without regard to any limits whatsoever.[147] He writes:

> [S]ince the Middle Ages, the mind of the West has lifted off like a rocket, starting slowly to raise itself above the ground, then picking up speed exponentially. . . . No other civilization shows this self-propelling explosive development. Seen in this light, the atom bombs and missiles of this century do not look like accidental by-products of our culture . . . but more like *the* symbol of the West as a whole. . . .[148]

That science and technology are pursued with such single-minded devotion can only be understood if we realize that they are not secular activities at all. What he says of the bomb can be applied to the universal scope of technology as a whole:

The nuclear bomb in its phenomenology is so immense and so inhuman that, although a man-made object, it nevertheless extends far beyond the merely human into the dimension of the ontological and theological, into the dimension of Being and of the Gods.[149]

Where do we look for the origins of this huge dynamic that threatens to overwhelm us all? There are two key events in Judeo-Christian history that are decisive. They are to be found in the Old Testament story of Moses and the Golden Calf, and in the New Testament narratives of the Incarnation.

Throughout his account, Giegerich contrasts what he regards as a characteristically Judeo-Christian experience of reality with an interpretation of that of the ancient Greeks. The story of the clash between them begins with Moses' destruction of the idol:

> This story is, so to speak, a story of the collision of two worlds. One is situated in the lowlands and is characterized by an animal-shaped image of God cast from metal to whom the worshipping people bring offerings and in whose honor they celebrate a holiday, releasing themselves playfully to the celebration. The other world is a mountain peak and is characterized by an invisible, transcendent God in the heights, by a code of moral laws engraved on stone tables, and, on the part of God as well as on the part of Moses, by a fierce wrath against the celebrating people.[150]

Moses came down from the mountain with the tablets of the Law, and in a rage pulverized the golden calf around which the people had celebrated and danced in his absence. He then forces a decision: "Who is on the side of the Lord?" and commands those siding with him to "slay every man his brother, every man his companion, every man his neighbor"[151] and so this is how they ordained themselves for the service of the Lord. This story, Giegerich says, has penetrated deeply into the soul of Western humanity for two thousand years, causing a permanent rift in our souls between the pagan dancer and the warrior in service to the transcendent God. It signals the birth of both the sin of idolatry and of the One God. For there can be no True God without false gods, and no idols without that Lord.

This story describes a schism in the experience of reality. The pagan, mythical, ritualistic experience of the world is dominated by the self-evident radiance of phenomena. The word phenomenon has its roots in the Greek *phainesthai*: to appear, to shine. For Giegerich, a psychologist in the Jungian tradition, this "shining" of things is what Jung has meant by the "image."[152] Avens writes, "Phenomena have no backs: they are what they mean and they mean what they are. What manifests itself and impresses the soul with a numinous effect is true by virtue of its shining." As Jung discovered in conversation with a Pueblo Indian Chief, the Sun that is God has nothing "behind" it. The Chief said, "The Sun is God, everyone can see that." "This is the Father, there is no

Father behind it."[153] This "pagan" god is a *theos,* and does not refer to a Supreme Being—it expresses a quality of existence, something "unheard of," "extraordinary," "wonderful."[154] In the case of the Golden Calf, "anybody could immediately *see* from the bull's radiating imaginal quality that this is God. The essence of God was in the pagan world to be sought in the radiation and in the numinosity of this metaphoric shine."[155] There is no question as to the existence of such deities—they *are* the self-evident fullness of sensuous reality.

But when Moses pulverizes the idol, God "pushes off from his animal base and takes off for the mountain."[156] This unprecedented, entirely unique event has enormous consequences. The meaning of divinity and the meaning of the world have changed utterly. Though it takes centuries for the effects to work themselves out, the die is cast. God becomes invisible, present only in faith and in the preaching of his word. God becomes wholly transcendent, his immanent shine now gone—he disappears even from the winds. God becomes *One:* no longer visible, but pure spirit, his particularity and plurality disappear. God's animal nature and concrete reality vaporize and we are left with an idealized Being. With no presence in the world, with no sensate epiphanies to speak for Him, there must be an unbroken string of Witnesses to keep the faith alive. Lastly, by pushing off any *image,* God becomes *literal:* the One, True, Positivist God. Only the literal can be *believed* in. Images show themselves—they are what they reveal, and as an essential part of this showing, they have their being in relation to other such images, and thus their boundaries are labile, indistinct, and sensuous. Only an ideal, abstract reality can be perfect, stable, and simple enough to be *literal.* In short:

> God was only able to acquire his literal existence by paying the price of his substantiality, self-evidence, and worldly embodiment. Only by abandoning his sensate reality, only through his mystification, was he able to become absolute spirit and true God.[157]

The effects on the world He leaves behind are just as radical. Idols and the True God are born simultaneously. Both are equally distant from the mythical, imaginal reality from which they emerge with the stroke of Moses' sword. Giegerich writes:

> Moses' pulverizing and melting down the Golden Calf is an assault on the imaginal quality of reality as such. . . . Moses reduces the reality of God to "mere matter": dust instead of divine image. Just as God becomes a literal God, so does matter in a positivistic sense originate here. . . . It is this act which gives rise for the first time to the idea of something earthly that is "nothing but" earthly, for it is deprived of its imaginal shine. As God becomes worldless by obtaining his ab-soluteness, so earthly reality becomes God-less.[158]

We are witnessing here the birth of positivism: literal, monotheistic religion, and literalist, monomaniacal secular scientism. It took centuries for the divine image of reality to be completely destroyed, and yet the seeds of the destruction are clear. In this biblical tale we are present at the birth of the literal and the "elimination altogether of the imaginal from the prevailing ontology."[159] For Giegerich the catastrophic event that leads to the modern world lies at the very heart of the Judeo-Christian experience of transcendence.

There are three new elements that appear at this birth: God as a transcendent, purely spiritual intensity, matter as a literalized, secular "dust," and, born out of the psychic energy released by this "first fission" of the West, the Will to Power, in the form of the *ego*.[160] This will to power is what drives modern scientific technology and has produced most emblematically the horror that is the Bomb.

There is a good deal more to Giegerich's story, but our focus is on the Incarnation. Given the radical split between God and the world, what is the meaning of the Incarnation for Giegerich? He stresses that Christianity alone of all the world's religions professes such a doctrine, and it is out of the Christian Middle Ages that the modern view of nature arises. What this uniquely Christian doctrine adds to the schism is the paradoxical union of its members. Speaking in psychological terms, Giegerich says that God must somehow compensate for his lack of Being, his disappearance into the empyrean. But given the gulf separating God from matter, the only way to effect a contact is through the necessarily paradoxical union, the *perichoresis* or reciprocal interpenetration of the divine and the human. Giegerich calls the burial of the Logos in earthly flesh the "somatization of Being" and says that it provides the only possible mythical basis for our modern sense of the objective reality of the world of things and facts.[161] It is significant that Giegerich should choose *perichoresis* from among all the various ways of understanding the doctrine of *kenosis*. As we have seen, this term was used by John of Damascus, and in his hands the doctrine threatened the full permeation of the human by the divine. It threatened the obliteration of human weakness "by the invasive leakage of divine power."[162] This understanding of *kenosis* raises the specter of a divine force destroying and controlling the human nature of Christ, and so His essential weakness. This is indeed the point that Giegerich is making. This is the kind of *kenosis* that is really at work in the Western psyche, in spite of all the disputations of the theologians.

When the Logos becomes flesh, the flesh is "logolized." The embodiment of the transcendent, abstract spirit, in compensation for its loss of reality and immanence, has three results. Avens summarizes:

> First, God's essence ceases to be only image-like, mythical. God wants to be positively "someone," a substantial being, a being in flesh. Second, the fact that this God . . . must become flesh, shows that from the very outset he lacks something—that he is incorporeal, insubstantial, unreal. The natural gods never need to become flesh because they carry their corporeality in their image-like or imaginal nature. Third, in the event of the incarnation a twofold change takes place: a change in the essence of flesh and a simultaneous change in the essence of nature. . . . [W]e are witnessing here an event of awesome

proportions: the flesh—in its oneness with the Logos—acquires a radically different nature. The very idea of flesh, earth, reality, is changed. The flesh is no longer natural, but flesh from above; indeed it is not flesh at all but, so to speak, a "logolized" abstract flesh.[163]

The world is forever changed. What counts as real is no longer the phenomenal real of the mythical, ritual world, but the abstract, manufactured "second nature" of what will become technology. Technology is Logos, and technology is flesh—and it is what defines what is really real: "[T]he flesh, after the Incarnation, has acquired a new meaning: it is 'made,' technological flesh, a second nature."[164]

Christianity attains to its truth only through the death of nature, through the dominion of the abstract and yet intensely, literally real world of technological devices whose actual purpose is to build God here on earth, in the flesh. This is what transcendence means for us: it is "a quality within reality, another style of reality" where the abstract, invisible "spiritual" laws of nature, the generalized abstractions of science, are given body through technique. The global domination of Western technology is also a fulfillment of Christian monotheism in its relentless attempt to unify, control, and dominate the various viewpoints of the plural, human world. The God's-eye view of the satellite in space, the all-encompassing reach of global capitalism, and the pervasive tentacles of consumer culture, TV, and the Internet: all of this points to the dominance of "one absolute, total, all-encompassing God—the God of technology." Giegerich says, "The event of technology as a whole means the end of eachness, the end of cosmos and the victory of universe. . . . Concrete objects, tables, cars, shoes, tin cans, plastic now have their nature in being throwaway objects, and only abstract Technology as a whole has divine value."[165] The aim of technology is a total obliteration of the human and of the natural. Avens comments, "Everything is a fusion of heaven and earth in one point. . . . In a word, the very being of the artificial (the technological) is power and violence-violation."[166]

The movement into the literal world of second nature is also an exteriorization of everything inner, interior. This is a turning inside out into a world of objects and history, a world of human-made devices that have undone the natural realm in its entirety—where we have given all the names. The Incarnation is the truth of the West, and can only be fulfilled by a total exteriorization of our inwardness—by a total immersion in earthly reality. We must learn to see, Giegerich says, that humanism, freedom, individuality, and interiority are the "untruth of the West." We are bound by destiny, by the new truth of Being which technology inaugurates, and our only redemption lies in giving ourselves over wholly to this new ontology, this more-than-human power that will sweep us along in its wake whether we will it or not. We have viewed the world of technology as a secular realm only because we have tried to deny its sacred power—the power of the one God among us—and we can be saved only by accepting the fact that for us, technology is God. "The nuclear Bomb *is* God."[167]

One can imagine Corbin's horror, were he to hear this account. This is just the catastrophe he feared, just what the failed initiation could produce, just what one could expect from a *fana* of God into the world. The perils of the Incarnation include just this divinization of the human. Corbin saw that the doctrine of the God-Man can go wrong in precisely this way, so that the two natures of Christ collapse together, and in a monstrous inversion of the monophysite doctrine, Man sets himself up as God on Earth.[168] Corbin would say that Giegerich has read the Judeo-Christian story from the point of view of the dominant tradition. By doing so, he has been able to show us what this tradition has done. But it has also led him into the errors of that tradition. Importantly, he misunderstands the *imaginal*. His interpretation of the "image" as well as his use of *imaginal,* differ essentially from Corbin's. In Corbin's theophanic cosmology, "image" always implies an interplay between immanence and transcendence; that is what guarantees the angelic function of beings and prevents idolatry. Giegerich views the origins of monotheism through the lens ground by the very technicians whose worldview is the result of the failed initiation. So he cannot understand the true meaning of theophany and of the *imaginal*. Thus, Giegerich reads a modern disaster back into the rift between the Greek and the Hebrew.

But it is not the Abrahamic tradition that is at fault, only the literal, dogmatic, "Hegelian" versions of it. What Giegerich has done is to reveal to us clearly what these interpretations of the Incarnation and kenosis have produced. Surely Corbin would say that Giegerich reads the Incarnation aright— this *is* what has happened, we do live under the dominion of the Will to Power, in the shadow of the domination of the individual, and the violation of the world of the *anima mundi* given in the primordial Revelation. It is a rape of Nature and of humanity as well. Giegerich's view of the Incarnation expresses precisely what Corbin was most worried about—Faustian science, demonic inflation, and the disappearance of the interiority of the individual. But for Giegerich this reality forces us to accept that Pan is in fact dead, Nature is violated, the air is fouled, and the forests will not regrow. This is our fate, we have all contributed to its development, and *we* are the very enemy we pretend to loath. He says that we have no choice. In an echo of Vattimo, he thinks this is our destiny and we have no other option. We must accept the world of technology. It is, he says, the place where our being truly is. He writes, "[F]or us technology is 'our place of soul-making' our form of alchemical opus and our place of theophany."[169] But where Vattimo's theophanies appear in the ephemeral being of transient things, Giegerich's appear in warheads and thermonuclear detonations.

There is sense in his "realism," for we cannot bury our heads in the sand. And yet to believe that technology is the inevitable embodiment of the Will to Power invites the darkest visions of a technological world run amok. Harraway, who as we have heard writes of the promise that *may* be found in the image of the cyborg, sees the demonic side quite clearly. In her words, the cyborg is the awful apocalyptic telos of the West's escalating dominations of abstract individuation, an ultimate self untied at last from all dependency, a man in space.... From one perspective a cyborg world is about the final imposition of a grid of control on the planet, about the final abstraction embodied in a Star Wars apocalypse waged in the name of defense, about the final appropriation of women's bodies in a masculinist orgy of war.[170]

We can envision a technological future as Vattimo does, and as Harraway hopes we may, as the birthplace of multiple interpretations that dissolve all global powers in a happy chaotic welter of local powers and local rationalities. There is a good deal of such theorizing within the scientific community itself.[171] Then technology can perhaps represent the culmination of *kenosis* as love. In that case there are some points of agreement with Corbin's theology. There are then ways of understanding the kenotic foundations of normative Christianity in line with Corbin's views. But coexisting with these tendencies are those that Giegerich describes. If, as I suspect, it is the latter that are likely to prevail, then Corbin's prediction of catastrophe has come true with a vengeance.

There are clearly truths in both of these accounts of the modern world. But whichever way we read technology, Corbin would stand firm against both Vattimo and Giegerich on one key issue: that there is no other option. Both Vattimo and Giegerich affirm our helplessness in the face of the Truth of Being. We are doomed either to accept "accomplished nihilism" or the inhuman powers of Second Nature. But to interpret this as the unalterable destiny of the West, as somehow the new Truth of Being[172] which we must accept in order to be in tune with our times—this invites the ultimate catastrophe, the ultimate Idolatry: worship of the Promethean human in the form of Technology and the complete and final occultation of even the memory of both the human being and of God. For Corbin the proclamation that our current sorry state is our destiny and in fact the truth of Being, is the greatest domination, the most dangerous dogmatism. Corbin stands for the freedom of the individual against the tides of the times. It is a stand against a world made by men, or a world, if so it be, made by the Fallen God, the absolute literalist, a God who is no longer hidden at all, whose body is the bomb, whose meaningless images now flood our lives. Corbin stands for the individual soul, in that community of beings accessible to us in the numinous shine and radiance of the Primordial Revelation.

FOR LOVE OF THE WORLD:
IMAGINATION, LANGUAGE AND
THE PRIMORDIAL REVELATION

I want to sketch out the rudiments of a response to these analyses of the history of the West, of technology, and of our sense of who we are. Surely we have been shaped by the prophetic tradition out of which Christianity was born, but I share Corbin's belief that we are not trapped within the confines of history as it has developed. The direction I want to pursue owes a great deal to Corbin's vision of the Religions of Abraham, the Religions of the Book, and to those elements within those traditions that he so passionately defended. But I find it difficult to embrace any of them. Their official forms have been too violent, too oppressive, too destructive. And the God of Abraham has been absent too long and too hideously in the century's genocides and catastrophes. And yet, I am profoundly stirred by Corbin's work, and want to count myself among "those who have chosen." I want to join in his battle against the forces of Ahriman, and in the search for glimmers of light in these dark times. Corbin's work on the roots of the Abrahamic tradition points the way toward an understanding of the relation between transcendence and immanence, thought and being, the spiritual and the ethical, that can perhaps allow us to begin formulate a response adequate to the conditions of humanity and the world in our time. We must pay close attention to what he has to tell us of the Imagination, the world, and the Word. Because the central question to be asked about the Religions of the Book is: After the unspeakable catastrophes of the twentieth century, what *can* we say?

THE PRIMORDIAL AND THE PRIMITIVE

We are in danger of becoming defined and dominated by our tools. Our powers and techniques are truly titanic: monstrous and divine at once. We are caught in a multitude of contradictions established by the powers we have unleashed. We are indeed made weak by what we have thought, for our tools *are* our thoughts "made flesh." We are overcome by these literally real abstractions in a global society of a generalized communication and the unfettered flow of *things*. This world without boundaries is wracked with violence, madness, and despair—for overhanging it all is that final abstraction made real, that infinite counterweight to any physicist's Theory of Everything, the nuclear bomb. We find ourselves caught between the abyss of a horrible "freedom" and the finality of an annihilating constraint, amidst the wreckage of nature and of human hopes.

It is time for each of us to make a choice. If we are not to perish in the flux of history we must follow Corbin's lead and take a stand against it. His entire work constitutes an invitation to choose, not for ourselves, but for our Angel and for the Angel of the Earth. In order to gain access to the experience of the soul of the world upon which our own souls depend we need a method, a *theoria*. To take a stand against the powers that threaten to engulf us we need a countertechnology. We need techniques to oppose the immense powers that threaten to annihilate all the rich diversities of the world, both cultural and natural. And we need the means to resist the perils of nihilism that threaten to weaken our determination, undermine our sense of the ultimate worth of the human soul, and that give support to the insidious darknesses that dissolve us from within.

Among the lovers of the world, among the ecologists, among the "greens," there has long been recognition that our species has overstepped its bounds, that our actions are disrupting the physical and biological systems upon which our lives depend. We need to reinvent human political economies, to move beyond the economic systems of the developed nations. Not in order to revert to an idealized nontechnological past, but to move toward a world where the human connection to the earth is understood, and given its due. We have to envision a post-technological world, a postmodern world where human culture is no longer conceived in separation from the natural world.

The attempt to establish humility, respect, and reverence for the matrix of life as the guiding principles for a new conception of human culture has been called "posthistoric primitivism."[173] *Posthistoric* because our vision of the enormous diversity of human cultures over vast expanses of time and space means that we can stand now outside the limits of a narrowly human conception of history. We can see ourselves as embedded in nonhuman nature, and our present lives as extensions of a prehistoric, Paleolithic past. *Primitive,* because we can recognize the primordial bases of human communal and individual life. As the anthropologist Stanley Diamond has said, "[T]he sickness of civilization consists . . . in its failure to incorporate (and only then to move beyond the limits of) the primitive."[174] Even Giegerich suggests that our situation would not perhaps have become so desperate had we been able from the outset to see our technologies not as part of the secular realm, and so merely utilitarian and unconnected to the life of the soul or the spirit, but as a living part of the psyche of the world. We might then have given them the attention due to any expression of the *anima mundi*. We might have taken the care to develop humane and appropriate technologies that could have helped to usher in a new kind of primitivism.[175]

The situation is very different from the perspective of traditional Islam. In Islam Nature itself is the primordial Revelation. Thus, as Corbin often repeats, God can say, "I was a Hidden Treasure and I longed to be known, so I created the world." The world itself is the original manifestation of the Face of Beauty. The Qur'an says, "Wherever you turn the face of God is everywhere."[176] The revealed Book is replete with cosmic imagery, more so perhaps than any other sacred text, and everything in that cosmos is a sign of God. As the last Revelation, part of the message of Islam is to restore the first Revelation, the miracle of creation, to center stage, since over time it has more and more come to be taken for granted.[177] But the return to the primordial in Islam does not signify what in the modern West is sometimes disparagingly regarded as a simplistic and utopian return to nature. The Islamic Revelation is a laying bare of the Face of God, by means of the "reminder" that is the Book.

To effect this transformation, to liberate the imagination from the control of the powerful who would manipulate all our thoughts and desires requires the moment of nothingness that is the result of the encounter with the *Deus abscon-ditus*. It requires the destruction of human meaning that Joyce called the "abni-hilisation of the etym."[178] This is part of the task of hermeneutics. In Corbin's vision, the soul and the world are not divisible, and hermeneutics is their simul-taneous development. Speech and song are the primordial technologies of the soul. A countertechnology based on this insight would consist in an attempt to reclaim the roots of language, of the soul, and of the world from their domina-tion by the powers of abstraction and universalization, whether these are tech-nological, economic, or political. These roots are to be sought not in the uni-versal, abstract, and general, but in the individual, the oral, the local, and the particular.[179] This provides the answer to the question that may be the central question of the Abrahamic prophetic tradition: Who is Khidr?[180] There is a hint of the answer in his name: Khidr is the "Verdant One."[181] He is the Green Man. He is the Angel of the Face and the Angel of the Earth as hermeneut: the *Verus Propheta* revealed to each soul in the form in which each is able to receive it.

It is to this hermeneutics that we now turn.

PSYCHOCOSMOLOGY: ALCHEMIES OF THE WORD AND OF THE WORLD

If we recognize the realm of the imaginal as the mediating world between the purely physical and the purely spiritual then the schism between them can begin to heal. Matter need no longer be confused with the demonic. Indeed, everything becomes material.[182] What had been conceived as spiritual reality becomes the realm of subtle bodies, and there is a continuum from the dense to the subtle that corresponds to an intensification of being. It is possible for any of the beings belonging to the world of Light to become more real, more themselves, more individual and intense in their very being. We begin to sus-pect then that the true meaning of the word *substance* is fading from our con-sciousness. We tend to think of the spiritual as disembodied, diaphanous, even abstract. We set spirit on one side, and matter on the other, and increasingly only the material, the manipulable, has any real importance, any "substance." But when priority is given to the imaginal, the dichotomy between substance and spirit collapses. The spiritual *is* substantial. It is not disembodied. It is here and now.[183] This is how we can reclaim a sense of the substantial presence and the concrete significance of human life. The "real work" for us is simultaneously a spiritual, ethical, and physical struggle. Like can only be known by like: this means that thought and being are inseparable, that ethics and perception are complementary. The form of the soul is the form of your world. This funda-mental unity of the faculties of human cognition and the world to which they give access *is* that eternal pagan substrate of all religion. As we saw earlier, Corbin speaks of the "cognitive function of sympathy" as basic to the revela-tion of correspondences, the "balances" between the worlds visible to the eyes

of flesh and the worlds visible to the eyes of fire. This sympathy is at once perceptual and cognitive and requires an attitude toward reality that the modern
world has nearly completely forgotten. It is a stance toward reality that gives
weight to the display of the image, denying the schism between the inner and
the outer, the subjective and the objective. All the prophets have been sent to
remind us of it. And in the Islamic view there have been no people to whom
there have not been sent messengers. We can trace this substrate right back to
the Paleolithic. In recalling the poetic or cognitive function of sympathy,
Corbin is calling us to recover what the poet Gary Snyder calls the "mythological present." Snyder writes:

> To live in the "mythological present" in close relation to nature and in basic
> but disciplined body/mind states suggests a wider-ranging imagination and a
> closer subjective knowledge of one's own physical properties than is usually
> available to men living (as they themselves describe it) impotently and inade-
> quately in "history"—their mind-content programmed, and their caressing of
> nature complicated by the extensions and abstractions which elaborate tools
> are. . . . Poets, as few others, must live close to the world that primitive men are
> in: the world, in its nakedness, which is fundamental for all of us—birth, love,
> death; the sheer fact of being alive. . . . In one school of Mahayana Buddhism,
> they talk about the "Three Mysteries." These are Body, Voice and Mind. The
> things that are what living *is* for us, in life. Poetry is the vehicle of the mystery
> of Voice. The universe, as they sometimes say, is a vast breathing body.[184]

In Ibn 'Arabi's cosmology, which was so crucial for Corbin, it is the Breath of
the All-Merciful that unites the Cosmos, God, and Language into a single
extraordinary animate system of perpetual descent and return. For Ibn 'Arabi,
"[l]anguage is an articulation of the breath. . . . It is an image of the self and of
the world outside the self."[185] The imaginal world of the breath and human
speech expresses the creative power of the divine form because the human self
is "a unique articulation of the divine Breath." This Breath speaks itself as both
the microcosm of the human self and the macrocosm of the cosmos.

It is essential for the hermeneutics we are seeking to grasp the fact of the
embodied spirituality of the Word in Islam.[186] The Qur'an is first and foremost
a *recited* text. The power of the word, its poetic force, is based first of all upon
public vocalization, not internalized, private reading. The Revelation of the
Qur'an to Mohammad occurred as *recitation,* and the revelations, which con-
tinued throughout his life, were physically overwhelming. Islamic spirituality
has retained this embodied character throughout its history. The very position
of the ritual prayer is said to have provided the archetype for the design of the
human body. Prayer and its orientation toward Mecca as the symbol of centrality celebrate the worshipping body.[187]

And there is no distinction between the sacred and the secular in Islam.
There cannot be a merely utilitarian realm where a secular technology can get

a foothold. There is no realm of life that is outside the religion. All the details of human existence are subject to ritual prescriptions.[188] In the figure of Mohammad we find an exemplar of the perfect human that Christians often find hard to understand, raised as they have been with the image of Christ as the archetype of holiness. Mohammad was a husband many times over, father, confidant, warrior, teacher, politician, businessman, prophet, and mystic: the fullness of human worldliness *and* spirituality, the perfection of that breathing body and microcosm of the world which is the human self. He provides a model for the substantial struggle of human life, for *gnosis* as the transformational, salvational knowledge that alters the networks of connections linking the microcosm and the macrocosm.

The phenomenology of the imaginal is in full accord with this essential embodiment of Islamic spirituality. "[I]magination embodies. It cannot conceive of God or anything else save in concrete terms."[189] It is characteristic of Qur'anic Arabic that it is concrete: "[T]he Arabic of the Qur'an . . . always has a concrete side to it, and this is true of Arabic in general. . . ."[190] The language of the Qur'an is the foundation of Islamic spirituality. And so it is that for Ibn 'Arabi "it is in the world's concrete realities that God is found, not its abstractions."[191] On his view both reason and imagination are required for adequate knowledge of the self, the world, and God. Without reason we can easily be misled into delusion. And yet for us it is his emphasis on the imagination and the way that it prevents the rupture between matter and spirit that is definitive of our tradition. Chittick writes:

> [I]magination perceives that the symbol is identical with what it symbolizes, creation is the same as the Creator, the form is none other than the meaning, the body is the spirit, the locus of manifestation is nothing but God as manifest, and the image is the object. This perception . . . is unmediated by any rational process—it is a tasting, an unveiling, a witnessing, an insight. . . . It is best exemplified in human experience precisely by concrete experience—tasting food, being carried away by music, falling in love. Theologically, imagination . . . achieves an incontrovertible understanding that the creature is God.[192]

> The mysteries of the universe do not lie primarily in the universal laws and principles, even though these are mysterious enough. What is most mysterious and miraculous about the universe is its concrete particularity, its every object and inhabitant, each of which is ultimately unfathomable.[193]

For Ibn 'Arabi language, imagination, and the concrete embodiment of the cosmos are linked together through the flow of the Breath of the All-Merciful. And perhaps by believing in the vitality and truth of this worldview we can begin to recover the meaningful substance of the work of human life. Perhaps we can, as Corbin did, learn from the way Islam safeguards the primordial unity of self and world in a sensate, imaginative sympathy. It is this that he saw as the primordial vision uniting the monotheisms of the West into one True Church, a living embodiement of the *Harmonia Abrahamica*.

We can perhaps begin by taking language very seriously indeed. We can acknowledge the psycho-cosmic reach of language and its ontological force, its ability to transform the soul and the world. There is ample precedent for this in the Christian tradition, especially in what Corbin called the "tradition of hermeneutics" that stretches from Jacob Boehme through J. G. Hamann and continues right up to Heidegger and the contemporary world.

To attempt to learn to speak a language based upon the cognitive sympathy that lies at the root of religion would provide a means of warding off the dangers of abstraction and the dogmas that accompany it. Such a poetics could help us to live in the mythological present, in what Corbin called a realized eschatology: that is, one that occurs *right now*. Recall the anecdote Corbin relates of the conversation with D. T. Suzuki in Ascona in 1954:

> [W]e asked him what homologies in structure he found between Mahayana Buddhism and the cosmology of Swedenborg in respect of the symbolism and correspondences of worlds: I can still see Suzuki suddenly brandishing a spoon and saying with a smile "This spoon *now* exists in Paradise. . . . We are *now* in Heaven. . . ."This was an authentically *Zen* way of answering the question. Ibn 'Arabi would have relished it.[194]

Corbin devoted many pages to the work of Immanuel Swedenborg. For Swedenborg as for Corbin, the *ego* must be opened to the influx of its angel. It must be opened, that is, to the world beyond its narrow personal confines, toward its true Self. In Heaven, whether we achieve it in this life or in the next, the form of your world is what you *are*, just as in the Sufism of Najm Kubra. David Loy, an authority on Buddhism, writes of Swedenborg: "To be spiritual is nothing more than being open to, and thereby united with, the whole. . . . We are in heaven right now if our internals are open, according to Swedenborg, and *nirvâna* is to be attained here and now, according to Śâkyamuni Buddha."[195]

We need to keep our internals open. I can think of no better way to express that freedom from hard-heartedness and dogma that is one goal of the human struggle. It is a psycho-physical Quest to be open to the world. Not curved in upon ourselves, but open to the tastes and textures of the world as the Manifestation of the Real. And the breath of our words is essential because they reflect the images that engender the angelic function of beings.

A language is concrete, like Arabic, when the words are pregnant with images.[196] Poetic language in any tongue can be concrete in this way. Image opens onto image, landscape onto landscape, stitching the inner and outer together and enacting the sympathies between beings by means of perceptions of the subtle relations that link all things. This requires subtlety and attention and perceptual skills that have atrophied in us from lack of use.

We have Freud and Jung to thank for taking seriously the procession of images, the theater of the life of the soul, for the "talking cure" that recognizes the power of language to transform, and for the *amplificatio* that extends our reach into the unknown places where our souls and the world interact. But, as James Hillman has argued for many years now, we need to move beyond the inner-directed emphasis of much psychotherapy to the complex and difficult task of working in that intermediate realm of the alchemical, of subtle bodies, where the geographies of nature and the landscapes of the human soul inter-penetrate.[197] We have to learn to inhabit a world where the human and the more-than-human meet in mutual presence.

We who live in a world of real abstractions have seen the products of abstract and dogmatic thought that have little sympathy for human or any other beings. Knowing the inhumanities and excesses of a world so constructed, we can turn to the more difficult task of transformation that the thing-like-ness of concrete thought implies. We can turn now back to the real work of being human.

READING THE WILDERNESS

We have lived too long within a world of our own making. We have lived too long within a language of the merely human. To keep our internals open we have to learn to read and write ourselves out of ourselves, and uncurl ourselves back into the world.[198] This is the task set to us by Khidr, the Green Man, the hermeneut at the meeting place of the two seas. Language is not a tool for communication that belongs to us. Language is not an exclusively human abil-ity at all. It is a field of meanings and intentions that we inhabit. Human lan-guage grows out of the world itself. We speak because the world speaks. And because language and the symbols upon which it depends are the Breath of God, it has the power to penetrate to the very heart of things. Language in the broadest sense is creative because the world was spoken into being. Because of this, reading can be, as Ivan Illich has told us, "an ontologically remedial tech-nique,"[199] a means of transformation, of *gnosis*.

It seems clear the habits and skills of literate culture are being lost. We may indeed be entering a time that George Steiner calls the After-word. The habits of reading and the culture of the book are on the decline in modern techno-logical society. Both Steiner and Illich have somewhat wistfully proposed that perhaps as the universities turn themselves into the handmaidens of business, technology, and the military, we may yet preserve cells of humanist resistance, "Houses of Reading" where the habits of mind of a bookish civilization can endure.[200] I believe with them that something like this is essential for the preser-vation of our humanity, essential if we are to take a stand against the ongoing violations that are the annihilation of the person and the rape of nature. But it is not enough. Khidr is not a humanist. He is a messenger from far beyond.[201] The world that he opens up to us is infinite. He announces that the cosmos itself is a "house of reading"—it is the Primordial Temple of the Word. The guardians of high culture, of literature and the humanities, have for a long time not read this book at all. They have been too curved in upon themselves. And when it is read, as it is by natural scientists, it is too often only in the most abstract languages of domination and control. The cultures of the After-word will not just be illiterate, but also denatured, dysfunctional, and condemned to occupy the world of Second Nature that Giegerich describes.

There are as many kinds of literature as there are kinds of attentiveness.[202] In 1907 the unorthodox psychoanalyst and physician Georg Groddeck made a distinction that is useful here.[203] He said that there is a kind of poetry, of literature, that seems to come from inside human consciousness and brings us "news of the human mind." Groddeck suggested that European culture after around 1600 became increasingly absorbed in this kind of attention, and that the resulting literature, having reached its apogee in Shakespeare, is now in decline and becoming more extreme in order to compensate for its essential bankruptcy. At the opposite end of the spectrum is a kind of poetics based on attentiveness, not to the human, but to the more-than-human, to what Groddeck calls *Gottnatur*, a divine instinctuality. This kind of attentiveness and the art it produces bring us "news of the universe." Groddeck found this attention sometimes in Goethe. He thought it represented something new beginning in the West. I hope he was right, and I think it is here that we may look for an element of the countertechnology we are seeking. Robert Bly comments: "Literature and art that attempt to reopen the channels between human beings and nature, and to make our fear of her dark side conscious, help us to see her without fear, hatred or distance."[204]

What are the techniques we need? We already know that we must be willing to allow the world to speak, willing to seek correspondences between human consciousness and what we might call the consciousnesses in the natural world. We already know that this means being open to images as the theater of the world. To open ourselves to the news of the universe requires a poet's hermeneutic attentiveness, and this requires some disciplines we are sorely lacking. We do need something like "houses of reading," to serve as cells of resistance to the dominion of those who control the postliterate culture of the wholly unnatural. But these would be half-open dwellings, opening outward beyond the confines of the *ego*, beyond the range of human culture and onto the mysteries of the more-than-human world. To fully understand the significance of the task we set ourselves, we must recognize with Jung that these untamed regions do not correspond to the boundaries we have set up between the inner and the outer. The wild is not identical with the world of physical nature. And the tame is not restricted to a protected enclave within the human person.

The reading of the world that we need to learn has to be active and engaged. It must take the form of a dialogue that begins with a careful listening to the voices that speak to us from beyond the bounds of the known. We have to engage in a gentle kind of call and response, a reading that calls in turn for speech, and perhaps for writing, or other kinds of making, and that always turns back to listening. We can learn aspects of this kind of discipline from children, from certain kinds of natural science, and from poets and artists. George Steiner's profound study of the grounds of meaning in language and art are of tremendous importance here. We need a theory, a *theoria*, not just of meaning in poetry and literature, but in the perception of all reality, and Steiner's suggestions are fertile. He recalls to us yet again the roots of *theoria*. "It tells," he writes,

> of concentrated insight, of an act of contemplation focused patiently on its object. But it pertains also to the deeds of witness performed by the legates sent, in solemn embassy, to observe the oracles spoken or the rites performed at the sacred Attic games. A "theorist" or "theoretician" is one who is disciplined in observance, a term itself charged with a twofold significance of intellectual-sensory perception and religious or ritual conduct. . . . Thus theory is inhabited by truth when it contemplates its object unwaveringly and when, in the observant process of such contemplation, it beholds, it takes grasp of the often confused and contingent . . . images, associations, suggestions, possibly erroneous, to which the object gives rise.[205]

All truth in perception begins with this "theory." This kind of attention is intensely relational because it is felt, it is sensuous, it is embodied. The encounter with intelligible form as presented in art requires that the object be experienced as a real presence, and in this encounter the "poem, the statue, the sonata are not so much read, viewed or heard as they are lived."[206] Art thus "makes sense" of the world. But *aesthesis* refers to the perception of the world we have not made, as much as to the world that we have. We who are so removed from the more-than-human need this kind of contact with the primordial grounds of life. And crucially, Steiner understands that the perception of any meaningful form is grounded in the encounter with a real presence, a transcendence, beyond the human. The perception of meaning in art, and we can extend this to the world as a whole, is based upon the "axiom of dialogue."[207] We are always, when we are truly paying attention, in communion with what lies beyond us. Steiner writes, "[I]t is, I believe, poetry, art and music which relate us most directly to that in being which is not ours."[208] As we begin to learn what it may mean to read and write the world, to hear the news of the universe, we would do well to hear these words.

Another feature of the reading we must learn is that it is attentive to *place*. Bodies occupy places, they are located. This we know from the ecologists. You need to know where you live: to know the trees, the flowers, the bedrock on which we build, where the water comes from and where it goes. But human beings are not only located; they *locate*. Corbin says,

> Orientation is a primary phenomenon of our presence in the world. A human
> presence has the property of spatializing a world around it, and this phenom-
> enon implies a certain relationship of man and the world, *his* world, this rela-
> tionship being determined by the very mode of his presence in the world.[209]

Both of these aspects of our place in the world must be given their due. The
inner and the outer interpenetrate. You cannot know who you are without
knowing the terrain you occupy; and yet you cannot truly know what your
orientation is within that terrain without knowing who you are. The ecologists
tell us we are defined by our world. Corbin tells us that our world *is* who we
are. Our inner landscapes define our orientation in the world just as surely as
the geographies of the outer world. The boundaries of the world as we have
learned to see them are disrupted. To realize this is threatening. There are few
safe havens in this task of being human.[210]

To cope with the threats and challenges of the encounter with the worlds
beyond the *ego,* what we would learn in the houses of reading would have to
include an ancient virtue: *ascesis.* There are three aspects of this discipline to consider. First, an asceticism of the body. Not the asceticism that Corbin so vehemently attacks, the furious, rejecting asceticism that creates a chasm between the
object of love and the transcendence that is immanent in it.[211] This asceticism
cannot be incompatible with a passionate love for the things of this world. An
asceticism of the body would, for us in the developed world, mean a refusal to
participate in the excesses of the consumer culture. But this is really the easy
part. Ivan Illich uses *ascesis* in another sense to mean "courageous, disciplined,
self-critical renunciation, accomplished in community." He proposes an "epistemological ascesis," a purging of corrupting concepts that give reality to abstraction, and tear us away from our roots in embodied, local, communal realities.[212]
When we live immersed in the modern world of generalized communication,
where every natural boundary is violated, we are constantly assaulted by images,
messages, ideas, *all* of them having their origins outside the boundaries of our
responsibility and control, all of them having been crafted by someone for some
purpose of their own, and all of which in the end serve to manipulate us. The
profound and magical news of the human that Shakespeare once brought, has
now degenerated, at the end of literacy, into advertising and mere "news."

Epistemological ascesis cannot entail a refusal to entertain novelty or new
ideas. But I have lived at the mercy of the tides of intellectual fashion for long
enough to know that the tremendously difficult task of renunciation is based
on an ability to discriminate and to refuse—to have a keen and attentive sense
for what is destructive, dangerous, and dominating. This requires a matured
sense of freedom and beauty. Is this teachable? Is it "art?" Perhaps it is the basis
for art; an art we have to learn in our half-open dwellings of reading.

The third aspect of ascesis is poverty: having little, needing little, living
rooted in the mystical poverty of the dervish. It is only through realizing the

poverty of the *ego* that attentiveness to the news of the universe is possible. There is an intimate connection between ascesis and aesthesis. Each requires subtle discrimination, silent attention with all the senses, and careful, watchful feeling. These operations can best be accomplished in spaces that open freely onto mystery and the unknown, that open onto darkness. Remember Sarah Coakley's call for an *ascesis* appropriate to contemplative, wordless prayer, that quiet vulnerable waiting that opens onto the dark knowing beyond speech.

The *psyche*, the *anima mundi* that we find in nature often has this openness to darkness evident as a kind of sadness. Bly writes, "The psychic tone of nature strikes many people as having some melancholy in it. The tone of nature is related to what human beings call 'grief,' what Lucretius calls 'the tears of things,' what in Japanese poetry is called *mono no aware,* the slender sadness."[213] We have encountered this before in Mir Damad's perception of the silent clamor of beings in their metaphysical distress. All things *are* only as made-to-be. All things exist in poverty and it is this that opens them to mystery, to the angelic function of beings. That is their ability to lead beyond themselves as symbols revealed to the lover, to the hermeneut, as tokens of transcendence. This may well be another way of saying that all things have some kind of consciousness, that there is a vast web of images tying together the inner and the outer. As consciousness is to supraconsciousness, so being is to mystical poverty.

The hermeneut and the lover, you see, must keep the darkness very close, always. For it is the function of the *Absconditum,* the forever and necessarily hidden God, to open the world for us at each instant, making everything new. The ever-present "moment of nothingness" hovering just beyond the horizon ensures the pervasive transcendence of the world. Only the *Deus absconditus* guarantees the eternal dissolution of dogmas and underlies the necessity of a "permanent hermeneutics," the unending reading and writing of the soul of the world, the ceaseless uncovering of harmonies between the worlds within and the worlds without. This provides the setting for the human journey toward itself and the world in which it is truly at home. We are not spirits lost in a world of matter. Both spirit and matter are abstractions born of reason. Closer to the mysterious and substantial truth is Corbin's image of a soul seeking its Angel, in an endless quest through immense landscapes in a cosmos that knows no bounds.

FIVE

HARMONIA ABRAHAMICA

The Lost Speech and the Battle for the Soul of the World

What is the source of our first suffering? It lies in the fact that we hesitated to speak. . . . It was born in the moment when we accumulated silent things within us.

—Gaston Bachelard

INTRODUCTION

WE ARE LIVING out the consequences of three great crises: a rupture between the individual and the Divine, a severing of the felt connection between human beings and the living earth, and a profound breakdown of long-held assumptions about the nature and function of language. In traditional terminology, we are witnessing a collapse of the structures that make sense of the relations among God, Creation, Logos, and the human person. Two of the catastrophes are fairly easily categorized; they are spiritual and environmental. The third, the crisis of Logos, is more diffuse and more fundamental. It is a crisis of meaning.

These crises may be understood together, as part of single, coherent story. I can't claim that this is the best story that can be told about how we arrived at our current situation, but I think it is a *good* story; that is, it is a fertile, living, open-ended story that suggests its own continuation, its own kinds of resolutions. And I must admit, my fondness for this story is born of a strong desire to find something *original,* that is, something at the origin, that can serve us all as a kind of common ground.

THE PROPHETIC TRADITION

In his late writings Henry Corbin articulated particularly clearly a powerful vision of the unity of the religions of Abraham. It is a mystical and esoteric view of these religions, in that it gives precedence to the inner significance of religious experience rather than to the social forms that contain and channel the potent forces to which religious experience can give rise. These logocentric religions share a story that centers on the revelation of the Word of God. Corbin writes,

> The drama common to all the "religions of the Book," or better said, to the community that the Qur'an designates as *Ahl al-Kitab,* the community of the Book, and that encompasses the three great branches of the Abrahamic tradition (Judaism, Christianity and Islam), can be designated as the drama of the "Lost Speech." And this because the whole meaning of their life revolves around the phenomenon of the revealed holy Book, around the true meaning of this Book. If the true meaning of the Book is the interior meaning, hidden under the literal appearance, then from the instant that men fail to recognize or refuse this interior meaning, from that instant they mutilate the unity of the Word, of the Logos, and begin the drama of the "Lost Speech."[1]

For Corbin much of Judaic, Christian, and Islamic history can only be understood if we see it as the theater in which the drama of the conflict between the literal and the hidden meaning of the Word is played out. To the degree that the Word becomes only public property, to that degree is the true meaning lost.

I think it is fair to say that all Corbin's work was at root devoted to illustrating deep commonalities between the mystical and often heretical traditions within Christianity and Islam, and of both with similar movements in Judaism. This effort he understood as akin to the attempts of early Christian hermeneuts to reconcile the stories in the four canonical Gospels. The original work of harmonization written by the Syrian Tatian in the second century took its name from Greek musical theory: his *Diatessaron* means "according to four." The traditional name for the underlying unity of the Gospels is the *Harmonia evangelica.* Corbin suggests that his own work is based upon an underlying *Harmonia Abrahamica.*[2]

One of Corbin's early influences, whose importance for his work can't be overemphasized, is Johann Georg Hamann. It is Hamann's view of language I want to single out. In a short but crucial essay that Corbin in fact translated, Hamann writes,

> Poetry is the mother-tongue of the human race; even as the garden is older than the ploughed field, painting than script; as song is more ancient than declamation; parables older than reasoning; barter than trade. A deep sleep was

the repose of our farthest ancestors; and their movement a frenzied dance. Seven days they would sit in the silence of deep thought or wonder;—and would open their mouths to utter winged sentences.

The senses and passions speak and understand nothing but images. The entire store of human knowledge and happiness consists in images. The first outburst of creation, and the first impression of its recording scribe;—the first manifestation and the first enjoyment of Nature are united in the words: Let there be Light! Here beginneth the feeling for the presence of things. . . .

Speak, that I may see Thee! This wish was answered by Creation, which is an utterance to created things through created things. . . . The fault may lie where it will (outside us or within us): all we have left in nature for our use is fragmentary verse and *disjecta membra poetae*. To collect these together is the scholar's modest part; the philosopher's to interpret them; to imitate them, or—bolder still—to adapt them, the poet's.

To speak is to translate—from the tongue of angels into the tongue of men, that is to translate thoughts into words—things into names—images into signs. . . .[3]

The language of poetry is as close as we can get to the language of the angels. It is a language of images, of imagination. And the imagination is central to the psycho-cosmology that Corbin describes in the Sufism of Ibn 'Arabi and in Shi'ism. Nature itself speaks, and it takes a special kind of attention to hear it. As Hamann wrote elsewhere,

It takes more than physics to explain nature. Physics is only the abc. Nature is an equation of unknowable grandeur; a Hebrew word of which only the consonants are written, and to which the understanding must add the diacritical vowels.[4]

Corbin's account of Western history traces the progressive loss of the Breath of Compassion that articulates those vowels and so gives life and soul to the world. He warns us that the history of the West has been the theater for the battle for the soul of the world.[5] He calls us to struggle in that long combat by turning toward the inner recesses where the Angel of the Earth and the Angel of Humanity dwell. His emphasis is on the light that illuminates the path of the mystic out of this world in which we are in exile. On his view, perhaps the most crucial event in this long history was the loss in the Christian West in the twelfth century, of the angelic hierarchies of Avicenna and Neoplatonism that had provided the connection between the individual and the divine. The loss of the intermediate world of the Imagination that they inhabit, of the realm of the *imaginal,* occasioned all the schisms that split the West: religion and philosophy, thought and being, intellect and ethics, God and the individual.

From the first to the last then, Corbin tells a tale of human life in which the place of language and the Word is central, and in which the quest for the lost language of God and the angels is the fundamental problem. It is *the* question that underlies the unity of the three branches of the Abrahamic tradition.

In his masterful treatment of the prophetic tradition, Norman O. Brown too relies on Corbin's work for insights into the history of these interconnected and tragically divided religions.[6] Islam is the last in the sequence of the great Revelations, and so sees itself as the end of the prophetic tradition. Following Louis Massignon, Brown takes Sura XVIII as the central book of the Qur'an, and the central episode of this Sura is the meeting between Moses and Khidr. Khidr is a mysterious figure, who acts as Moses' Guide and initiator into the secret meanings of the Law and of the world. He is *the* archetypal hermeneut whose speech is the lost poetry of Creation. In the Islamic tradition he is identified with the Old Testament figure of Elija. Khidr is the personal Guide, and Corbin says, equivalent to the Paraclete and the Hidden Imam, to the Christ of the Cross of Light; he is the *Verus Propheta,* the inner guide of each person, the celestial Anthropos and Angel of Humanity whose appearance to every person is *each time unique.*

Brown writes that the question posed by Islam, at the end of the prophetic tradition, after Moses, Jesus, and Mohammad, is, What comes after the Prophets? In Brown's words, "The question is, *Who is Khidr?* And, *What does it mean to be a disciple of Khidr?* . . . Pursuing that question, Ibn Arabi said that he had plunged into an ocean on whose shore the Prophets remained behind standing."[7]

This question is equivalent to asking how we may recover the Lost Speech.

AFTER THE WORD

In order to have any chance of answering this question we must examine very closely the state of language for us now, at the end of the prophetic tradition. Norman O. Brown has suggested parallels between the revealed language of the Qur'an and, astonishingly, *Finnegan's Wake.* The Qur'an, by means of its pulverization of human language, is more avant-garde, more postmodern than *Finnegan's Wake.* In its structure, its allusiveness, its ambiguities, its imagery, and its poetry "the Qur'an reveals human language crushed by the power of the divine Word."[8] God's Word unmakes all human meanings, all the proud constructions of civilization, of high culture, and returns all the luxuriant cosmic imagery back to the lowly and the oppressed, so that in their imaginations it can be made anew. Brown says,

> The Islamic imagination, Massignon has written, should be seen as the product of a desperate regression back to the primitive, the eternal pagan substrate of all religions—that proteiform cubehouse, the Ka'ba—as well as to a primitive pre-Mosaic monotheism of Abraham. The Dome is built upon the Rock.[9]

The way to start a new civilization, Brown says, "is not to introduce some new refinement in high culture but to change the imagination of the masses. . . ."[10]

The world is shattered. Language is crushed by the Word. We return to the Origin out of which alone new worlds can be made. But what is this soil out of which the luxuriant cosmic imagery grows? The return to that pagan substrate is not without danger. It suggests as well the *Blut und Boden* of Aryran supremacy, and the genocide of the very people who provide the root and origin of the entire Tradition of the Word.

Is that truly the meaning of the end of the prophetic tradition? Is it bounded by Abraham and Auschwitz? What *is* the meaning of the Word, of Logos, after the unspeakable catastrophes of the twentieth century? Is there any hope of recovering the Lost Speech now? What kind of meaning is possible in the absence of the God of Belief? What can the human response be to the long history of failures to embody the Breath of Compassion? In order to answer the fundamental questions posed by our place in the prophetic tradition, we must grapple with the enormity of our situation. I know of no more powerful and uncompromising analyst of our predicament than George Steiner. In his work we find a prolonged and intense concentration on the confrontation of creative imagination with inhumanity and evil. In Steiner's treatment of the relation between Paul Celan and Martin Heidegger all our themes come together with an intensity of focus that is staggering: Language, God, Logos, Earth, and the human person.

The poetry of Paul Celan is the result of the encounter of the creative power of human language with the unbearable bestiality of the Holocaust. Celan's late verse exists on the edge of intelligibility, where human meaning shades off into the unknown reaches of the soul and of the world. Though fluent in several languages he chose German for his poetry, the language in which the inhuman and the demonic was, for his time, given expression and reality. The darkness of the unknown sources of language and human meaning and that of the unbearable demonic are thus brought together in a terrible tension in his writings at every moment. His work represents a stunning example of the awe-ful struggle in which human creativity and the reach of the soul toward light contend with the monstrous evil of which we are capable and that threatens to negate every breath of love and compassion that we take. As Corbin has taught us, there are two darknesses, and to confound them is a disaster of cosmic proportion: there is the darkness of the evil that refuses the Light, and the Luminous Darkness at the approach to the Divine.

Heidegger too struggled with the relation between language and being throughout his life. His work unquestionably stands as a towering monument to human thought. But his legacy is as deeply ambiguous as his writings are difficult and perplexing. It is not merely that he was, however briefly, an enthusiastic supporter of National Socialism. As Steiner argues, it is his almost total silence about the Holocaust *after* 1945 that is damning and nearly impossible to understand. Is it possible to reconcile this silence with the deeply lyrical writings of his late works?

In Steiner's view, Heidegger's metaphysics is throughout an effort to think immanence without transcendence. From early on he categorically refused the theological. His work is an attempt to think Being without recourse to categories of transcendence. Much of his writing is indeed "pagan" and full of references to the earth, to the soil, to tradition, and to the gods, and seems deeply rooted in the immediate realities of a pastoral life. His attempt to return to "the eternal pagan substrate" that is the origin of religion has been much praised by various ecologically minded philosophers for these reasons. His writings are deeply suggestive for anyone involved in trying to rethink the modern Western relation between the human person and the earth. Much of his work is also profoundly antitechnological in character, and this as well has made him attractive to environmentalists of many kinds. His critiques of modern instrumental thought and action are profound and stirring. And yet there is a certain hollowness, a profoundly "abstract" character to his work that is troubling to say the least. There is an impersonal and inhuman tenor to his thought that is at times revelatory and entrancing. Yet from *Being and Time* on there is, as Steiner says, nowhere for an ethics to take hold, except perhaps one based on an impersonal aesthetics of nature. Heidegger's "mystical" tendencies are rooted in a realm beyond the ethical. Steiner writes, "Far beyond Nietzsche, Heidegger thinks, feels in categories *outside* good and evil."[11] And increasingly in the later works, in strong contrast to the early talk of *authenticity* and *resolve,* his categories are beyond *action* and he speaks in a "poetic" language only of letting-be.

Paul Celan's struggles with language, thought, and being are in many ways parallel to Heidegger's. But the great Jewish poet's existence is defined by the Holocaust. Steiner writes,

> Together with Primo Levi (and both men chose suicide at the height of their strengths), Paul Celan is the *only* survivor of the Holocaust whose writings are, in some true degree, commensurate with the unspeakable. Only in Levi and Celan does language, in the exact face of subhuman yet all too human enormity and finality, retain its reticent totality.[12]

Celan was deeply immersed in and constantly preoccupied by Heidegger's writings, and his readings of Hölderlin, George, and Trakl. The intensity of the relation between the two is not "merely" a mark of intellectual interest, but of deep spiritual affinity: "What is absolutely clear is the degree to which Paul Celan's radically innovative vocabulary and, at certain points, syntax are Heideggerrian."[13]

This relation was not one-way. Heidegger knew Celan's work well and "in a rare public act, attended Celan's readings. Even on the basis of incomplete documentation, the intensity and depth of the inward relationship is palpable. . . ." And yet, there is a chasm separating these two men that is of vast historical, spiritual, and ethical implications; a chasm that is unbridgeable. Steiner narrates a drama of epochal significance:

> The two men were present to each other with rare force. The crystallization of that reciprocal presentness was Celan's visit to Heidegger's famous hut at Todtnauberg a few years before Celan's suicide. . . . Of the encounter we know only what Celan's enigmatic recall tells us, or, rather, elects not to tell us. That there came to pass a numbing, soul-lacerating deception . . . is unmistakable. . . . Celan came to question . . . Heidegger's perception or non-perception of the *Shoah,* of the "death-winds" that had made ash of millions of human beings and of the Jewish legacy which informed Celan's destiny. . . . Celan was taking the risk of an ultimate trust in the possibility of an encounter, of the renascence of the word out of a shared night. . . . So far as we know . . . that trust was violated either by trivial evasion . . . or by utter silence. . . . Either way, the effect on Celan can be felt to have been calamitous. But the issue far transcends the personal. Throughout his writings and teachings, Martin Heidegger had proclaimed the deed of questioning to be of the essence; he had defined the question as the piety of the human spirit. Whatever happened at Todtnauberg, when the foremost poet in the language after Hölderlin and Rilke sought out the "secret king of thought," blasphemed against Heidegger's own sense of the holiness of asking. *It may, for our epoch at least, have made irreparable the breach between human need and speculative thought, between the music of thought that is philosophy and that of being which is poetry.* Much in Western consciousness has its instauration in the banishment of the poets from the Platonic city. In somber counterpoint, Heidegger's denial of reply to Celan . . . amounts to a banishment, to a self-ostracism of the philosopher from the city of man.[14]

And so we arrive at the final, horrible outcome of that rupture in Western culture between thought and being which was the constant and central theme of Henry Corbin's life of theological meditation. When the cosmology of angelic mediation between the individual and the divine is shattered, and the mediating function of the *anima mundi* and Imagination destroyed, then the breach is opened separating thought and being, God and humanity, knowledge and ethics, imagination and knowledge, human language and the Word, spirit and matter.

What is lacking in the thought beyond metaphysics that Heidegger provides is that Breath of Compassion which breathes life and sympathy into the world. And this Breath is the substance of the soul of a Person. In the Abrahamic Tradition it is the trace of that Person in all things that gives them their being. Heidegger tried to erect a philosophy denying the need for the category of the Person and the transcendence implicit in that Being, and it is this that is ultimately responsible for his failure, for the emptiness and inhumanity of his work. Paul Celan experienced in an almost unimaginable degree the loss of this Person, and his work resounds in the emptiness of that Absence. But it is only because of the anguish at the loss and the exile that results from the withdrawal of God that his search for language, so close to Heidegger's on the surface, is a deeply human cry for meaning betrayed.

If the prophetic tradition is not to conclude with finality in this moment of immeasurably tragic drama, then a means must be found of learning to speak again, of learning to think again, to feel again, of bringing these shattered fragments of a life into some wounded yet living whole. Perhaps it is more than we can hope that we will be able to succeed. And yet there is no question that the attempt must be made. We must try, in the face of all that is darkest in this night of the world, to learn what the Sufis call "the thought of the heart." And we must do this by struggling to learn again the languages of the world.

NOTES

CHAPTER ONE
"WE ARE NOW IN HEAVEN"

Epigraph, CW9i, §65.

1. Dr. Ferdinand Edward Cranz (1914–1998) was Rosemary Park Professor of History at Connecticut College. See Cranz, "1100 AD: A Crisis for Us?," also "The Reorientation of Western Thought circa 1100 A.D.—Four Talks," unpublished manuscript.

2. *de Anima* III, 8 432b20. Cranz's unpublished translation.

3. See for example Shepard, *Nature and Madness* and *The Others: How Animals Made Us Human;* Baring and Cashford, *The Myth of the Goddess;* Oelschlager, *The Idea of Wilderness: From Prehistory to the Age of Ecology;* on the general issue of disjunction, Berman, *The Re-enchantment of the World* and *Coming to Our Senses: Body and Spirit in the Hidden History of the West.*

4. See Illich and Sanders, *ABC: The Alphabetization of the Popular Mind;* Illich, *In the Vineyard of the Text: A Commentary to Hugh's Didascalicon;* Abram, *The Spell of the Sensuous: Perception and Language in a More-Than-Human World.*

5. See Merchant, *The Death of Nature: Women, Ecology, and the Scientific Revolution;* also Berman, *Re-enchantment* and *Coming to Our Senses,* and Oelschlager, *The Idea of Wilderness.*

6. See especially Corbin, *Creative Imagination in the Sufism of Ibn Arabi.* For an introduction to his work see Shayegan, *Henry Corbin: La topographie spirituelle de l'Islam Iranien,* and Cheetham, *The World Turned Inside Out: Henry Corbin and Islamic Mysticism.* On Illich, see "Consuming Passions" below.

7. For these categories and much else, I am indebted to Toulmin, *Cosmopolis: The Hidden Agenda of Modernity.*

8. This view of theory in biology is influenced by familiarity with work at the Santa Fe Institute; see for example, Kauffman, *At Home in the Universe: The Search for the Laws of Self-Organization and Complexity.* On the relations between recent trends in science and the those in the humanities, the writings of N. Catherine Hayles are important, and I think, support my claims. See Hayles, *The Cosmic Web: Scientific Field Models*

and Literary Strategies in the Twentieth Century; Chaos Bound: Orderly Disorder in Contemporary Literature and Science; Chaos and Order: Complex Dynamics in Literature and Science; and *How We Became Posthuman: Virtual Bodies in Cybernetics, Literature, and Informatics.*

9. Minsky, "Will Robots Inherit the Earth?"

10. CW6, §78. This claim of Jung's provides one of the basic tenets of archetypal psychology. See Hillman, *Re-visioning Psychology, Anima: An Anatomy of a Personified Notion, The Thought of the Heart and the Soul of the World.*

11. *Timaeus,* 51–52, quoted in Illich, *H₂O and the Waters of Forgetfulness: Reflections on the Historicity of Stuff,* 17.

12. P. Berry, "What's the Matter with Mother?"

13. Illich, *H₂O and the Waters of Forgetfulness,* 22.

14. Ibid.

15. *Physica* IV, 209b.

16. Quoted by Thomas Moore in Hillman, *A Blue Fire: Selected Writings by James Hillman,* v.

17. See Heidegger, *The Question Concerning Technology.* Avens, *The New Gnosis* provides a fine analysis of Heidegger's relationship to mythic, or archetypal experience.

18. Robert Duncan, "The Truth and Life of Myth," 20.

19. Hillman, *Kinds of Power: A Guide to Its Intelligent Uses,* 210–11. His source is Scholem, *Major Trends in Jewish Mysticism.*

20. Duncan "The Truth and Life of Myth," 1–2.

21. Corbin, *Creative Imagination,* 206.

22. Ibid., 354–55, n. 41.

23. Jung, *Memories, Dreams, Reflections,* 247–48.

CHAPTER TWO
CONSUMING PASSIONS

Epigraph, Fisher, *The Art of Eating,* 353.

1. Qur'an 2: 74.

2. Bachelard, *The Poetics of Space,* 222.

3. See Hillman, "In," 15–20 and references therein to Farnell, *Cults of the Greek States;* Paris, *Pagan Meditations;* Pignatelli, "The Dialectics of Urban Architecture: Hestia and Hermes"; and others. On Hermes and Hestia, see also Hillman, *Kinds of Power: A Guide to Its Intelligent Uses,* 233–38.

4. Hillman, "In," 15.

5. Ibid., 17–18.

6. Ibid.

7. Ibid., 20.

8. Ibid., 18.

9. Ibid.

10. Alexander et al., *A Pattern Language: Towns, Buildings, Construction*, 697.

11. Merton, *The Living Bread*, 126–27, quoted in Alexander et al., *A Pattern Language*, 698.

12. Oxford English Dictionary, *s.v.* converse.

13. Shepard, *The Others: How Animals Made Us Human*, 30.

14. Ibid., 327.

15. Ibid., 29.

16. Ibid., 30.

17. Ibid., 29.

18. Hillman, *The Dream and the Underworld*, 172.

19. Ibid., 53.

20. Alexander, *A Timeless Way of Building*, 397–98.

21. W. Berry, "The Pleasures of Eating," 152.

22. Hillman, *The Thought of the Heart and the Soul of the World*, 101.

23. Corbin, *Spiritual Body and Celestial Earth: From Mazdean Iran to Shi'ite Iran*, 81.

24. Corbin, "The Science of the Balance and the Correspondences between Worlds in Islamic Gnosis," 68.

25. Corbin, *Creative Imagination in the Sufism of Ibn 'Arabi*, 114.

26. Ibid., 115–16.

27. Ibid., 125.

28. Ibid., 129.

29. Ibid., 130.

30. Ibid., 131.

31. Genesis 13: 1–15. The same event occurs in the Qur'an, 11: 72.

32. Corbin comments on the fifteenth-century icon of this event by Andrei Rublev in Corbin, *Creative Imagination*, 130–31 and 315–16, n. 75. See below, "Within This Darkness." See Evdokimov, *The Art of the Icon: A Theology of Beauty*, ch. 24, for an Orthodox reading of the icon. For Eastern Orthodoxy, the three "Angels" represent the three Persons of the Holy Trinity and the Communal Feast represents the inner movement of self-giving love that occurs within the depths of the Triune God.

33. Hillman, *Re-visioning Psychology*, 9–10.

34. Nasr, "Oral Transmission and the Book in Islamic Education: The Spoken and the Written Word," 57.

35. Corbin, "The Force of Traditional Philosophy in Iran Today," 13.

36. Ibid., 16.

37. Rothenberg and Joris, *Poems for the Millennium, Volume 2: From Postwar to Millennium,* 449, 72, 798; Rothenberg and Joris, *Poems for the Millennium, Volume 1: From Fin-de-Siecle to Negritude,* 378.

38. Illich, *In the Vineyard of the Text: A Commentary to Hugh's Didascalicon.*

39. Ibid., 14.

40. Ibid., 17.

41. Ibid., 18, n. 32.

42. Ibid., 17–18.

43. Ibid., 11.

44. Ibid., 54.

45. Ibid.

46. Ibid., 56–57.

47. Ibid., 57, and n. 25.

48. Ibid.

49. Abram, *The Spell of the Sensuous: Perception and Language in a More-Than-Human World,* 241.

50. Ibid., 242–43.

51. Rodman and Cleaver, *Spirits of the Night: The Vaudun Gods of Haiti,* 3.

52. Diggs, "Alchemy of the Blues," 34.

53. Quoted in Ibid., 35.

54. Quoted in Ibid., 33.

55. William Seabrook, quoted in Rodman and Cleaver, *Spirits of the Night,* 9.

56. Steiner, *Real Presences,* 226.

57. Ibid., 198.

58. Quoted in Senghor, "Speech and Image: An African Tradition of the Surreal," 565.

59. Ibid.

60. Quoted in Snyder, *The Real Work: Interviews and Talks 1964–1979,* 79.

61. CW 8, §389–90.

62. CW 8, §390.

63. CW 8, §392.

64. Corbin, *Alchimie comme art hieratique,* 12.

CHAPTER THREE
BLACK LIGHT

Epigraph, CW 12, §439.

1. Hillman, "The Seduction of Black," 8.

2. Ibid., 7.

3. Ibid., 5.

4. Neumann, *The Origins and History of Consciousness,* 157–58. My emphasis. The quote from Jung can be found in CW9i, §183.

5. See Berman, *Coming to Our Senses: Body and Spirit in the Hidden History of the West,* ch. 1.

6. Hillman, *Anima: An Anatomy of a Personified Notion,* ch. 6.

7. Ibid., 81.

8. Ibid., 109.

9. Ibid., 113.

10. See for instance, Griffin, *Woman and Nature: The Roaring Inside Her, The Eros of Everyday Life;* Merchant, *The Death of Nature: Women, Ecology, and the Scientific Revolution;* Oelschlager, *The Idea of Wilderness: From Prehistory to the Age of Ecology.*

11. Quoted in Whitmont, *The Symbolic Quest: Basic Concepts of Analytical Psychology,* 79.

12. Corbin, *Creative Imagination in the Sufism of Ibn 'Arabi,* 142.

13. CW14, §34, n. 228.

14. Freud, "Civilization and Its Discontents," 738.

15. McLuhan, *Understanding Media: The Extensions of Man,* ch. 4.

16. CW14, §106.

17. Ibid.

18. CW12, §413.

19. CW14, §101.

20. CW12, §425.

21. CW12, §332.

22. CW12, §394.

23. CW14, §35.

24. CW14, §503.

25. CW14, §125.

26. CW14, §35.

27. Jung, *Jung Speaking: Interviews and Encounters,* 227–29.

28. CW14, §261.

29. CW14, §251–52.

30. CW13, §448.

31. CW13, §449.

32. CW14, §262.

33. CW14, §404.

34. CW14, §307.

35. CW14, §252.

36. CW14, §381.

37. CW14, §252.

38. CW14, §200.

39. CW14, §180.

40. CW14, §306.

41. CW14, §364.

42. CW14, §318.

43. CW12, §440.

44. CW14, §410.

45. CW14, §106.

46. CW14, §388.

47. Ibid.

48. CW14, §284.

49. CW14, §354.

50. Ibid.

51. CW14, §11.

52. CW12, §404.

53. CW14, §36.

54. CW14, §12.

55. CW14, §5.

56. CW12, §472.

57. CW13, §162.

58. CW14, §50.

59. CW14, §46.

60. CW14, §47.

61. CW13, §162.

62. CW14, §372.

63. CW14, §374.

64. CW12, §432.

65. CW14, §22.

66. CW14, §238.

67. Ibid.

68. CW14, §86.

69. CW12, §342, n. 1.

70. CW12, §332.

71. CW14, §446.

72. CW13, §149.

73. CW14, §150.

74. CW12, §432.

75. CW13, §149.

76. CW14, §344.

77. Ibid.

78. CW13, §149.

79. CW13, §163.

80. CW13, §155.

81. CW13, §154.

82. CW13, §163. My italics.

83. CW13, §164.

84. CW14, §296.

85. Ibid.

86. CW14, §309.

87. CW14, §151.

88. Ibid.

89. CW14, §142. See CW14, §134 ff.

90. CW14, §153.

91. CW14, §152.

92. Ibid.

93. Ibid.

94. Ibid.

95. Jung, *Memories, Dreams, Reflections,* 343–44.

96. Hannah, *Jung: His Life and Work, A Biographical Memoir,* 76.

97. CW13, Section IV.

98. CW13, §300.

99. CW13, §301.

100. Ibid. My italics.

101. CW13, §302.

102. See above, "Matter: An Essay in Mythology."

103. See Corbin, *Creative Imagination,* Introduction; and Cheetham, "Dogmas, Idols, and the Edge of Chaos" and *The World Turned Inside Out: Henry Corbin and Islamic Mysticism.*

104. Murata and Chittick, *The Vision of Islam,* 144.

105. Najm Kubra in Corbin, *The Man of Light in Iranian Sufism,* 77.

106. Ibid., 96

107. Murata, *The Tao of Islam: A Sourcebook of Gender Relationships in Islamic Thought,* 8.

108. Ibid., 9.

109. Ibid., 8–9.

110. Quoted in Ibid., 10.

111. It could be argued that contemporary science is replete with concepts that stress polarity, and this is true to a large extent, at least in the sciences of complex systems. But what these lack from the point of view discussed here is any sense of hierarchies or modes of being.

112. This is the meaning of the parable of Khidr in Sura 18. See Jung, CW9i, §240ff.; Corbin, *Creative Imagination,* 55ff., and Brown, "The Apocalypse of Islam."

113. Corbin, *Man of Light,* 47.

114. Unfortunately these confusions are rampant in other strains of Islam. On this general issue see Murata, *The Tao of Islam,* and Murata and Chittick, *The Vision of Islam.*

115. Quoted in Shayegan, "Le Sens du Ta'wil," 84–85.

116. Murata and Chittick, *The Vision of Islam,* 99.

117. Corbin is perhaps not always careful to distinguish satanic darkness from the material that receives it. Nonetheless, he is quite clear that matter is required for theophany in our world. On the general issue of the relation between the masculine and the feminine in Islamic thought, Murata, *The Tao of Islam* is indispensable.

118. Schuon, *The Essential Writings of Frithjof Schuon,* 359.

119. Corbin, *Man of Light,* 3.

120. Ibid.

121. Ibid., 5.

122. Ibid., 6.

123. Corbin, *Avicenna and the Visionary Recital,* 159.

124. Corbin, *Man of Light,* 6–7.

125. Ibid., 10.

126. Ibid., 11.

127. CW14, §401–402.

128. Corbin, *Man of Light,* 47.

129. Ibid., 91.

130. Ibid., 92.

131. Ibid., 94.

132. Ibid., 95–96.

133. Ibid., 51; also Cheetham, *The World Turned Inside Out.*

134. Chittick, *The Self-Disclosure of God: Principles of Ibn 'Arabi's Cosmology,* 152, 201.

135. Corbin, *Man of Light,* 100.

136. See Ibid., 103–10 and 155, n. 109. And see below, "Within This Darkness."

137. Ibid., 150, n. 64.

138. Ibid., 102.

139. Ibid., 102–103.

140. Ibid., 102.

141. Ibid., 108.

142. Ibid.

143. Ibid., 116.

144. Ibid., 102.

145. CW14, §129.

146. Corbin, *Man of Light,* 108.

147. Ibid., 111. Alaoddawleh Semnani was a major figure in Iranian Sufism, born in Semnan, east of Teheran, in 1261. After undergoing a spiritual crisis at the age of fifteen, he devoted his life to Sufism. He spent most of his life in Semnan and died in 1336. See Corbin, *Man of Light,* chapter VI and Corbin, *En Islam Iranien: Aspects spirituels et philosophiques, Tome III: Les fideles d'amour et Shi'isme et sufisme,* 275–355, and below, "Within This Darkness."

148. Mir Damad (d. 1631) was an Iranian theologian of the School of Isfahan. See Corbin, *En Islam Iranien: Aspects spirituels et philosophiques, Tome IV: L'Ecole d'Ispahan— L'Ecole Shaykhie—Le Douzieme Imam,* 9–53.

149. Corbin, *Man of Light,* 112.

150. Rilke, "Eighth Elegy," *Duino Elegies,* 61.

151. Corbin, *Creative Imagination,* 106.

152. Corbin. *Man of Light,* 115.

153. Ibid., 117.

154. Iranian Shaykh of the Nurbakhshiyah Order of Sufis, died in 1506 and buried at Shiraz.

155. Ibid., 117–18.

156. Ibid., 118.

157. Ibid., 119.

158. Ibid., 120.

159. Ibid., 123–4.

160. Ibid., 125. The Paraclete is understood to be Mohammad, or by the Twelver Shi'ites, the Hidden Imam.

161. Ibid., 126.

162. Ibid., 127.

163. Ibid.

164. That is, that Jesus and God are the "same nature."

165. Early Iranian Sufi, died martyred for this claim in 922. Subject of the massive 4 volume masterwork by Louis Massignon who was Corbin's teacher and predecessor at the Sorbonne. See Massignon, *The Passion of Al-Hallaj: Mystic and Martyr of Islam.*

166. Corbin, *Man of Light,* 127–8.

167. Ibid., 128.

168. Ibid., 136.

169. Ibid., 132.

170. Corbin, *Creative Imagination,* 125. See above "Consuming Passions: The Science of the Balance and the Mystic Supper."

171. Jung, *Memories, Dreams, Reflections,* 352.

172. Ibid., 355.

CHAPTER FOUR
WITHIN THIS DARKNESS

Epigraph, see Corbin, *The Man of Light in Iranian Sufism,* 111 and 156, n. 117. Mahmud Shabestari (d. 1320) was a renowned Azerbaijani Shaykh.

1. Corbin, "Théologie au bord du lac," 62–63.

2. Corbin, "Post-Scriptum biographique à un Entretien philosophique," 41. On Suhrawardi see Corbin, *Creative Imagination in the Sufism of Ibn 'Arabi, Spiritual Body and Celestial Earth: From Mazdean Iran to Shi'ite Iran,* and especially Corbin, *En Islam Iranien: Aspects spirituels et philosophiques, Tome II: Sohrawardi et les platoniciens de perse;* also Cheetham, *The World Turned Inside Out.*

3. Corbin, *Man of Light,* 7.

4. See Waley, "Najm al-Din Kubra and the Central Asian School of Sufism (The Kubrawiyyah)."

5. See Corbin, *Man of Light,* ch. IV. Born in Khiva in what is now Uzbekistan in 1146, he traveled widely before returning to Khiva, where he was killed defending the town against the Mongols in 1220.

6. One of Kubra's twelve chief disciples, he fled west at his master's insistence, eventually to Asia Minor where he had contacts with Rumi and his followers. He died in Baghdad in 1256.

7. See above "Black Light," n. 147.

8. Corbin, *Spiritual Body*, 81.

9. Corbin, *Man of Light*, 60.

10. Najm Kubra quoted in Waley, "Najm al-Din Kubra and the Central Asian School of Sufism (The Kubrawiyyah)," 84.

11. See Ibid., 83.

12. Ibid., 73.

13. See Nasr, "Oral Transmission and the Book in Islamic Education: The Spoken and the Written Word," also Sells, *Approaching the Qu'ran: The Early Revelations.*

14. Corbin, *Spiritual Body*, x.

15. Corbin, *Man of Light*, 75.

16. Corbin, *Spiritual Body*, xi.

17. See Corbin, *Man of Light,* 124–25.

18. Ibid., 125.

19. Corbin, *Creative Imagination,* 55.

20. Although there are some significant differences in the various doctrines of the masters these are outweighed by the similarities. Najm Razi notably places the Black Light at the summit of the path.

21. See above, "We Are Now in Heaven," and "Black Light: A Cosmology for the Soul."

22. See Corbin, *Spiritual Body,* 10, 13.

23. Williams, "Zoroastrianism and the Body," 156.

24. Corbin, *Man of Light,* 65–66.

25. Corbin, *Creative Imagination,* 143.

26. Ibid., 282.

27. Corbin, *Man of Light,* 103.

28. Ibid., 150, n. 64.

29. Corbin, "De la théologie apophatique comme antidote du nihilisme," 234.

30. Corbin, *Man of Light,* 112.

31. Ibid., 112–13.

32. Corbin, *Spiritual Body,* xiv.

33. Corbin, *Man of Light,* 127. On *ta'wil* see Cheetham, *The World Turned Inside Out.*

34. Corbin, *Man of Light,* 120.

35. Ibid., 127.

36. Ibid., 128.

37. Corbin, "De la théologie apophatique comme antidote du nihilisme," 243–44.

38. Mark 15:33–34 (RSV).

39. Matthew 27:51 (RSV).

40. Qur'an 4: 156.

41. Corbin, *Creative Imagination*, 292, n. 10.

42. Corbin, *Avicenna and the Visionary Recital*, 92.

43. Corbin, "Harmonia Abrahamica."

44. Ibid., 11.

45. Ibid., 15.

46. Corbin, *Spiritual Body*, 106.

47. Corbin, *Creative Imagination*, 107.

48. Ibid., 134.

49. Ibid., 292.

50. Corbin, "Le paradoxe du monothéisme," 73.

51. Sells, *Mystical Languages of Unsaying*, 226, n. 5.

52. Corbin, "Post-Scriptum biographique à un Entretien philosophique," 39.

53. Sells, *Mystical Languages*, 31.

54. Corbin, *Creative Imagination*, 327, n. 16.

55. Quoted in Sells, *Mystical Languages*, 44.

56. Ibid., 47.

57. See Pelikan, *The Christian Tradition: A History of the Development of Doctrine. Vol. 1. The Emergence of the Catholic Tradition (100–600)*, ch. 4.

58. Corbin. *Man of Light*, 133.

59. Corbin, "De la théologie apophatique," 250. Also Corbin, "Harmonia Abrahamica," 13–14.

60. Corbin, "De la théologie apophatique," 250.

61. Corbin, *Spiritual Body*, 14.

62. CW6, §62.

63. *de Anima* III 8 432b20. Trans. F. E. Cranz. See above, "We Are Now in Heaven."

64. *Ennead* VI, 5, 7. Trans. F. E. Cranz.

65. See Sells, *Mystical Languages*, ch. 1, esp. 17–32.

66. Partridge, *Origins: A Short Dictionary of English Etymology, s.v.* theater.

67. Deck, *Nature, Contemplation, and the One: A Study in the Philosophy of Plotinus*, 126.

68. Corbin, "Emblematic Cities: A Response to the Images of Henri Stierlin," 12. See Liddell and Scott, *A Greek-English Lexicon, s.v. peplum.*

69. Corbin, "Emblematic Cities," 12.

70. Ibid.

71. CW 12, §403 and n. 3.

72. CW 15, §37–38 and n. 46.

73. CW 16, §486.

74. Corbin repeatedly cites Jung on the issue of the subtle body. See Corbin, *Spiritual Body,* 11 and 274, n. 24, also 98 and 300, n. 69; Jung CW 12, §393 ff. and CW 15, §173 ff.; On the *physika* and the *mystika* see, e.g., CW 12, §332.

75. Corbin, *Man of Light,* 135.

76. CW 12, ch. 5.

77. Corbin, *Man of Light,* 137–38.

78. Corbin, "Harmonia Abrahamica," 14.

79. Philippians 2: 5–11. (RSV).

80. Corbin, *Man of Light,* 127 and 159, n. 133a.

81. For what follows see Coakley, "Kenosis and Subversion: On the Repression of 'Vulnerability' in Christian Feminist Writing."

82. Ibid., 85.

83. Ibid., 87.

84. For reasons of simplicity and organization, I do not follow Coakley's numbered list of meanings of *kenosis.* I combine her numbers one and two and omit her number four until later.

85. Ibid., 90.

86. Ibid. The interesting question from Corbin's point of view would be precisely why the docetic interpretation lost out to the Incarnationist.

87. Ibid., 91.

88. Ibid.

89. CW 12, §29.

90. Coakley, "Kenosis and Subversion," 92.

91. Ibid.

92. Ibid., 93.

93. Ibid., 94.

94. Quoted in Loofs, "Kenosis," 687. This is a translation of the original German article that Corbin refers to in his footnote.

95. McGrath, *Christian Theology: An Introduction,* 355.

96. Coakley, "Kenosis and Subversion," 88.

97. Ibid., 89.

98. Ibid., 99.

99. See Murata and Chittick, *The Vision of Islam.*

100. McGrath, *Christian Theology: An Introduction,* 331–32.

101. See Hampson, *Swallowing a Fishbone?: Feminist Theologians Debate Christianity;* Loades, *Feminist Theology: A Reader;* Russell, *Feminist Interpretation of the Bible.*

102. Quoted in Papanikolaou, "Person, Kenosis, and Abuse: Hans Urs von Balthasar and feminist theologies in conversation," 42.

103. Hampson, "Luther on the Self: A Feminist Critique," 218–19.

104. Coakley, "Kenosis and Subversion," 84.

105. Ibid., 108.

106. Ibid. It is not surprising that this "driving of wedges" should occur in the twelfth century, since this marks the point in the history of reading where an embodied textuality open to the Word of God began to be replaced with a more modern experience of "text" and reading. See Illich, *In the Vineyard of the Text: A Commentary to Hugh's Didascalicon;* Cheetham, *The World Turned Inside Out,* and above, "We Are Now in Heaven" and "Consuming Passions."

107. Coakley, "Kenosis and Subversion," 109.

108. Ibid., 110, and 2 Corinthians 12: 9.

109. Papanikolaou, "Person, Kenosis, and Abuse."

110. Quoted in Ibid., 52.

111. Ibid., 47.

112. Ibid., 48.

113. Ibid., 49.

114. Corbin, *Creative Imagination,* 129.

115. Genesis 18: 1–8; Qur'an 11: 72.

116. An illustration of this work can be found in Stokstad (2002), 340.

117. Corbin, *Creative Imagination,* 315, n. 74.

118. Ibid., 315–16, n. 75. For an Eastern Orthodox view also see Evdokimov, *The Art of the Icon: A Theology of Beauty,* ch. 24. Corbin's own note on this refers to the 1929 Russian original of Sergei Bulgakovs' *Jacob's Ladder.* A short excerpt of this work can be found in English in Bulgakov, *A Bulgakov Anthology,* and it has since been translated in its entirely into French. See Bulgakov, *L'Échelle de Jacob: des anges.* It is of deep significance for Corbin's theology that in the Islamic tradition the Holy Spirit is often understood to be feminine. For an explicit reference to Alaoddawleh Semnani and the doctrine of the Trinity, see Corbin, *En Islam Iranien: Aspects spirituels et philosophiques, Tome III: Les fideles d'amour et Shi'isme et sufisme,* 285, n. 102.

119. Corbin, *Creative Imagination,* 131.

120. Nichols, *No Bloodless Myth: A Guide Through Balthasar's Dramatics,* 3.

121. Nichols, *The Word Has Been Abroad: A Guide Through Balthasar's Aesthetics,* 16.

122. Quoted in Greeley, *The Catholic Imagination,* 5.

123. Ibid., 1. On Luther's influence on Corbin, see Cheetham, *The World Turned Inside Out.*

124. Nichols, *The Word Has Been Abroad,* 2.

125. Quoted in Ibid., 3.

126. Ibid., 43. Notice that this does not mean that Balthasar is an advocate of the sufficiency of the "historical Christ."

127. My reading of Vattimo is based on the analysis presented by Frascati-Lochhead, *Kenosis and Feminist Theology: The Challenge of Gianni Vattimo.*

128. *Thus Spoke Zarathustra,* 124, in Nietzsche, *The Portable Nietzsche.*

129. Cohn, *Cosmos, Chaos, and the World to Come: The Ancient Roots of Apocalyptic Faith.*

130. *The Gay Science,* 447, in Nietzsche, *The Portable Nietzsche.*

131. Ibid., 448.

132. See Heidegger, *The Question Concerning Technology.* Vattimo has his own novel interpretation of Heidegger, and of Heidegger's understanding of Nietzsche, as well as of the way both of them understand modern science and technology. See Frascati-Lochhead, *Kenosis and Feminist Theology.*

133. Frascati-Lochhead, *Kenosis and Feminist Theology,* 154.

134. See Hayles, *How We Became Posthuman: Virtual Bodies in Cybernetics, Literature, and Informatics,* xxxx, for a discussion of this contrast.

135. Frascati-Lochhead, *Kenosis and Feminist Theology,* 140–47.

136. Vattimo, *Beyond Interpretation: The Meaning of Hermeneutics for Philosophy,* 48. Quoted in a different translation in Frascati-Lochhead, *Kenosis and Feminist Theology,* 156.

137. Ibid., 48. Quoted in a different translation in Frascati-Lochhead, *Kenosis and Feminist Theology,* 156.

138. Ibid., 49.

139. Ibid., 49–50. Translation slightly altered in accordance with that given by Frascati-Lochhead, *Kenosis and Feminist Theology,* 157.

140. Corbin, *En Islam Iranien: Aspects spirituels et philosophiques, Tome IV: L'Ecole d'Ispahan—L'Ecole Shaykhie—Le Douzieme Imam.,* 443–44.

141. Quoted in Frascati-Lochhead, *Kenosis and Feminist Theology,* 158.

142. Ibid.

143. He is following Heidegger's use of some similar key terms.

144. Quoted in Frascati-Lochhead, *Kenosis and Feminist Theology,* 193.

145. Corbin, "Post-Scriptum biographique à un Entretien philosophique," 36.

146. My analysis relies on Giegerich's writings in English, and especially on Avens's paraphrase of Giegerich, "Das Begräbnis der Seele in die technische Zivilisation." See Giegerich, "The Nuclear Bomb and the Fate of God: On the *First* Nuclear Fission," "Saving the Nuclear Bomb," "The Invention of Explosive Power and the Blueprint of the Bomb—A Chapter in the Imaginal Pre-History of Our Nuclear Predicament," and Avens, "Reflections on Wolfgang Giegerich's 'The Burial of the Soul in Technological Civilization.'"

147. Giegerich mentions China in particular, but the Islamic world also had the requisite wealth and knowledge.

148. Giegerich, "The Invention of Explosive Power," 1.

149. Giegerich, "The Nuclear Bomb and the Fate of God," 2.

150. Ibid., 4.

151. Exodus 32: 27.

152. Giegerich thus stands within that part of the phenomenological tradition that sees common ground between Jung and Heideggerian phenomenology. See Roger Brooke, *Jung and Phenomenology.* Brooke comments that "what analytical psychology calls images, phenomenology, following Heidegger, calls things." Brooke, *Jung and Phenomenology,* 149.

153. Avens, "Reflections," 37.

154. Ibid., 38.

155. Giegerich, "The Nuclear Bomb and the Fate of God," 8.

156. Ibid., 6.

157. Ibid., 9.

158. Ibid., 9–10.

159. Ibid., 11.

160. Vattimo, and Frascati-Lochhead following his lead, provide critiques of the idea of technology as Will to Power in Nietzsche and Heidegger and in modern feminist epistemologies. See esp. Frascati-Lochhead, *Kenosis and Feminist Theology,* ch. 5. This is pertinent here since there is much in Giegerich's account that is evidently influenced by Heidegger's view of technology.

161. Avens, "Reflections," 39.

162. Coakley, "Kenosis and Subversion," 92–93.

163. Avens, "Reflections," 39.

164. Ibid., 40.

165. Ibid., 47.

166. Ibid.

167. Giegerich, "The Nuclear Bomb and the Fate of God," 23.

168. Corbin, "De la théologie apophatique," 229.

169. Quoted in Avens, "Reflections," 50.

170. Quoted in Frascati-Lochead, *Kenosis and Feminist Theology*, 142–43. N. Catherine Hayles has thought very deeply about these issues and treats Harraway's views at some length; see Hayles, *How We Became Posthuman: Virtual Bodies in Cybernetics, Literature, and Informatics.*

171. A "postmodern" view of scientific culture stressing the inherent pluralism of scientific thought is found in the works of Jacob Bronowski, Paul Feyerabend, Clifford Geertz, Stuart Kauffman, and Stephen Toulmin, for example.

172. Giegerich's style is reminiscent of Heidegger's later ontology. For a critique of the essentialism of the later Heidegger's view of technology see Caputo, *More Radical Hermeneutics: On Not Knowing Who We Are.*

173. Oelschlager, *The Idea of Wilderness: From Prehistory to the Age of Ecology*, ch. 1.

174. Diamond, *In Search of the Primitive: A Critique of Civilization*, 129.

175. Avens, "Reflections," 52–53.

176. Qur'an 2: 115. Ali's translation has "glory" but notes that the literal rendering of the word is "Face."

177. Lings, *What Is Sufism?*, 23.

178. *Finnegan's Wake*, cited in Brown, "The Apocalypse of Islam."

179. See Toulmin, *Cosmopolis: The Hidden Agenda of Modernity.*

180. Brown, "The Apocalypse of Islam."

181. Corbin, *Creative Imagination*, 56.

182. Jambet, *La logique des Orientaux: Henry Corbin et la science des formes*, 312.

183. Corbin took just this position from the very first. In 1931 he and a small group of friends founded a short-lived review *Hic et Nunc.*

184. Snyder, "Poetry and the Primitive: Notes on Poetry as an Ecological Survival Technique," 91.

185. Chittick, *The Self-Disclosure of God: Principles of Ibn 'Arabi's Cosmology*, xxxii–xxxiii.

186. See above, "Consuming Passions."

187. Sells, *Early Islamic Mysticism*, 11.

188. See Chittick, *Faith and Practice of Islam: Three 13th Century Sufi Texts.*

189. Chittick, *Self Disclosure of God*, xxxvi.

190. Ibid., xxxv.

191. Ibid., xxxvi.

192. Ibid.

193. Ibid., xxxvii.

194. Corbin, *Creative Imagination,* 354–55, n. 41.

195. Loy, in Suzuki, *Swedenborg: Buddha of the North,* 98.

196. See Senghor, "Speech and Image: An African Tradition of the Surreal," 565.

197. See for instance Hillman, ". . . And Huge is Ugly," and *The Thought of the Heart and the Soul of the World,* and Hillman and Ventura, *We've Had a Hundred Years of Psychotherapy and the World's Getting Worse.*

198. This is the conclusion reached by David Abram, *The Spell of the Sensuous: Perception and Language in a More-Than-Human World.* I am much indebted to his work.

199. Illich, *In the Vineyard of the Text: A Commentary to Hugh's Didascalicon,* 11. See above, "Consuming Passions."

200. Illich, *Vineyard of the Text,* 3 and Steiner, "The End of Bookishness?"

201. This is of course not an antihumanism of the sort that George Steiner finds in Heidegger, since it based on a perception of transcendence of the sort that Heidegger cannot admit. See Steiner, *Martin Heidegger. With a New Introduction.*

202. It is as unfair to scientists to lump them all together as apologists for the dominion of technology, as it is to making sweeping generalizations about "the humanists," but there is no space for finer distinction here.

203. Groddeck's essay is discussed by Bly, *News of the Universe: Poems of Twofold Consciousness,* 280–85.

204. Ibid., 285.

205. Steiner, *Real Presences,* 69.

206. Ibid., 143.

207. Ibid., 198.

208. Ibid., 226.

209. Corbin, *Man of Light,* 1.

210. The work of Paul Celan, which reveals the struggle to speak again, after the Holocaust, is one place to look for the lineaments of such landscapes. See "Harmonia Abrahamica" below, Steiner, *Martin Heidegger,* and the introductions by Pierre Joris in Celan, *Breathturn, Threadsuns,* and Lyon, "Paul Celan's Language of Stone: The Geology of the Poetic Landscape."

211. Corbin, *Creative Imagination,* 292.

212. Cayley, *Ivan Illich: In Conversation,* 49–51.

213. Bly, *News of the Universe,* 286.

CHAPTER FIVE
HARMONIA ABRAHAMICA

Epigraph, Bachelard, *Water and Dreams: An Essay on the Imagination of Matter,* 195. This translation is that of Colette Gaudin in the Preface to Bachelard, *On Poetic Imagination and Reverie,* lvix.

1. Corbin, "L'Initiation Ismaèlienne ou l'Esoterisme et le Verbe," 81.

2. Corbin, "Harmonia Abrahamica."

3. Hamann, "Aesthetica in nuce," 141–42.

4. Hamann, *Hamann's Schriften,* I (509), ed. Friedrich Roth, Leipzig, 1821–1825, quoted in Corbin, *Hamann, philosophe du lutheranisme,* 47. My translation from Corbin's French. Corbin's essay on Hamann was written in 1937, thirty-three years before he wrote *Harmonia Abrahamica.* Corbin says that Hamann had a deep understanding of the Semitic languages, as of course he did himself.

5. Corbin, *Spiritual Body and Celestial Earth: From Mazdean Iran to Shi'ite Iran,* xvii.

6. Brown, "The Prophetic Tradition," and "The Apocalypse of Islam."

7. Brown (1991b), 93.

8. Seyyed Hossein Nasr quoted in Brown, "Apocalypse," 90.

9. Brown, "Apocalypse," 92.

10. Ibid.

11. Steiner, *Martin Heidegger,* xxxiv.

12. Ibid., xxxi–xxxii.

13. Ibid., xxxi.

14. Ibid., xxxi–xxxiii. My italics.

WORKS CITED

Abram, David. *The Spell of the Sensuous: Perception and Language in a More-Than-Human World*. New York: Pantheon, 1996.

Alexander, Christopher. *A Timeless Way of Building*. New York: Oxford University Press, 1979.

———, Sara Ishikawa, Murray Silverstein, Max Jacobson, Ingrid Fiksdahl-King, and Schlomo Angel. *A Pattern Language: Towns, Buildings, Construction*. New York: Oxford University Press, 1977.

Ali, Ahmed. *Al-Qur'an: A Contemporary Translation*. Princeton: Princeton University Press, 1984.

Avens, Roberts. *The New Gnosis*. Dallas: Spring Publications, 1984.

———. "Reflections on Wolfgang Giegerich's 'The Burial of the Soul in Technological Civilization.'" *Sulfur: A Literary Tri-Quarterly of the Whole Art* 20 (Fall 1987): 34–54.

Bachelard, Gaston. 1964. *The Poetics of Space*. Boston: Beacon Press.

———. *Water and Dreams: An Essay on the Imagination of Matter*. Translated by Edith Farrell. Dallas: The Dallas Institute of Humanities and Culture, 1983.

———. *On Poetic Imagination and Reverie*. Translated with a Preface and Introduction by Colette Gaudin. Dallas: Spring Publications, 1987.

Baring, Anne, and Jules Cashford. *The Myth of the Goddess: Evolution of an Image*. London: Penguin, 1991.

Berman, Morris. *The Re-enchantment of the World*. New York: Bantam Doubleday, 1984.

———. *Coming to Our Senses: Body and Spirit in the Hidden History of the West*. New York: Bantam Books, 1989.

Berry, Patricia. "What's the Matter with Mother?" In *Echo's Subtle Body: Contributions to an Archetypal Psychology*, 1–16. Dallas: Spring Publications, 1982.

Berry, Wendell. "The Pleasures of Eating." In *What are People For? Essays by Wendell Berry*, 145–52. San Francisco: North Point Press, 1990.

Bly, Robert, ed. *News of the Universe: Poems of Twofold Consciousness*. Chosen and Introduced by Robert Bly. San Francisco: Sierra Club Books, 1980.

Brooke, Roger. *Jung and Phenomenology.* London: Routledge, 1991.

Brown, Norman O. "The Prophetic Tradition." In *Apocalypse &/or Metamorphosis,* 46–68. Berkeley: University of California Press, 1991.

———. "The Apocalypse of Islam." In *Apocalypse &/or Metamorphosis,* 69–94. Berkeley: University of California Press, 1991.

Bulgakov, Sergius. *A Bulgakov Anthology.* Edited by Nicolas Zernov and James Pain. Philadelphia: Westminster Press, 1976.

———. *L'Échelle de Jacob: des anges.* Translated by Constantin Andronikof. Lausanne: Editions L'Age d'homme, 1987.

Caputo, John. *More Radical Hermeneutics: On Not Knowing Who We Are.* Bloomington: Indiana University Press, 2000.

Cayley, David. *Ivan Illich: In Conversation.* Concord, Ontario: Anansi, 1992.

Celan, Paul. *Breathturn.* Translated and Introduced by Pierre Joris. Los Angeles: Sun and Moon Press, 1995.

———. *Threadsuns.* Translated and Introduced by Pierre Joris. Los Angeles: Sun and Moon Press, 2000.

Cheetham, Tom. "Dogmas, Idols, and the Edge of Chaos." *Human Ecology Review* 7(1) (2000): 68–71.

———. *The World Turned Inside Out: Henry Corbin and Islamic Mysticism.* Woodstock, CT: Spring Journal Books, 2003.

Chittick, William. *Faith and Practice of Islam: Three 13th Century Sufi Texts.* Translated, introduced, and annotated by William Chittick. Albany: State University of New York Press, 1992.

———. *The Self-Disclosure of God: Principles of Ibn 'Arabi's Cosmology.* Albany: State University of New York Press, 1998.

Coakley, Sarah. "Kenosis and Subversion: On the Repression of 'Vulnerability' in Christian Feminist Writing." In *Swallowing a Fishbone? : Feminist Theologians Debate Christianity,* ed. Daphne Hampson, 82–111. London: SPCK, 1996.

Cohn, Norman. *Cosmos, Chaos, and the World to Come: The Ancient Roots of Apocalyptic Faith.* New Haven: Yale University Press, 1993.

Corbin, Henry. *Avicenna and the Visionary Recital.* Translated by Willard Trask. Bollingen Series LXVI. Princeton: Princeton University Press, 1960.

———. "The Force of Traditional Philosophy in Iran Today." *Studies in Comparative Religion* (Winter 1968): 12–26.

———. *Creative Imagination in the Sufism of Ibn Arabi.* Translated by Ralph Manheim. Bollingen Series XCI. Princeton: Princeton University Press, 1969.

———. *En Islam Iranien: Aspects spirituels et philosophiques, Tome II: Sohrawardi et les platoniciens de perse.* Paris: Gallimard, Bib. des Idees, 1971.

———. *En Islam Iranien: Aspects spirituels et philosophiques, Tome III: Les fideles d'amour et Shi'isme et sufisme.* Paris: Gallimard, Bib. des Idees, 1972.

————. *En Islam Iranien: Aspects spirituels et philosophiques, Tome IV: L'Ecole d'Ispahan—L'Ecole Shaykhie—Le Douzieme Imam.* Paris: Gallimard, Bib. des Idees, 1972.

————. "Emblematic Cities: A Response to the Images of Henri Stierlin." Translated by Kathleen Raine. *Temenos Journal* 10: 11–24. French original in: Henri Stierlin. *Ispahan: Image du Paradis.* Geneva: Editions Sigma, 1976.

————. *Spiritual Body and Celestial Earth: From Mazdean Iran to Shi'ite Iran.* Translated by Nancy Pearson. Bollingen Series XCI: 2. Princeton: Princeton University Press, 1977.

————. "Harmonia Abrahamica." Preface to Luigi Cirillo and Michel Frémaux. *Évangile de Barnabé: Recherches sur la composition et l'origine,* 5–17. Paris: Éditions Beauchesne, 1977.

————. "Le paradoxe du monothéisme." In *Le Paradoxe du Monothéisme,* 11–96. Paris: l'Herne, 1981.

————. "De la théologie apophatique comme antidote du nihilisme." In *Le Paradoxe du Monothéisme,* 211–55. Paris: l'Herne, 1981.

————. "Théologie au bord du lac." In *Henry Corbin,* ed. Christian Jambet, 62–62. Paris: Cahier de l'Herne, no. 39, 1981.

————. "Post-Scriptum biographique à un Entretien philosophique." In *Henry Corbin,* ed. Christian Jambet, 38–56. Paris: Cahier de l'Herne, no. 39, 1981.

————. "L'Initiation Ismaèlienne ou l'Esoterisme et le Verbe." In *L'Homme et Son Ange: Initiation et Chevalerie Spirituelle,* 81–205. Paris: Fayard, 1983.

————. *Hamann, philosophe du lutheranisme.* Paris: Berg Internationale, 1985.

————. "The Science of the Balance and the Correspondences between Worlds in Islamic Gnosis." In *Temple and Contemplation,* 55–131. Translated by P. Sherrard and L. Sherrard. London: KPI, 1986.

————. *Alchimie comme art hieratique.* Edited and introduced by Pierre Jory. Paris: l'Herne, 1986.

————. *The Man of Light in Iranian Sufism.* Translated by N. Pearson. New Lebanon, NY: Omega Publications, 1994.

Cranz, F. Edward. "1100 AD: A Crisis for Us?" In *De Litteris: Occasional Papers in the Humanities,* ed. M. Despalatovic, 84–108. New London: Connecticut College Library, 1978.

————. "The Reorientation of Western Thought circa 1100 A.D.—Four Talks." Unpublished manuscript.

Deck, John. *Nature, Contemplation, and the One: A Study in the Philosophy of Plotinus.* Toronto: University of Toronto Press, 1967.

Diamond, Stanley. *In Search of the Primitive: A Critique of Civilization.* London: Transaction, 1974.

Diggs, Stephen. "Alchemy of the Blues." *Spring Journal* 61 (1997): 16–50.

Duncan, Robert. "The Truth and Life of Myth." In *Fictive Certainties: Essays by Robert Duncan,* 1–59. New York: New Directions, 1985.

Evdokimov, Paul. *The Art of the Icon: A Theology of Beauty.* Crestwood, NY: St. Vladimir's Seminary Press, 1990.

Farnell, Lewis Richard. *Cults of the Greek States.* Oxford: Clarendon Press, 1896–1909.

Fisher, M. F. K. *The Art of Eating.* New York: Vintage Books, 1976.

Frascati-Lochhead, Marta. *Kenosis and Feminist Theology: The Challenge of Gianni Vattimo.* Albany: State University of New York Press, 1998.

Freud, Sigmund. "Civilization and Its Discontents." In *The Freud Reader,* ed. Peter Gay, 722–72. New York: W. W. Norton, 1989.

Giegerich, Wolfgang. "Das Begräbnis der Seele in die technische Zivilisation." *Eranos Jahrbuch* 52 (1983): 211–76.

———. "The Nuclear Bomb and the Fate of God: On the *First* Nuclear Fission." *Spring 1985:* 1–27.

———. "Saving the Nuclear Bomb." In *Facing the Apocalypse,* ed. Valerie Andrews, 96–108. Dallas: Spring Publications, 1987.

———. "The Invention of Explosive Power and the Blueprint of the Bomb—A Chapter in the Imaginal Pre-History of Our Nuclear Predicament." *Spring 1988:* 1–14.

Greeley, Andrew. *The Catholic Imagination.* Berkeley: University of California Press, 2000.

Griffin, Susan. *Woman and Nature: The Roaring Inside Her.* New York: Harper and Row, 1978.

———. *The Eros of Everyday Life.* New York: Doubleday, 1995.

Hamann, Johann Georg. "Aesthetica in nuce." Translated by H. B. Nisbet. In *German Aesthetic and Literary Criticism: Winkelmann, Lessing, Hamann, Herder, Schiller, Goethe,* H. B. Nisbet, 140–50. Cambridge: Cambridge University Press, 1985.

Hampson, Daphne. "Luther on the Self: A Feminist Critique." In *Feminist Theology: A Reader,* ed. Ann Loades, 215–25. Louisville: Westminster/John Knox Press, 1990.

———, ed. *Swallowing a Fishbone?: Feminist Theologians Debate Christianity.* London: SPCK, 1996.

Hannah, Barbara. *Jung: His Life and Work, A Biographical Memoir.* Boston: Shambhala, 1991.

Hayles, N. Katherine. *The Cosmic Web: Scientific Field Models and Literary Strategies in the Twentieth Century.* Ithaca: Cornell University Press, 1984.

———. *Chaos Bound: Orderly Disorder in Contemporary Literature and Science.* Ithaca: Cornell University Press, 1990.

———. *Chaos and Order: Complex Dynamics in Literature and Science.* Chicago: University of Chicago Press, 1991.

———. *How We Became Posthuman: Virtual Bodies in Cybernetics, Literature, and Informatics.* Chicago: University of Chicago Press, 1999.

Heidegger, Martin. *The Question Concerning Technology.* Translated and introduced by William Lovitt. New York: Harper, 1977.

Hillman, James. *Re-visioning Psychology.* New York: HarperCollins, 1975.

———. *The Dream and the Underworld.* New York: Harper and Row, 1979.

———. *Anima: An Anatomy of a Personified Notion.* Dallas: Spring Publications, 1985.

———. *A Blue Fire: Selected Writings by James Hillman.* Edited and introduced by Thomas Moore. New York: HarperCollins, 1989.

———. "...And Huge is Ugly." *The Bloomsbury Review* 12(1) (1992).

———. *The Thought of the Heart and the Soul of the World.* Dallas: Spring Publications, 1992.

———. *Kinds of Power: A Guide to Its Intelligent Uses.* New York: Doubleday, 1995.

———. "The Seduction of Black." *Spring 61* (1997)—*Haiti or the Psychology of Black:* 2–15.

———. "In." *Spring 63* (1998)—*Mom and the Kids:* 9–22.

———, and Michael Ventura. *We've Had a Hundred Years of Psychotherapy and the World's Getting Worse.* San Francisco: HarperSanFrancisco, 1992.

Illich, Ivan. *H_2O and the Waters of Forgetfulness: Reflections on the Historicity of Stuff.* Dallas: Dallas Institute of Art and Humanities, 1984.

———. *In the Vineyard of the Text: A Commentary to Hugh's Didascalicon.* Chicago: University of Chicago Press, 1993.

———, and Barry Sanders. *ABC: The Alphabetization of the Popular Mind.* New York: Random House, 1988.

Jambet, Christian, ed. *Henry Corbin.* Paris: Cahier de l'Herne, no. 39, 1981.

———. *La logique des Orientaux: Henry Corbin et la science des formes.* Paris: Éditions du Seuil, 1983.

Jung, Carl Gustav. *Memories, Dreams, Reflections.* New York: Vintage Books, 1965.

———. *The Collected Works.* Translated by R. F. C. Hull. Bollingen Series XX, vols. 1–20. Princeton: Princeton University Press, 1953–92.

———. *Jung Speaking: Interviews and Encounters.* Edited by W. McGuire and R. F. C. Hull. Bollingen Series XCVII. Princeton: Princeton University Press, 1977.

Kauffman, Stuart. *At Home in the Universe: The Search for the Laws of Self-Organization and Complexity.* New York: Oxford University Press, 1995.

Liddell, H. G., and Robert Scott. *A Greek-English Lexicon.* Oxford: Clarendon Press, 1968.

Lings, Martin. *What Is Sufism?* London: Unwin Hyman, 1981.

Loades, Anne, ed. *Feminist Theology: A Reader.* Louisville: Westminster/John Knox Press, 1990.

Loofs, Friedrich. "Kenosis." In *Encyclopedia of Religion and Ethics,* Vol. VII, ed. James Hastings, 680–87. New York: Scribner's, 1915.

Lyon, James K. "Paul Celan's Language of Stone: The Geology of the Poetic Landscape." *Colloquia Germanica* 8 (1974): 298–317.

Massignon, Louis. *The Passion of Al-Hallaj: Mystic and Martyr of Islam.* 4 vols. Translated by Herbert Mason. Bollingen Series XCVIII. Princeton: Princeton University Press, 1982.

————. *The Passion of Al-Hallaj: Mystic and Martyr of Islam.* Abridged Edition. Translated, edited, and abridged by Herbert Mason. Bollingen Series XCVIII. Mythos Series. Princeton: Princeton University Press, 1994.

McGrath, Alister. *Christian Theology: An Introduction.* Oxford: Blackwell, 1997.

McLuhan, Marshall. *Understanding Media: The Extensions of Man.* New York: McGraw-Hill, 1964.

Merchant, Carolyn. *The Death of Nature: Women, Ecology, and the Scientific Revolution.* San Francisco: Harper and Row, 1980.

Merton, Thomas. *The Living Bread.* New York: Farrar, Straus and Cudahy, 1956.

Minsky, Marvin. "Will Robots Inherit the Earth?" *Scientific American,* 271 (4) (October 1994): 108–14.

Murata, Sachiko. *The Tao of Islam: A Sourcebook of Gender Relationships in Islamic Thought.* Albany: State University of New York Press, 1992.

————, and William Chittick. *The Vision of Islam.* New York: Paragon House, 1994.

Nasr, Seyyed Hossein. "Oral Transmission and the Book in Islamic Education: The Spoken and the Written Word." In *The Book in the Islamic World: The Written Word and Communication in the Middle East,* ed. George N. Atiyeh, 57–70. Albany: State University of New York Press, 1995.

Neumann, Erich. *The Origins and History of Consciousness.* Bollingen Series XLII. Princeton: Princeton University Press, 1970.

Nichols, Aidan. *The Word Has Been Abroad: A Guide Through Balthasar's Aesthetics.* Washington, DC: Catholic University of America Press, 1998.

————. *No Bloodless Myth: A Guide Through Balthasar's Dramatics.* Washington, DC: Catholic University of America Press, 2000.

Nietzsche, Friedrich. *The Portable Nietzsche.* Edited and translated by Walter Kauffman. New York: Viking, 1982.

Oelschlager, Max. *The Idea of Wilderness: From Prehistory to the Age of Ecology.* New Haven: Yale University Press, 1991.

Papanikolaou, Aristotle. "Person, Kenosis, and Abuse: Hans Urs von Balthasar and feminist theologies in conversation." *Modern Theology* 19(1) (January 2003): 41–65.

Paris, Ginette. *Pagan Meditations: The Worlds of Aphrodite, Artemis, and Hestia.* Translated by Gwendolyn Moore. Dallas: Spring Publications, 1986.

Partridge, Eric. *Origins: A Short Dictionary of English Etymology.* New York: Macmillan, 1966.

Pelikan, Jaroslav. *The Christian Tradition: A History of the Development of Doctrine. Vol. 1. The Emergence of the Catholic Tradition (100–600).* Chicago: University of Chicago Press, 1971.

Pignatelli, Paola Coppola. "The Dialectics of Urban Architecture: Hestia and Hermes." *Spring 1985:* 42–49.

Rilke, Rainer Maria. *Duino Elegies.* Translated by C. F. MacIntyre. Berkeley: University of California Press, 1961.

Rodman, Selden, and Carole Cleaver. *Spirits of the Night: The Vaudun Gods of Haiti.* Dallas: Spring Publications, 1992.

Rothenberg, J., and Pierre Joris. *Poems for the Millennium, Volume 1: From Fin-de-Siecle to Negritude.* Berkeley: University of California Press, 1995.

————. *Poems for the Millennium, Volume 2: From Postwar to Millennium.* Berkeley: University of California Press, 1998.

Russell, Letty M., ed. *Feminist Interpretation of the Bible.* Philadelphia: Westminster Press, 1985.

Scholem, Gershom. *Major Trends in Jewish Mysticism.* London: Thames and Hudson, 1955.

Schuon, Frithjof. *The Essential Writings of Frithjof Schuon.* Edited and introduced by S. H. Nasr. Shaftesbury, MA: Element Books, 1986.

Sells, Michael. *Mystical Languages of Unsaying.* Chicago: University of Chicago Press, 1994.

————. *Early Islamic Mysticism.* Edited, translated, and introduced by Michael Sells. Classics of Western Spirituality. Mahwah, NJ: Paulist Press, 1996.

————. *Approaching the Qu'ran: The Early Revelations.* Ashland, OR: White Cloud Press, 1999.

Senghor, Leopold. "Speech and Image: An African Tradition of the Surreal." In *Poems for the Millennium, Volume 1: From Fin-de-Siecle to Negritude,* J. Rothenberg and Pierre Joris, 564–65. Berkeley: University of California Press, 1995.

Shayegan, Daryush. "Le Sens du Ta'wil," In *Henry Corbin,* ed. Christian Jambet, 84–87. Paris: Cahier de l'Herne, no. 39, 1981.

————. *Henry Corbin: La topographie spirituelle de l'Islam Iranien.* Paris: Editions de la Difference, 1990.

Shepard, Paul. *Nature and Madness.* San Francisco: Sierra Club, 1982.

————. *The Others: How Animals Made Us Human.* Washington, DC: Island Press, 1996.

Snyder, Gary. *The Real Work: Interviews and Talks 1964–1979.* New York: New Directions, 1980.

————. "Poetry and the Primitive: Notes on Poetry as an Ecological Survival Technique." In *Symposium of the Whole: A Range of Discourse Towards and Ethnopoetics,* ed. Jerome Rothenberg and Diane Rothenberg, 90–98. Berkeley: University of California Press, 1983.

Steiner, George. "The End of Bookishness?" *Times Literary Supplement,* 8–14 July 1988, 754.

————. *Real Presences.* Chicago: University of Chicago Press, 1989.

————. *Martin Heidegger. With a New Introduction.* Chicago: University of Chicago Press, 1991.

Stokstad, Marilyn. *Art History.* 2nd ed. Upper Saddle River, NJ: Prentice-Hall, 2002.

Suzuki, D. T. *Swedenborg: Buddha of the North.* Translated and introduced by Andrew Bernstein; Afterword by David Loy. West Chester, PA: Swedenborg Foundation, 1996.

Toulmin, Stephen. *Cosmopolis: The Hidden Agenda of Modernity.* New York: Free Press, 1990.

Vattimo, Gianni. *Beyond Interpretation: The Meaning of Hermeneutics for Philosophy.* Translated by David Webb. Stanford: Stanford University Press, 1997.

Waley, Muhammad Isa. "Najm al-Din Kubra and the Central Asian School of Sufism (The Kubrawiyyah)." In *Islamic Spirituality: Manifestations,* ed. S. H. Nasr, 80–104. Vol. 20 of *World Spirituality.* New York: Crossroads, 1991.

Whitmont, Edward C. *The Symbolic Quest: Basic Concepts of Analytical Psychology.* Princeton: Princeton University Press, 1969.

Williams, Alan. "Zoroastrianism and the Body." In *Religion and the Body,* ed. Sarah Coakley, 155–66. Cambridge: Cambridge University Press, 1997.

INDEX